Spiritual Perspectives

Spiritual Perspectives

Maharaj Charan Singh
Answers Questions:
1960 – 1990

Volume III
Living the Life

RADHA SOAMI SATSANG BEAS

Published by:
J. C. Sethi, Secretary
Radha Soami Satsang Beas
Dera Baba Jaimal Singh
Punjab 143 204, India

First edition 2010

17 16 15 14 13 12 11 10   8 7 6 5 4 3 2 1

ISBN 978-81-8256-933-1

Printed in India by: Thomson Press (India) Ltd.

CONTENTS

Volume III
Living the Life

Volume I
Understanding the Basics

Volume II
Walking the Path

Spiritual Perspectives

Volume III
Living the Life

∝ 12 ∞

Master and Disciple

1   *Master, you have mentioned that the soul – or an individual – has to come to the eye centre here, and the master takes charge of him once he meets him at the eye centre. Coming to the eye centre seems to be the hard part of it.*

Well, brother, to be very frank, we become conscious that master has taken charge when we come to the eye centre; actually, master takes charge right from birth. Those people who have come to the path, master takes charge of them right from birth – he will never allow them to go so astray that he cannot pull them back to the path. You have seen a kite flyer flying a kite. He keeps loosening the string, but when he thinks the kite is going out of his control, he pulls it back. He will never lose sight of the kite; he will always keep pulling it, keeping it straight in the sky. But we become conscious that we are being taken care of only when we see the master within – then we know that we are being helped, we are being taken care of. Before that, we are not conscious of it.

As Christ has explained in the parable, a shepherd has so many sheep, but if one sheep goes down into some big ravine, he leaves the ninety-nine sheep and runs after the one, and brings that sheep back to the fold.[57*] And if that sheep is incapable of walking back, he will even physically lift that sheep and bring it back to the fold because he's concerned with all the sheep, not only the ninety-nine sheep. He will not be happy if one sheep has strayed. He's concerned with all the sheep; he has to account for all the sheep to the owner. So the ninety-nine sheep can't be jealous that he has neglected them and run after one sheep; even when he is running after that one sheep his whole attention is towards the ninety-nine sheep. But they have reached to that standard that he knows that they will not go astray, so he can give more attention to the others who have gone astray. But he loves all the hundred sheep and he is concerned about all of them.

Christ in the end prayed to the Lord that not a single sheep be lost: Father, I don't want a single sheep to be lost, because you have allotted them to my care.[58] So mystics, when they initiate, want every soul to go back to the Father. Some stay in the fold, but some try to go out and it takes time to bring them back to the fold again, but the shepherd doesn't lose sight of any of the sheep; he's responsible for all the hundred sheep which have been allotted to his care.

That sheep which has gone astray will become conscious only when the shepherd physically lifts the sheep and brings it back to the fold. But even before that the shepherd is running after that sheep, keeping an eye on where that sheep is going.

The master always keeps an eye on us and never lets us go so astray that he cannot pull us back to the path again. Sometimes the winds of karmas do blow very strong, and we stagger and become lame and can't walk straight; but again we get a

*References to Bible quotes are numbered according to their order in the Bible and appear in a separate index. The Ten Commandments appear in their entirety at the end of the index.

push and strength to walk straight again. When a child starts learning to walk, he falls, but he gets up again; he falls again, but ultimately he learns to walk.

That is why Christ has given so many examples about healing lame people, sick people. This was not physical healing – it was spiritual healing. People who don't know how to walk straight in life, who don't deal straight in this world – they are the lame people; they don't know how to walk at all so they get help to walk straight. We are all diseased by becoming victims of the senses, so we are washed, we are cured of all these diseases, and again the soul shines. That is the miracle which the mystics perform. It is no miracle to get rid of a certain disease or cure somebody of leprosy; even the doctors can do that with strong drugs.

So Christ didn't come here as a doctor. As he said, I have not come to create peace – I've come with a sword.[39] He did not come to improve the lot of people in this world but to take them from this creation back to the Father. That is the greatest miracle mystics perform. What difference does it make to the world if there are a hundred lepers less from the time of Christ till now? That was not his greatness; his greatness was that he took those souls who came to him, who were allotted to him, back to the Father.

2   *When someone is brought to the path and until the time of initiation, does the living master stay with him if he strays from the path while he is still seeking? And then after his initiation, if he strays from the path again, does the living master still stay with his disciple?*

I will explain this to you with a parable by Christ, from Saint Matthew. If a shepherd has a hundred sheep and one sheep goes astray – runs down to the ravines – the shepherd leaves the

5

ninety-nine sheep and runs to that lost sheep, lifts that sheep on his shoulder and brings it back to the fold.[57] This holds true with all initiates. The master initiates so many people. Some people will go off the path or will be led astray, but the master does not leave them at all. He is responsible for taking the initiated soul back to the Father, so he ultimately brings that sheep back to the fold. Once the master initiates a person, he never leaves that disciple.

Christ gives another beautiful parable. A farmer sows good seeds into fertile ground. But tares also grow in the field along with the crop. The farmer does not remove the tares. When the harvest is ready, the tares are cut and burned and whatever is left of the crop is harvested and brought back.[50]

Similarly, when the master initiates a person, that is a good seed in receptive ground. But the enemy, the mind, tempts the disciple to go astray. The mind leads him to sense pleasures. Or it tries to deceive him. So the mind starts sowing tares. Now, the master knows this, but the master does not like the tares to be removed because if the tares are pulled out, the roots of the crop may be damaged.

In other words, if you make a disciple conscious of his weaknesses, he may leave the path completely. He may not even attend to meditation. He may become shy even to come to the master. But at the time of death the tares will be taken care of, balanced with the meditation he has done, the path he has followed. Ultimately the soul will shine and go back to the Father.

Once the seed has been sown, it cannot be destroyed. Once the disciple has been accepted, he must go back to the Father. The seed must sprout; whether it takes one rain, two rains or ten rains, the seed must sprout. Initiation is never wasted. Even if the disciple goes astray, ultimately he will again come back to the path and will again be led by the master. The master will not leave the disciple. He is responsible to take that soul back to the Father.

sowing seeds

3   *Master, in* Spiritual Gems *it says that without complete*
devotion to the physical form of the master, we don't have
a possible chance of going across. What does that mean?

As I often say, devotion brings faith in us, faith will enable you
to put in effort, and effort will take you out of this ocean of
existence. Without love there can be absolutely no faith at all,
without faith there can never be an effort at all, and without
effort we can never succeed.

You see, if I have faith in a professor, love for a professor
and respect for a professor; if I believe that he knows his subject,
that he is the master authority of whatever he is teaching me; if
I have respect for him, I'll listen to him very attentively. I will
try to please him by learning my lesson, and I will try never to
displease him. When I gain respect for him, then I have faith
in him. Whatever he tells me to do, I do it. I make that effort.
Then I also become a professor like him. If you don't respect a
professor, you will never listen to what he says; and if you don't
listen to what he says, you will never follow what he says. And
then we remain blank – we don't learn anything.

It is the same in Sant Mat. If we have respect, reverence
for the master, automatically we will have faith in him and will
listen to what he says, and then we will try to live in the teaching that he is trying to explain to us. We will put in an effort to
follow the teachings. Effort will help us to cross the ocean. So
they are all interconnected with each other. Soami Ji says: First
comes love. If we have no love, we can have no faith at all; and
if we have no faith, we will never be able to put in any effort.[*]

If a servant has reverence for you, respect for you, love for
you, then whatever you ask him to do, he is so happy to do it.
He knows that his master will be happy with what he has done.

---

[*] *Preet parteet guru ki karna, nam rasaayan ghat mein jarna.* Sar Bachan,
p. 123.

But if he has no respect for you, he will never obey you. He will never be able to complete what you want him to do and thereby please you. That can never be achieved.

4   *I was reading in* Science of the Soul, *the South African magazine, that if we do our meditation, you will take us by the hand, and if we don't, you will take us by the ear. [Laughter]*

Then what is the problem? As long as you are taken to the Lord, what difference does it make? Haven't you seen a shepherd dragging a lamb by one leg or sometimes taking the lamb on his shoulder? It depends upon the individual lamb. For some lambs, he just whistles and they automatically run to the flock. Others see the stick and they run to the flock. Others are probably waiting for the dog to bark and then they'll run to the flock. And some have to be physically lifted – some have to be dragged to the fold. But the fold is one, and as long as you come to the fold, it is okay. It is for the shepherd to see how he brings us to the fold.

5   *Maharaj Ji, in the books they talk about certain disciples that have had a personal relationship with the master, like Shadi with the Great Master [Maharaj Sawan Singh]. A lot of times I've had a desire to have a personal relationship with you, more than I can have living in the United States. I know that you are my master, but you seem so far away from me in my day-to-day life that I've really wanted to be able to talk with you as a person.*

Brother, every satsangi has a personal relationship with his own master, and he's never away from his master. Neither is the master away from the disciple. We should never feel our master is somewhere at a far distance. He is the one nearest to us. He's always with us.

6   *Master, in reading* Spiritual Letters, *we can fairly easily see the communication and the relation between Baba Jaimal Singh and the Great Master. Could you say anything about how we can expect to relate with you, in our meditation and our daily lives?*

Our relationship with the master is that of love and devotion, of meditation. It is not any worldly relationship; it's only a spiritual relationship. And the more we are filled with love and devotion for the master, the nearer we feel to him. The master is always near to us; it is we who are away from the master. The more we are filled with love and devotion for the master, the nearer we feel to him and the more we feel that he belongs to us and we belong to him. Actually, that is our own feeling. We come to that level of consciousness where we feel the nearness of the master. Otherwise master is always near every disciple.

7   *Great Master used to say that if you come to satsang even with a stony heart, at least that stone gets to sit in the cool water for a little while. But the problem for us is that we take that stone and put it in the sunlight, and the effect of satsang is gone right away.*

But as long as it remains in the water, at least it has saved itself from the heat.

So we should stay here and never leave?

Even if you want to leave, you cannot leave. We are so much tied down with these iron chains that in spite of our best efforts we cannot get released. But his hands are very strong and he has *kite + string*

a long reach. The one who plays with the kite has the string in his hand. He lets it go and lets it go and lets it go. When he sees that it is going out of his control, he pulls it back and holds it tight. So when the master, the Lord, has put us on the path, no matter what we do, he will not let us go astray. Ultimately he will bring us back to the path. As Christ said, ultimately there is one shepherd and one fold.[107] That is our only hope.

8   *What does it mean when Christ said, no man can serve two masters?*

Your devotion to your master should be one-pointed. "A rolling stone gathers no moss." If you run from or shift from master to master, from place to place, you will get nowhere. We have got to build definite faith and devotion in our guide who is to lead us. Unless we develop that faith, our mind will not let us practice, as we will have so many doubts coming in our mind, and then we will make no progress. So, what Christ meant was that we must have implicit faith in our master. The other master is our mind and senses. It is not possible to be a slave of the senses and serve the Lord simultaneously, for the one is the exact opposite of the other, and we cannot go in two directions at the same time. Either we are bound down by the mind and senses, or we serve the master by doing the spiritual practice and thus going back up and merging into the Lord. Christ also said, ye cannot serve God and mammon,[24] meaning that it is impossible to go up and merge back into him as long as we have any attachments down here, whether they are possessions, wealth, family, friends. Anything that keeps our attention away from him is mammon. That must not be our master if we want to make any progress at all. Only our spiritual master can help us reach our goal.

9   Master, does the master sometimes send us situations to test us, or is this just our own karmas coming to us?

Why test us – doesn't he know us, how strong we are? Doesn't the professor know the quality of his student? Does he need an examination for that? What is there to test? We are all full of weaknesses, we're all struggling souls. Christ said, somewhere in the New Testament, that I will not condemn you to my Father because we are already condemned.[80] We are already miserable with our weaknesses. What is there to test us about? Guru Nanak says: If you go on scratching the earth, you will never reach the bottom, no matter how much effort you keep putting in. So similarly, he says, if you go on scratching your weaknesses, there would be no end to it.* We live only on the Lord's grace, on his mercy. If we think that we are ready for the examination or that we have become fit for the examination, that is impossible. So what is there to test us about? The saints help us. Sometimes when we feel quite egoistic about ourselves – then situations arise in which we may realize where we stand. But it's not that the master is testing us; he has just made us conscious of where we stand. It's not that he doesn't know anything about us. We are all struggling souls.

10   Master, you said the other day that if the master told a disciple that an elephant was a donkey, a good disciple would immediately believe that to be true. Does the master ever tell the disciple that an elephant is a donkey?

You will reach that level of consciousness where you do not discriminate whether it is a donkey or an elephant – where whatever comes from him is right – only when you have merged

---

* *Maati ka kya dhopay swaami, maanas ki gat eihee.* Guru Arjun, Adi Granth, M5, p. 882.

11

yourself into the master, when you have become one with him and have lost your own identity. Only then will this stage of faith come. And then there's no question – the question does not arise – because then you are one; there's nobody to ask and nobody to answer. You are the one who is saying and you are the one who is hearing what is said because you have no identity of your own. You have lost your identity, your individuality, and become one with the master. It's only when you become one with the master that you can have so much faith. Then this question doesn't arise.

11   *Master, I understand that after initiation the master takes on some of our karma. Does that mean master actually takes some of our karma or just that we become stronger?*

Sister, who told you that master takes the karma after initiation?

I have just read that karma seems to be a lot lighter after initiation.

You have to help yourself to make those karmas lighter. The master gives you a sword and a helping hand to fight your enemies. Then you have something to lean on when you fight your enemies, fight your karma. But you have to do it yourself. You are not to throw your whole load on the master.

Then that just means that master makes us stronger?

He will help you. When you have confidence in someone, when you feel you can depend upon someone, you can always face a situation in a much better way. If you have nobody to lean on, you just get confused. So, when the master puts us on the path, he gives us certain methods and techniques to clear or lighten our karmas. These initiation instructions tell us how to clear our sins. And the master helps us also in many other ways. But we shouldn't just think that since we have been initiated, he will share our karma, so why should we bother about it? We ourselves have to work to make our soul free from the mind and the senses. We have to put in effort in order to do that. But we get help and grace from the Lord.

12 *If we're in love with the Lord, with the master, why do we keep doing things that are displeasing to him?*

Because we are more in love with the senses than with the master. If we are really in love with the Lord, we will always do what pleases him and we will never do anything which displeases him. We intellectually feel that we are in love with the Lord, but actually our whole heart is in this creation. We're attached to the world; we're attached to worldly faces and worldly objects more than we are attached to the Lord. So we think more about the creation, we try to please the creation more than the Creator. Intellectually, we want to feel that we are in love with the Lord, but actually we're not. And even if we try to love the Lord, it is for our own selfish purposes in order to get the maximum out of him from this creation. We're so attached to this creation that we worship him so that we may get more wealth, more love, more honours from this world. That is why we worship him. We don't worship him because we love the Lord, we worship him because we want gifts from him, worldly graces from him. So actually we're in love with this creation. We only want to use him as a medium to give us the gifts of the creation. We don't love him at all.

How do we ever get that love?

In some tribes and countries, people worship snakes. It's not that they're in love with snakes but they're frightened of the snakes' poison. Most of our worship is just to avoid the Lord's curse, so that misfortune may not fall on us – so that we may not lose in our cases, our promotions, our health, our worldly riches, worldly fame. We worship him so that we may not be deprived of these things or because we want more and more of them, not because we are in love with the Lord.

If we are really in love with him, then the question of pleasing or displeasing him doesn't arise. Then you have no will of your own. You have merged your will in the will of the Father. You feel neither happy nor unhappy about anything which happens to you in your life because you have become one with the Father. You have lost your own identity, your own individuality. You have merged your individuality into the Father, and you have become one with him. So you don't feel anything at all. Neither the ups nor the downs of the world upset you then because you have merged, you have lost your identity and you've become one with the Father.

Then you always please him, and you won't bother about whether you have pleased him or displeased him because you're so much in love with him. You have no other thoughts except love and devotion for the Father. And we become better humans, too, because the nearer we are to the Lord, the nearer we are to his creation. Then we see the Creator in every part of the creation. Then we are in love with the creation also – we're helpful to people, we're humble before them. We develop a loving nature towards everybody when we see the Creator in every part of the creation. When you are in love with him, then you are in love with everything that he has created in this creation.

So the nearer we become to him, the nearer we become to his creation because only then do we see the Creator in the creation. Then we are not attached to the creation but to the one who has created it, the one who permeates everything in this world.

14

13   *So has the master been pleased or displeased with our behaviour?*

You see, the professor loves all the students in the class, but some students are not attentive; some students don't work hard at all, and unless they are given seats in the front, they won't be attentive. It doesn't mean that the master doesn't love the students sitting on the back benches and is only considerate of the students who are sitting in the front. He wants them to be attentive. Because he loves all the students, he wants everybody to pass. So this is a wrong way of judging things. The professor does not discriminate among his students; he only wants to teach and see that every student passes.

14   *How does the satsangi know when the master is pleased with him or displeased with him?*

Well, to be very frank, the master is never displeased with any soul. If he were displeased, why would he put us on the path? It is our own conscience which pricks us. He knows our sincerity, and he's here to help us to rise above those weaknesses, to help us to go beyond those weaknesses. He's not here to hurt us or to be displeased with us. He's never displeased. It's our own conscience which hurts us.

15   *If we feel that we've displeased the master, is there any way to make up for that?*

First, let me assure you, we never displease him. How can we displease him? We can only displease a person when we do something which he never expected. When he knows how helpless we are, what victims we are of our mind, that at every step we are full of failures, it's nothing new for him to know about us; he already knows us. That is why Christ said: If you won't follow me, won't live my teaching, I won't condemn you to the Father, because we're already condemned.[80] How much more can we be condemned than to be separated from the Father and be part and parcel of this creation? He tells us that he won't complain to the Father. So the question of displeasing the master doesn't arise at all, but definitely we can please him by living the Sant Mat way of life, by attending to our meditation. This definitely pleases him, but nothing displeases him.

16   *In the* Sar Bachan, *there is great emphasis on the importance of pleasing the master. How can we tell when we have pleased or displeased the master?*

When you have been able to please yourself by attending to meditation, you can think your master is very happy with you. When you are not in a position to please your own self, when you're at war with yourself, you're not happy with yourself, how can you think that you are happy with the master or that you have been able to please him? In order to please the master, first please yourself; be happy with yourself. Attend to your meditation. That is the only thing which pleases the master, and that will please you, too. You will feel that bliss and peace and that love and devotion within you, and you will also feel that your master is happy with you.

17   *I'd like to ask you a question. I've asked you this before, but it still bothers me. It's about fear, being frightened of the master.*

What frightens you about the master? Actually we are always frightened of our own self. It's not the other person. We're frightened of our own weaknesses, of our own handicaps, and that becomes a barrier between us and the master. There's nothing to fear about the master. He comes to create love, to strengthen love, to help it to grow and to absorb a disciple within himself. He doesn't create fear. Our own weaknesses stand in our way. But fear is also a part of love, as I have explained many times. We are afraid lest we do something to offend him, and to offend him is also our own weakness. We are frightened of ourselves, that we may do something which may offend him. But there is nothing to fear because he never sits in judgment. He doesn't judge anybody. What is there to judge? He knows us. We are all struggling souls, full of weaknesses. What is there to judge? We are all imperfect. That is why we are here. It is our own mind which tries to create barriers.

As I said, some fear is a part of love. Fear of offending is a part of love, but that doesn't keep us away from the master. That helps us to follow the teachings, to live the teachings and to always take positive steps to please him. That fear of offending doesn't become a barrier in our way.

18   *What is the difference on the inside with regard to how stern the master is with the disciple? Is a master more stern on the inside than on the outside?*

As an example: A mother loves her child more than anyone – I don't think there is a stronger love than that between a mother and child. But doesn't the mother spank the child if the child doesn't behave, doesn't remain disciplined? The mother wants the child to be a model of absolute discipline and love, and she has to train him to come to that level. For that she may even spank him, and even turn him out of the house for a time or not feed him. But what is the purpose behind it? It is all love. If the child is sick and he wants toffee, the mother will never give it to him. You can't say the mother is stern. We don't understand why the mother is not giving the toffee to the child. But the mother understands even if the child doesn't understand.

So the mother is most loving, most kind. But we don't understand that type of love and kindness. Our concept of love and kindness is that whatever we want, we should get. But sometimes the mother has to put bitter quinine in the mouth of the child. And the child has to swallow it, in his interest. But there can be no better love than the mother for the child. If he is dirty, the mother may give him a cold wash. But if the child misbehaves or commits a crime, the mother never will send him to the police. A mother will always shield the child in spite of all the crimes he may commit, because she loves that child.

Similarly, master always loves his disciple. He will never hand him over to Kal, no matter what he does. But definitely, he has to improve that soul to take it back to the Father. That soul must shine because he loves that soul. Christ gives an example: One sheep runs away from the fold and goes astray. The shepherd himself runs after that one sheep, even physically lifts that sheep and brings it back to the fold,[57] because he loves that sheep and is responsible for all the sheep entrusted to him. So is the master responsible for all the allotted souls entrusted to his care. But he has to discipline them so they can become one with the Father – he has to make them pure.

Our concept of love and kindness is to fulfil all our worldly desires, all our worldly ambitions. Whatever we want, we should get. That is not love and kindness. But for the master's love and kindness for the disciple, he would never put the disciple on the path at all. He is not charging any money. He is not being paid for his services. But he has a certain responsibility and duty to make us good citizens of the Father. He loves us; otherwise, why would he bother about us? But our outlook on love and kindness is very different. We don't want to point out each others' weaknesses – we say that may hurt someone's feelings. We'd like to be kind and try to avoid that. But the master has to tell us where our fault lies, where our weaknesses lie, because he wants us to get rid of them and he wants to keep us straight on the path.

We have been brought up by our parents, and now we realize how much they did for us to make us such good human beings. But when we were younger we resented them, we were all rebellious, we did not want to stay at home, we did not want to read any books. We never wanted to be disciplined. We thought that our parents were cruel and unkind. But now we appreciate what they did for us. Similarly, we have to grow spiritually to understand the master's kindness and love for us.

19   We know our pain, but what is your pain, as master?

Well, your pain is my pain. When you go to a happy person, he will make you happy. If you deal with a miserable person, he'll make you miserable. So if you want to relieve my pain, you should all become happy. And when you're happy, I'm happy. If you tell me painful things, naturally it will affect me. I have no pain of my own.

20   Maharaj Ji, don't the masters feel some pain on our behalf?

Don't worry about the suffering of the master; the body may suffer, but the soul never suffers at all. The body belongs to Kal, the prince of this world. Masters don't bother about that at all. Their soul never suffers. The soul is always at peace and happy. Masters help the disciples by sharing their burden sometimes.

21   I have a sort of inner rebellion against belonging to a group. I feel there is a great spiritual freedom between the master and the individual. May not a person just have his master, without any organization? Is it really necessary to belong to a group?

No. The relationship of a master with a disciple is just a personal relationship of the individual. It does not come through society; it does not come through groups; it does not come through organizations. It is a personal contact of a disciple with a master, and nobody comes in the way at all.

22 *Master, does the master sometimes communicate with his disciples in ways other than through his radiant form or verbally? You often hear of mystic stories where people get messages from their master via other people.*

Why should the master use other people to reach you? Why can't the master reach you himself directly? If we can't reach the master, the master has no barrier preventing him from reaching us. Why would he use another medium to reach us? The relationship of the disciple with the master is individual and direct, not through anyone at all.

23 *Master, you've said that we must learn to walk on our own feet. Is that self-realization?*

Self-realization is going beyond the realm of mind and maya. Whether you walk on your own feet or you have to lean on somebody's shoulder, that is a different question. But the real question is to go beyond the realm of mind and maya.

When I try to walk on my own feet, I've found that I only stumble. But when I keep my mind on the fact that master is doing the walking, I seem to move forward more easily.

You see, the expression "walking in the footsteps of the master" means that whatever teaching the master has given us, we have to follow it. We have to adhere to those teachings, live that way of life and attend to our meditation. That is walking in the footsteps of the master – changing our way of life, the pattern of our life and attending to meditation as explained to us by our master. Don't take it literally. To follow the teachings, to live the teachings, to make them part and parcel of our life – that is walking in the footsteps of the master.

All the help that we need, we always get within. We are never left alone. We are not orphaned. There's somebody to guide us, somebody to lead us, somebody to pull us forward, somebody to push us forward within. Walking on your own feet or in the footsteps of the master is one and the same thing. These are just expressions.

24   *Master, this question of loneliness – we're very lonely, and then immediately upon reaching our master at initiation, this loneliness seems to disappear completely. Our quest seems to be finished, as it were, in the master.*

Well, when you're searching for your home, and you have lost the way in the wilderness, and suddenly you find somebody who can lead you to your home in the darkness or in the wilderness, you have not reached home yet. You have only found somebody who can lead you to your home, but that anxiety about the quest absolutely leaves you. Then you are sure that you have a guide now, he knows the way home and is going to lead you to your home, so naturally contentment comes at once.

The real bliss and happiness will come only when you reach your home, not before that. But if you become sure that this man knows my home and he can lead me out of this wilderness, out of this darkness, naturally your anxiety leaves you, your worry leaves you. This is what happens on the path.

When we find living guidance and we have faith in this living guidance that now I am on the path and I am going to be led back to my home, naturally that worry and anxiety leaves us. But if there's a lack of faith that the guide is right, that he knows the way home – will I ever be able to reach my home? – naturally your anxiety won't leave you. So not everybody gets that peace or contentment after initiation. It depends upon the individual. It depends upon our attitude towards the guide. And we only get real happiness when we get back home, not before that.

25 *Could you say something about faith and devotion and why mystics expect faith from their disciples when they are the creators of that faith?*

Unless we have love for somebody, we don't have any faith in them. Love creates faith in the person, and faith leads us to the practice of obeying the instructions of that person. So they're all essential. If we have love for the master, we naturally will have faith in him. And if we have faith in him, then we'd like to please him by following his instructions. Then we practice what he teaches. The whole remedy lies in practice; but for that, faith and love are required.

> *I was looking through* Sar Bachan *and came across the expression "when the love for the master becomes perfect." I was wondering when that would occur?*

'Perfect' means when we don't love anybody else. As Christ said in the Bible, if you love your father and mother more than me, you are not worthy of me.[42] 'Worthy of me' means to become me, to merge in me. We can only become the master when we have no attachment with anybody else in this creation. That is a perfect love – when it's one-pointed. If it is scattered, it has no depth. It has depth only when it is one-pointed.

26 *The scale on which we weigh our love, I believe, is the experiences we see around us. If we see others shedding tears for you, if we see others captivated by your physical presence, and yet we don't feel those things ourselves, I think that basically we feel that we are empty-hearted, hard-hearted.*

Well, brother, I don't think that would be the right analysis because everybody has his individual way of expression. Some people know how to digest. Some people can't digest; their emotions overflow. Those who digest, it doesn't mean that they have no emotions. Everybody has an individual relationship with the Lord. We cannot know our emotions for the Father by looking at others. We are made differently from each other. We have different backgrounds, different ways of expression. We have come from different cultures, different atmospheres, different societies, so our expression is also different.

We should be concerned only with ourselves, not with the conviction of others. We shouldn't base our conviction on the conviction of others. We have to stand on our own legs, not on the legs of others. We must have our own base to stand on and it must come from within. We don't need any support from outside, conviction from outside. Where we stand has to come from within.

Don't the tears come from within?

Tears do come from within, but sometimes they are absorbed within. Sometimes they overflow.

27   *In Delhi, Mr Sethi was reading, I think from Soami Ji*
     Maharaj. He brought up a point that was brought up
     to me several years ago here that I don't think has been
     really clarified. He said that when the lover is completely
     immersed in the master, there is no desire to get anything.
     One is just happy to be with the master, to be in the
     company of the master, to be in that radiance. Now I am
     worried, because when a master and a disciple have a
     wonderful relationship and it grows with the years – even
     when the disciple is nothing, the master is everything,
     the master is beautiful and the whole life of the disciple
     is the master, even though the disciple is not perfect and
     has silly little things that come up – but, Master, is it
     wrong if we would like for you to look at us?

He said the lover has no other desire but to love the master.
His only desire is to love the master. The lover doesn't want to
calculate his love from any other angle. He is happy in his love
for the master. He has no other desire in him except to love
him. He doesn't want anything else from the master but that
he lets him love him.

The disciple will never love the master unless the master
plants that seed of love in the heart of the disciple, unless he
nourishes that seed in the disciple, strengthens that seed in
the disciple, pulls the disciple towards him. His inner hand of
strengthening that seed of love is always there at the back.

Words are a very poor expression for the lover. He doesn't
want to waste words unnecessarily or even express them. His
expression is not by words. He has another way of expressing his
love. It is his tears and eyes. The expression on his face shows his
love, not words. When we express it, when we try to dramatize
it, we lose its depth. A lover never advertises that love. He digests
it within himself. When a girl falls in love with some man – I

don't know about in your country – she tries to hide it from everybody in the family. She tries not to share it with anybody; she tries to keep it to herself as much as she can.

28   Is it true that Great Master used to say that the master is
      a mirror to his disciples?

Yes, generally we say that the master is just like a looking glass, a mirror. If we go to him with devotion, we find devotion in him. If we go with a critical mind, then we have so many things which bother us. It is your own receptivity with which you approach the master that determines what you get out of the master. Whatever faces you make in the mirror, the mirror reflects them back to you. Some saints have said that the master is just like a mirror. If you go with a closed mind, you will have a hundred and one doubts in the master. You will find many faults and defects. If you go with love and devotion, you will find him full of love and devotion, and you'll find yourself more receptive to his teachings and to the way of life. So that is why it is generally said that he is just like a mirror. Great Master used to always give this explanation.

29   I hear that the master conceals our defects – I read that
      somewhere.

The master doesn't want to take the lid off; otherwise nobody would come to the master. If we are exposed by him publicly, nobody would come to him. And even in a private interview, no one likes to hear something against himself because we always justify our weaknesses, and we would like the master to accept our justification. Moreover, there is no reason for the master to expose us. He has come to redeem us, to help us to rise above those weaknesses, not to expose our weaknesses. What would he get by exposing our weaknesses? His main object is to pull us out of these weaknesses and take us back to the Father. But for our weaknesses, we wouldn't be here. We are part of this creation due to our weaknesses. And our weaknesses are not hidden from anybody, especially not from him, so what is there to expose? He's only here to help us go back to the Father.

As Christ said, I will not condemn you to my Father because you are already condemned.[80] What is there to condemn? How can we condemn a condemned person? When we are part of this creation, we're already condemned. We're already full of weaknesses, so what is there to expose about them? The moment we rise above these weaknesses, we rise above the creation because it is our weaknesses which are pulling us down to the level of creation. Rather, the masters always come to help us.

30 *Master, on the subject of unconditional love for the guru, something has been on my mind for the last few years. The fact of the matter is that it's easy for a human being to love somebody as a brother or sister. For example, if my brother was mean or lied to me, I would always love him no matter what, because he is my brother. The same goes for my mother or my father. Sometimes on the path when we take the master to be God – I've noticed that sometimes satsangis at one moment think that the master is God and then the next day they leave the path. Is it better, Master, to love you as we would love a brother or sister, unconditionally, so that no matter who or what ...*

The Great Master used to say that when you love the master as a brother, as a friend, then automatically you will realize that he is within. Have as much faith in him as a brother and as a friend, and then, in your practice, you will realize what the real situation is. God is also our own concept. We say we love God, but what do we love? How can we love someone whom we have never seen? Our mind only loves what it sees, some form, some association – mental association – and then, slowly and slowly, we fall in love with that object, with that person. It is just our mental concept that we love God. What do we love about him? How can we love him when we haven't seen him, when we don't know what he looks like? We just think we love God.

If we really loved God, we'd never do anything bad in this creation. If we know that God is one and that God is within us and we are sure about our love for God, then why is there so much turmoil in the whole creation? We'd never do anything bad or heinous if a five-year-old child were standing before us, but what do we not do while thinking that God is within us and professing that we are in love with him? We only intellectually think that he is within us and that we love him. This is no love at all. It's abstract love. You cannot fall in love with anyone unless you see him, unless you meet him, unless you know what he looks like. That is the nature of the mind. You cannot fall in love with a man who was living a thousand years before you and whom you've never seen. How can you fall in love with him?

31   Could you tell us some of the ways that could allow us to be in the presence of the masters or the master?

Brother, just be in his presence as you are in the presence of any other human being, with a relaxed mind and no nervousness, as all are struggling souls on the same path.

Master, I think he means, what are the qualifications that we must build within ourselves in order to be in the presence of a living master?

The necessity to meet him is a sufficient qualification to go to the master.

*Well, in my case – I speak about myself – I feel ardently
that I should please meet that master.*

Most welcome, brother.

*I want to know how, in my meditation every day, in my
recollection of the evening, all the time, I can feel that I
am closer and closer to the master.*

Brother, I assure you that when we are honest, when we are
sincere seekers, we put the whole burden on the Lord to put us
on the right path. You are doing your duty, and he will do his
duty. You should not worry about it.

32 *Maharaj Ji, if mentally we talk to our satguru as if we
    were talking to a friend, does that give us any spiritual
    enrichment, or not?*

The only advantage is that when you are talking mentally to
your master, you are not talking mentally to other people,
and in that way you do not let your thoughts be scattered into
the world. Then it will be easier for you to concentrate, spiritually, at the eye centre. If you let your thoughts spread out
into the whole world, naturally it will take time to withdraw
your consciousness to the eye centre. So it is always better to
remain within our own self or to remain within our master, to
live within.

Even if it is just a chat with him in our mind?

Whatever it may be. It is always good; at least we always feel
happy about it.

Is it a substitute for bhajan?

No, there is no substitute for bhajan.

*33   Maharaj Ji, how did you succeed in creating love for your
      own master?*

How to create love for your master? If one honestly thinks about
it, I don't think you can succeed in this unless he gives you his
love. He gives his love. But we can make ourselves receptive by
meditation. By living in the commands, leading our lives the
way he wants us to lead them, and by attending to our meditation, we are just being receptive and provoking his love. But
otherwise, it is all given as a gift by him.

*34   Maharaj Ji, no love appears more difficult than the love
      for the master. In the beginning the master's love is dif-
      ferent from what we expected and we suffer as a result. It
      appears that only after we have fully accepted the meth-
      ods he uses that we begin to understand what it means to
      love the master. Is it correct to say that love for the master
      grows in the time of purification?*

You see, actually, we can only have love for the master when we
see his radiant form within. That is so catching that automatically the mind doesn't go to anybody else at all. Christ said, you
will come unto me, and I will come unto you.[122] You will merge
into me and become one with me. Love makes us lose our own
individuality, our identity, and helps us to merge into the radiant
form of the master. That is real love for the master. Before that,
by love for the master we mean that we follow the teaching. We
live the Sant Mat way of life, we build our meditation on the
foundation given to us by the master and do not compromise
with our principles; we attend to our meditation diligently,
honestly and truthfully. Then automatically you create love for
your master. That helps to create love, and meditation helps to
strengthen that love, and by meditation that love grows and
grows to the extent that we become one with the master.

That is why Christ said that to sin against the holy ghost can never be forgiven,[46] because meditation will automatically fill you with love and devotion for the Father. Automatically it will detach you from this creation and attach you to the Creator. If you sin against the holy ghost – you don't attend to meditation – then even if you have love for the master, it is going to fade out sooner or later, and you may even lose it – because that love has no depth; it is superficial, just on the surface. Real love comes only by meditation.

35 *Yesterday, Professor was saying that we must fall in love with the body form of the master. What I am finding is that love for the physical master comes and goes. Is there any way to develop that love and help it grow so that it stays?*

Definitely – by meditation. Meditation creates that love; without meditation you cannot create love even for the physical body of the master. Meditation helps you to develop it; it helps you to grow it. If you say you love the master without meditation, you are just deceiving yourself. It is just an emotional deception. In real love, we feel an experience, and then this turns us inward to the level of the shabd master within. Then we feel more love for the outside master also. And that love is real. Otherwise, today we feel love, tomorrow we feel absolutely dry and vacant. We are trying to convince ourselves that we are in love, but probably we are not. Experience within gives your love depth.

36 *Maharaj Ji, is it possible for a disciple to submit to a master without meditation?*

I don't think it is practical at all. The question is, what is the master? As I've told you, the master is not the body, he is the shabd within. How would you merge in that without meditation?

Master is that shabd, that divine melody which is within every one of us, and we have to merge in that, to become that being. How can we do it without attending to meditation? Love helps you to meditate – love forces you to meditate. If you love somebody, you always want to be with the person concerned. If we love the master and he's within us, we will put our efforts toward being with the master because we become restless without him. We want to be with him. As Christ said, see, now you know the way.[118]

When we know the way towards our destination, towards our home, we have to follow the way in order to reach our home. I can't say that I am not going to follow the way, but I want to go home.

Meditation is the only way to follow the path. And love will definitely push us and pull us towards our destination. That is very essential. But love without meditation is just emotion – sometimes you feel it, sometimes you don't feel it. Sometimes you feel you're full of devotion, other times you feel you're absolutely blank. By meditation you develop love that comes with experience, with conviction. Meditation takes our roots very deep in love; nobody can shake us then.

37 *Would you talk to us about the love of the master for his disciple?*

Love of the master for the disciple? That's what I've been saying, that it is the master's love that creates the disciple's love for the master. It is the master who creates that love in the disciple for him. He's the one who is pulling the disciple from within. Then the disciple becomes helpless to love the master; he starts feeling that probably he's in love with the master. But actually it is the master who has filled him with his love. Otherwise, but for the grace of the Lord, we are so much attached to the senses and to worldly faces and worldly objects that we would never be able to love the master. He is the one who is pulling us from within.

38   Master, is it possible to love the master?

It is possible! You see, there are so many relationships of love, but no relationship is stronger, no bond is stronger than that of the disciple and the master. No love is stronger than that of the disciple and the master.

SHABD IS THE REAL MASTER

39   We are led to believe, and I believe you say it, that the master is God, is the Lord. How can we know this? How can our minds really know this? We see you there and it's very difficult to realize that the master and the Lord are one.

Our real master is shabd; it's not the body. And our creator is also shabd; it's not any entity. The soul is also part of that shabd, a spark of that shabd. So that is why every soul has the potential to become God, just like the ray and the sun. The real master is not the body; it's that creative power which has created the creation. You call it God. And that very power is also within our body – we are connected to it, and that is our guide within. The disciple will leave the body and the master will leave the body. No body will go to the final abode, neither the master's nor the disciple's. The soul is the real disciple and the shabd is the real master. Once the soul is brought in touch with the shabd, it pulls the soul to the level of the Father.

And this knowledge the satsangi gets from the perfect living master?

You can only get knowledge by experience, by going through that process. Otherwise it's all intellectual.

And how do we get this experience?

By meditation; by developing your level of consciousness to that level.

40 *I read somewhere in a book that the body isn't the disciple and the mind isn't the disciple, but the soul is the real disciple.*

Yes, the real disciple is the soul, not the mind. The mind we have to carry with us so that the soul can go back to the Father. You can't leave the mind back and take the soul in the initial stages, which is Trikuti. After Trikuti the mind stays back. The real disciple is the soul and the real master is the shabd and nam within. That is why Christ said, I'll send you the Comforter when I go.[121] It means, I'm not leaving you, because I'll be in touch with you through that Comforter which will give you peace and bliss, no matter whether I leave the body or not. So our real Comforter is the shabd. The real master is the shabd.

41 *We are taught that an advanced disciple can see his master within himself and in all others. In the time of contemporary gurus like Kabir Sahib and Guru Nanak, what did each of them see in the other?*

Our real master is not the body; it is the word which is in the body. That word is our master, not the flesh. Nor is the flesh of the disciple the disciple. The soul is the real disciple and the shabd is the real master. Whatever master we see within ourselves – the radiant form of the master – takes that shape from the shabd. That is why it is known as the radiant form of the master. It is not the flesh as we see it outside, though we see him just as we see him outside. Since the real master is the word, the shabd, the nam, the logos, so all masters are the same. All masters are a wave of the same ocean. Therefore, if you see your master within, it means you see all masters.

42 *Master, I'm having a great deal of trouble understanding the difference between the physical master and the master within. I wonder if you could maybe try to make it a little bit clearer?*

The physical master is required so that we may be able to find and seek our real master within. Our real master is the word, that holy ghost, which ultimately has to pull our soul back to its source. But unless that word or holy ghost is in the flesh like us, we cannot make contact with it within ourselves. When that word comes into the flesh at our level, then only through it can we be connected within ourselves with that holy word, that holy ghost. That holy ghost is our real master. Flesh is not the master. Neither is the body of the disciple the real disciple.

The real disciple is the soul; the real master is the word within every one of us. The disciple will leave his body here just as the master will leave his. The master never dies, but his body remains here. This means the master is not the body. The real master is that word which is in the body. Unless we are in the flesh and the master is in the flesh, the soul cannot be brought in touch with that word which the Lord has kept within every one of us. We need somebody in the flesh like us, who has access to that word, so that through him we may be brought in touch with that word, that holy ghost, within ourselves. So that is our real master, which ultimately will pull us back to the Father.

Christ says: I will raise up at the last day only those who have seen me and who have faith in me.[92] Now we can only see the master when he is at our level, when both of us are in the flesh, in the human form. When the master is in the human form, then we are able to see him, to know him and to have faith in him. 'Faith' means that only through him can we withdraw our consciousness to the eye centre and be one with that word and that shabd. Faith in the master means to follow and live according to his teachings. That is faith. Christ implied that the master never dies.[117] He will always be living and will never die. But he has left the body. It has decomposed. Therefore, the body cannot be the master. That word which is in the body, that is our master. So for the disciple, the master is always living.

43 *If a satsangi had a master in the previous life, and when he leaves the body forever, for good, leaves the earth, which master will meet him? The present one or the one he had in his previous life?*

All masters are the same. They are all waves of the same ocean. The body is not the master. Master is that power, that shabd, that nam. Our real master is that shabd, which is here at the eye centre. Saints have taken on a human body just to explain the teachings to us. So we see them as we see any other body in this world, but actually they are made of nothing but shabd itself. So shabd is there to look after them. It is therefore immaterial which body comes because the saint does not merge into the body; but through his master, he merges back into that shabd. Every soul which has the seed of initiation ultimately merges back into that Lord through the master. All masters are one; there is no difference.

44 *Does that mean that one soul will have more than one master if it takes it more than one lifetime to go back?*

All masters are the same. There is no difference between the masters. They are all waves of the same ocean. And there is no difference between one wave and another wave because the master is the word, not the body. Master is not the body, master is not the flesh. The master is that holy ghost, that word. The 'living master' means the word in the flesh. When the word takes on flesh, he becomes our living master. Every master has left his body behind. It doesn't mean the master has died, because the word is the master. The word never dies. When that word comes in the flesh, it becomes our living master. So ultimately the word, which is the inner master, will pull the soul back to the Father. So all masters are the same. There is no difference between one master and another master.

45 *It says that in three or four incarnations we return to our home, or find our way back home, or want to go back home, and that in walking the path, we will meet the same master after all those incarnations. Is that true?*

Well, brother, we must understand that all true masters are the same. They are all waves of the same ocean. Our real master is the audible life stream, the logos, the word of God which is within every one of us. That is our real master, and whatever master comes from that word, his reality is just that word, that shabd. So you will meet many masters from the point of view of the physical body, but actually it will be the same master to you because all masters are absolutely the same. The same physical form will not come again for a seeker, for an initiate who takes another birth, but the same master will come to him in the sense that all masters are the same.

> *But what about the form that we see inside, the radiant form? Would we recognize that as you, for instance, or*

*some other personality, such as Maharaj Sawan Singh or
Sardar Bahadur Jagat Singh?*

The master who initiates you will come within you, in his radiant form. He takes his form from the shabd, from that light, from that sound, whatever name you give it. You will see him as you see your own master outside, and he may bring his own master with him; that is different, but you are only concerned with your own master. Without your master, you are not to give any attention to anybody else within yourself, if you happen to see anybody at all, because then you are likely to be deceived sometimes. So we are to give attention inside to our own master only, and no one else, unless accompanied by our own master.

*Yes, but what I meant was, supposing a person had been
initiated in a previous lifetime, and he came back and
was initiated again, which outwardly is probable – when
he goes inside, will he see the one who initiated …?*

He will see the master who has initiated him in his present physical body.

He may also see the other one, I would think?

He may, yes, but they are all one.

46   *Is it necessary to become attached to the physical master
in order to become attached to the spirit within?*

Ultimately, Christ tells us, we have to leave the physical form and attach ourselves to the word within.[122] The purpose of the physical form of the master is simply to fill us with love and devotion for the Father, to put us on the path and to bring us in touch with the spirit. With the help of the physical form, we are finally able to attach ourselves to the word and become one with the spirit within.

*47   Is just being in the master's presence enough, or must you
     look directly at a disciple?*

The master is always within us and always looking at us. As I
have often said, master is not the body. Master is the spirit which
is in the body, and when he connects us with that spirit, with
that word within, he takes his abode within every one of his disciples. Therefore you have to look within to find the real master.
That is why Christ said: When you lift up your eyes to the son
of man,[97] meaning that you have to lift up your consciousness
to the level of the son of man to see him.

A disciple will not be able to take the physical body with
him, nor will the master be able to take his with him. The soul
is the real disciple and the word is the real master. So in order
to see the master, we should try to look within ourselves. We
must raise our level of consciousness to that level where we can
find our real master within, which is the radiant form of the
master. That is real darshan; that is real dhyan. So we should
try to divert our energy within.

*48   Why does the master speak of the master inside as being
     a separate being?*

This is due to modesty. This is humility. No master will say, "I
am the master." This is the humility you will find in the teachings of all the saints. They never like to assert themselves, never
like to say "I." They always say "thou." So it may be confusing
from that point of view.

*49   Is the astral form of the master one astral form that all
     initiates see when they go in? Or is there one astral form
     within each initiate?*

It is very difficult to say what you see. Actually, it is what you know, what you feel, what you realize. When you come back into physical consciousness, you may not be aware whether you have seen the eyes, or the head, or the feet, or anything. Yet you know that you have seen the master. There is nothing physical about it, though we feel, we think we have seen him physically inside; but it is not physical. It is more of a realization. Yet we feel we have seen him and we try to analyze that, but we cannot say that we have seen him; we cannot describe what we have seen. Yet we actually see him. So the master will be the master. There is no question of changing form. But if you say he will be in the same clothes, or the same car, that is just a question of your own individual way of thinking, because we cannot describe what we have actually seen.

What I meant was – the astral form of the master – is there just one astral form for all the initiates?

It is just one power. The sun is one. You have a thousand pitchers of water, and you see the same sun reflected in each one of them. Every pitcher does not reflect a different sun. The sun is the same in all the pitchers – what you see is the reflection. The master is one. The Lord is in every one of us. That does not mean we have many Lords. The Lord is just one. For all disciples, there is just one. He is in every one of us and yet he is separate from every one of us.

50 *Maharaj Ji, I heard that in India people have vans with a big picture of you on the side, and some people here have necklaces with your picture on them. Is this proper, to have something like that? And also, is it all right to bring Sant Mat books with us when we're around people who aren't familiar with the path?*

If it were in my hands, I would like people to keep their pictures in the house only, not hang me in cars or trucks or in trains, or even around their necks. But since people are independent, they do what they feel like doing, so I can't do anything about it. [Laughter] This should not be any ritual or ceremony.

The real image of the master should be within, not outside. These pictures are just to remind us about the master, about his love, his devotion, his teachings. As Christ says: Lift up the son of man. Lift up your consciousness to the level of the son of man.[97] That son of man, the radiant form of the master, is within every one of us, and we have to lift up our consciousness to that level within ourselves. That is the real picture, it seems to me, that you should always take with you.

FINDING THE MASTER WITHIN

51   Master, how can we communicate with the inner master?

When you are sitting before your beloved, how do you communicate? Is it through language? Does your language rightly express your feelings, what your face, your eyes or other things express? There's no language here at all. The soul doesn't need any language to communicate with the Father. It is a language of understanding and love that you automatically develop spiritually when you go to that level of consciousness. In love there is no language at all.

52   Should our love for the inner master be stronger than our love for the outer master?

Your love for the outside master *is* your love for the inner master.

53 *You say that shabd is the real master. When one hears the sound, so compelling, so enchanting, so elevating, one begins to love that shabd. Does that mean, sir, that an initiate directly or indirectly loves his master?*

The purpose of love for the outside master is to lead us to that love and devotion to the shabd within. It's a means to that end. We can always love one who's like us, but we can never love one who's not like us. Who's not like us, we can never love. When we are in the body, we are in love with the body master; when we are at the level of the soul, we love the shabd because that is like us, that is a drop of the ocean. So this love here is automatically transferred to that love and devotion there. And that is our real self. That is why Christ said somewhere that you can kill the body, but you can't kill the soul.[37]

54 *Could you talk about the disciple's relationship with the master?*

What is there to talk about? Who is the disciple and who is the master? Neither the body of the disciple is the disciple, nor the body of the master is the master. The soul is the real disciple, and the shabd or the word is the real master. So the real relationship of the disciple with the master is attaching the soul to the shabd within.

The soul filled with love and devotion for that shabd or spirit within is the real relationship because the disciple will leave the body here and the master will leave the body here. The real guru is the shabd within every one of us, and the real disciple is the soul within every one of us. So unless we go to some flesh where the shabd has taken abode, our soul cannot be brought into touch with the shabd within. We cannot know our real master within unless we go to some flesh where the shabd

41

has taken abode. So that is the necessity of the living master. And after that, we have that living master within ourselves.

As Christ says: I will come unto you.[122] After baptism, after initiation, master comes unto us. That means his radiant form comes unto us, and that is our real master. And the soul is the real disciple. The relationship between that inner master and the soul is that of love and devotion, which ultimately will make the soul merge into the master within. Merging into that divine melody or divine spirit within is the real relationship of the disciple with the master. The physical relationship is only to create that intensity or desire or longing to merge into that divine spirit within. That is the purpose of the physical master. Ultimately the real master is the sound within every one of us. That will pull our soul back to the master, back to the Father.

55   *I can't seem to grasp the idea of you being within me, at the eye centre. I read in all the books that you're there, waiting for me to come to the eye centre, and I would just like to hear you talk about it.*

You see, the difficult thing to understand is when we think that probably the body of the master will come into our body. It's not the body which is the master. It is the shabd, that creative power, which is the master. Our real master is the shabd, which is within every one of us. The inner master projects himself from the shabd when we see the radiant form of the master.

As Christ says, I have taken abode in you – now I am in you and you will be in me, and then both of us will be in the Father.[122] When the master initiates us, he takes abode in us in the sense that our soul is connected with the sound within, and the sound is our master. That creative power which has created the whole creation, that is the real master, and we get connected to that. Whenever we see the radiant form of the master, the master projects his form from the shabd within us. It's not the physical form of the master which has come within us; it is the radiant form of the master, and he projects that form from the shabd. That is our real master.

Even the disciple has to leave the body; even the master has to leave the body. The soul is the real disciple and the shabd is the real master. Once the soul is connected with the shabd, the shabd never leaves the soul until it pulls it to its own level. In that way, master is within every one of us.

And that is what Christ is referring to when he says that unless you drink my blood and eat my flesh, you cannot become part of me.[94] He's referring to the blood of that inner master, the flesh of that inner master. It's not the physical blood or the physical flesh of Christ. The spiritual body of Christ is shabd, the word made flesh – that is the real body of Christ. This reference is given just to make us understand because blood and flesh give life to this body. So similarly, the blood and flesh of the spiritual body of Christ is the shabd. Unless we drink that nectar within us, unless we merge into that shabd within us, we cannot become part of Christ and get everlasting life. That reference is to the mystic within, the master within every one of us.

We all know that God is within every one of us. If God can be within us, then why can't the master be within us? He's a wave of the same ocean. It is that power which is within every one of us, and we look to that power within us. Since we are not acquainted with that power and are only acquainted with the physical body of the master, we get acquainted with that power through the radiant form of the master because we can recognize our master. As Christ said: My sheep know me and I know my sheep. They recognize my whistle and I know them.[104] So the master knows us and we know the master, and then we can recognize him within. And he manifests himself from that power, that shabd within us.

So he says, ultimately you come in me and I come in you.[122] It means that we lose our identity and merge into that being, into that shabd, into that creative power – call it the master, call it God; ultimately it comes to the same thing. We have to merge into that being and lose our own individuality, our own identity.

Our problem is that we think only of the physical form of the master; naturally, he can't come within us. We have no other concept of the master. The real concept is that of shabd, the radiant form. For example, when you sleep, you see so many people within you in your dreams. Where are they? We are in the body when we sleep – we don't leave our bed or bedroom and go out. Yet when we are dreaming, we meet so many people within us – but where are they? We talk to them, we laugh, we enjoy, we weep, we cry – where are they? Where are we? This must be happening at some level of consciousness. So if they can be within us, why can't the master be within us?

56 *Is the physical master aware of all the initiates' inner experiences?*

Our real master is the shabd and nam, and when we are connected with that shabd and nam, it takes care of us. The physical master, of course, is aware of all that. But, you see, it is shabd and nam which is our real master, which takes care of everything.

57 *Will you speak a little bit more about the function of the inner and the outer master?*

We can never know the inner master without the outer master. Unless the outer master's teaching is there, unless his body is there to explain to us about the inner master, we're not even conscious of the inner master. Our inner master is nothing but the Lord. It's just a level of consciousness. And the outer master leads us to the inner master. The inner master has no form. So we cannot love that inner master without the outer master because we can only love that which has form, which we can see, we can touch, we can possess, we can feel. Otherwise, we can never love something abstract. But ultimately they're the same. So the love of this body automatically leads us to the love of the inner master, which leads us to become one with the Lord.

58   *I am a seeker and agree with the principles of Sant Mat. For me, the master is a teacher advanced in spirituality. But to think of him as God in flesh creates problems. Can I ask for initiation when I have this attitude?*

Sister, even if we say our master is God, we are just deceiving ourselves. We want intellectually to think that he is God, but unless we experience him within, we can never say he's God. We can say he's God only intellectually. Sometimes you will say he is, sometimes you will deny it. The main thing is to experience him within. Ultimately, master and God are one. But to begin with, we have to take the master as a teacher, an elder, one who can guide us, one who can help us. And then when you progress within, you may call him anything you feel like. These are just mere words. Even if we say it, we don't mean what we are saying.

59   *Does the soul have a will of its own to come closer to you? And can we make use of this will, or is there not much in it?*

You see, everybody wants to come closer to the master, but that master is within. By doing our meditation, we are becoming closer and closer to the master. Ultimately we merge into the master and we become the master, we become another being;

we lose our own identity and we merge into the identity of the master. As Christ said, you have come in me and I have come in you.[122] That is becoming one with the master, and you can do that only by meditation. One body can't enter into another body. Christ means that the soul has come into the shabd and shabd has taken possession of the soul. The shabd is the real master, and the soul is the real disciple. So this desire to be near the master is the desire of the soul to become one with the shabd within. And the main purpose of meditation is to achieve that. Christ says, the flesh quickens nothing; it is the spirit which matters.[95] It is the shabd which matters.

60 *Maharaj Ji, when several hundred satsangis may be med-itating in different parts of the world, can you actually be in touch with them all, whenever they happen to be meditating or needing help?*

Well, brother, our master is not the flesh. Our master is the word, the shabd, the logos, which is within every one of us, and we are in touch with that. So everybody has his own master within himself. We have to look to him within for guidance. So the question of my looking at anybody doesn't arise. We each have our own master within us and he looks after us.

61 *When we want guidance from within, but we're not able to contact the radiant form, how do we receive this guid-ance? We may feel like we're getting an answer, but is this the mind? How do we know that the master within is guiding us?*

You are only supposed to attend to your meditation. The rest of the guidance automatically will come from within. Your mind automatically will be moulded accordingly; you will think accordingly; you will act accordingly; your whole approach and attitude automatically will change. You don't have to do anything at all.

62 *Did you say that the disciple is always conscious of the guidance of the master?*

A person may not be conscious, but the guidance may still be there in an indirect way. The helping hand is still there. For example, for a disciple who hasn't come to the path yet, a guiding hand is still there, but he's not even conscious of the master's existence.

DARSHAN

63 *Master can you speak to us of darshan, please?*

There are no secrets at all. You see, darshan for a disciple is nothing but his helplessness to look at the master because he's in love with the master. Love compels him to look at his loving face – that is darshan. If you try to calculate its gain – that I have looked for ten minutes, how much have I gained? – then you gain nothing. Because one who is still conscious of darshan gets no benefit from it. Those who are lost in seeing the beloved, who don't know where they are, they have the advantage. So who's to calculate the gains? Why do we look at the face of people whom we love? We always like to gaze at them, talk about them, because we love them, and a lover never thinks what advantage he gains by looking at his beloved's face and by talking to her. His advantage is that he has been able to express his love or experience his love – that is the advantage.

It's the same way in Sant Mat. If we look at the master and try to calculate what advantage we have gained from that, then we have gained nothing. If we love him so much that we cannot help looking at him – it is the helplessness of a disciple to look at the master – then automatically he gets benefits from that.

How important is it for the master to look at the disciple?

Our gazing at the master is more essential. Master is already gazing at us because he is pulling us from within to look at him. He creates a love from within – that is why we become helpless to look at the master. So he has already done his duty; otherwise no disciple would fall in love with the master – unless the master wants him to fall in love with him. He sows the seed, then it sprouts, then it grows; so he is the one who is already pulling us from within. He is the one who is creating his love in our heart, strengthening it, and helping us to grow it. He's doing everything from within. Whether he looks at you from the outside or not doesn't make any difference at all.

64   *After having partaken of the darshan by gazing upon the countenance of the master in person, can one get approximately the same results after he is gone, by gazing upon his picture or photo?*

I will explain to you what the meaning of darshan is. Why do we look at our beloved? We love him. We do not want to take our gaze away from him because we are in love with him. We always want to see and see and see him. If we try to analyze why, perhaps we can find no explanation for it. But we look at him, have his darshan, just to have a mental association, or because it is something we just cannot help. It comes from within ourselves.

The purpose of having the master's darshan is that when we sit in meditation, we should try to be able to contemplate on his form when we have seen it. We should never try to contemplate on a photo. Photos are only for refreshing our memories.

We have photos in our houses of our friends and relatives. We never contemplate on them. When we are moving about and glancing at them, they are just to remind us of that friend or that relative, of our affection for them, of the good deeds that they have done and of our obligations towards them. That is the purpose of our keeping photos in our houses. We do not worship these photos. They just remind us of those individuals and our affection for them. So we generally keep a photo of our master in our house so that it may keep us reminded of him in the sense that we remain reminded of his teachings, of the principles of Sant Mat which he has taught us to follow. These teachings, as given by him, should always remain fresh in our mind. That is the purpose of the photo.

Is there an advantage in looking at the photo?

No. There is absolutely no advantage at all. When I was still a child, the Great Master for a very long time did not permit himself to be photographed, lest people start worshipping his photo, as many people do of the saints who have departed, and start meditating on the pictures, which is against the principles of Sant Mat. The first photo of the Great Master was taken for the public when Dr Brock wrote from America persistently, "I want to see what my master looks like, outside." So the Great Master's first picture was taken just to be sent to America. From there, slowly and slowly, a picture was given to a few others, restricted to only a few people in India. I still remember the occasion. It was a great problem for people to get a copy of that picture because in those days photography was not so common that everybody could bring a camera for a snap. But later, when the Mahattas became satsangis and other professional photographers, too, came in, the master could not conceal himself any longer. Wherever he went, everybody began taking his photograph. But he always insisted that these pictures or photos should never be used for meditating purposes. We should never contemplate on photos.

65 *Master, I was just wondering, how does the physical darshan of the master help a satsangi?*

Darshan is not just seeing the master. Darshan means the help-lessness of the disciple to look at the master.

So it doesn't have anything to do with distance, how close or how far from the master you are?

Even if you are a thousand miles away from him, darshan is something within which is pulling you towards him. Just seeing anybody is not having his darshan.

66 *When one is asking for darshan, is it asking for the Father or is it merely a gift of the Father?*

Real darshan of the Father is within. Darshan is seeing. When you see the Father within, you are having the darshan of the Father within. So we should try to have darshan of the Father within. You ask the Father and he will give you darshan, or work for it and he will give you darshan. Asking or working for it is the same thing.

67 *Master, can satsangis get darshan from their master's successor?*

You see, it will always remind him of his own master. No matter how much he looks at his master's successor, it always strengthens his faith in his own master. There is no betrayal of love. This is just reminding you or reviving your love for your own master.

68   *Is it literally true that if you look at a master, thousands of karmas are washed off?*

You can't calculate it mathematically. The question is, when do we look at the master? How to look at the master? The whole secret is in the word 'look'. When you really love the master, then you look at him. And if you're really full of love and devotion for the master, then of course you inculcate the teachings. You can never have that love and devotion without meditation. Merely looking doesn't help you at all if there's no love and devotion behind it. And love and devotion can only come by meditation – there's no other way. So ultimately, meditation will wash away our karmas. There's no other short cut.

So then meditation is better than looking at the master?

Well, when you are attending to the meditation, you can't help looking at the master. Then meditation is definitely better than looking at the master. But then you can't help looking at the master. Meditation forces you to look at the master. When you fall in love with somebody, you can't help looking at that particular face. You can't say, "I am in love with you, but I don't want to look at you." It's impossible. Both things go together. If you love, you definitely look, you stare, you gaze – you never want to lose sight of your beloved. But what makes you do all that is love. So similarly, if you love the master, you can't help looking at him. And that love can come only by meditation – there's no other way to achieve that love.

69   *What is the difference between outer and inner darshan?*

Inner darshan is permanent. It can stay with you forever. Outer darshan can't. Outer darshan should lead you to reach to that level of consciousness where you can get the inner darshan, which is your constant companion. Outer darshan only fills us with love and devotion so that we can reach to that level where darshan can always be with us. Outer darshan can't remain with us always.

70 *Master, in* Words Divine, *it says, "All bonds of worldly hopes and desires and the pleasures and pains of the past twenty-one lives are sundered at the very moment one gets the darshan of a perfect master." Is that true?*

This is perhaps an extract from some satsang. The main thing is, what is darshan? Darshan doesn't mean physically staring at the master. First we must come to that level where we are in a position to have that darshan. Darshan is of the radiant form of the master. Physically seeing a master isn't darshan. Darshan means the helplessness of the disciple to look at the master. That is darshan – that love, that devotion. That love and devotion only develops when you go to that level of consciousness where you see the radiant form of the master. It is not just physically seeing a man.

71 *In the big satsang in Chattarpur, there are so many people who are sitting very far away from you who have your darshan from a video screen. Someone asked me if the benefit of that darshan is different from the benefit people receive when they are sitting nearer to you.*

Love doesn't diminish if you are far away. Probably the people who are trying to sit very near the dais are trying to count my wrinkles or count the hairs in my beard and nothing else. Otherwise it makes no difference. Darshan means the helplessness of the lover to look at the beloved. It is the pull which is within every one of us. That is darshan. Whether you are sitting near or whether you are sitting far away, it comes to the same thing.

72 *Sometimes, during darshan, we're lucky enough to get eye contact with the master, and we feel very special inside. When you are looking at us in darshan, are you thinking of the person that you are looking at, or is that feeling often in the heart of the disciple?*

The master always looks at every disciple, wherever they may be. He is right within every one of us, and he is always looking at us. Sometimes we are not very happy that he is looking at us.

73 *Maharaj Ji, can you tell us something about darshan?*

Actually, darshan means to be in the company of your love, nothing else. What is darshan? Why do you want to see? Why don't you see everybody? It means you always like to remain in the company of the person you love. That is darshan. What do you get from remaining in the company of the person you love? If you try to analyze what you are getting, you get nothing. But still you don't want to be away from that company. That is darshan. You want to remain in that person's company. I don't think anybody bothers to even think about what benefit he's getting. It's not calculated. You want to be there because you can't help being there. That is real darshan – when you're drawn to somebody's company and you want to remain in that company and you never think about any of the advantages or disadvantages. All that you need is the company. That is darshan. If one tries to calculate, "If I have darshan for ten minutes, I'll get this advantage; or for twenty minutes, I'll get this advantage," then I don't think you've got darshan at all. He's not getting anything. Darshan has to be from within; the pull has to be from within, and the one who's being pulled doesn't calculate these things.

74   *Master, why did the disciples of, say, the Great Master, who saw their master inside, still long to see his physical form? Is that greedy?*

Yes, why not? Because that physical form has pulled them out of the mud, out of the senses, out of the worldly ditches. They love that physical form too. They see him inside, but that doesn't mean that love for the physical form has gone. It is always there. Rather, it increases, it grows.

75   *The disciple is told to look into the master's eyes with as much attention as he can. You have already said that if you love somebody, you're going to look at them anyway. Well, there are some times that the love isn't really felt in the heart but we're advised to go on looking as hard as we can. So when the master's eyes capture the disciple's eyes, what is taking place then?*

I personally think darshan can't be forced. You can't be advised to look at the master if you have no love in you, no love for him at all. There's no question of advising. Darshan can't be forced; love can't be forced on anyone. It has to come from within.

You see, love comes from within; then it grows with the help of darshan. But love must come from within. You can't be advised just to look at the master and then think that will create love – no, love will create the desire for darshan. But for that you won't feel the necessity of darshan at all.

The question is, how do we succeed in visualizing the form of the master? The face of whomever you love automatically appears before you. Without love, I don't think you can succeed in dhyan at all; the mind will always be wandering about. So ultimately you can't eliminate love and have darshan.

76 *I have just been reading* Spiritual Letters, *and Number
    26 says that darshan of the master destroys the karmas
    of the last twenty-one lives. Is this inner darshan or outer
    darshan?*

Sister, real darshan is when you see none else in the world
except your own master – when you have surrendered yourself
to the master, when you have concentrated your love in the one,
withdrawing it from all the other things in the world, and you
become the master, merge into him, lose your own identity,
become another identity. The background of darshan is the love
which pulls you towards the master, which makes you helpless
to be with him and to merge into him and to become one with
him. That is real darshan. And that not only destroys the karmas
of twenty-one lives, but that destroys all the karmas. Because
then nothing stands between us and the master.

77 *Maharaj Ji, could you please explain the difference between
    inner darshan and outer darshan?*

Outer darshan is when you see the master outside and inner
darshan is when you see the master inside. When you see the
radiant form, that is inner darshan, and when you see his physical form, that is outside darshan. But both should create that
faith and love and desire for meditation in you, the desire to be
one with the master within.

> *Does that mean, Master, that once you have contacted
> the radiant form it's no longer necessary to see the outer
> form?*

I think you feel like seeing the outer form more and more.
You see, this love is such that the more you get, the more it
grows – there is no satisfaction in it. It just grows.

You are saying that if I go to the company of a beloved, perhaps then I don't need to see her again. No – then you need to see her more and more. So when we are inside with the master, we also want to be with him outside. And when we are outside with the master, we want to be with him inside. So love for the outer form doesn't diminish at all; rather, it grows.

78 *Perhaps you could explain this passage from* Spiritual Letters *to me. It says: "Even after a hundred years of bhajan, one does not get so purified as by an intense longing for darshan." And it continues: "Bhajan does not purify so soon as does true love for the master and a true longing for his darshan. Rather, satguru himself is Sat Purush."*

You see, longing for darshan will only come out of meditation; otherwise this emotional upheaval doesn't lead you anywhere. Sometimes you feel, sometimes you don't feel. Sometimes in the master's presence you don't want to even talk or look. Sometimes being far away, you are very anxious to go back to the master. It's the meditation that will create real longing in you for darshan, and that darshan definitely is much better than anything else. But it's meditation that will create a desire for that real darshan within.

And then there is darshan and darshan. If you really have darshan of the master, thinking him to be God, then I don't think you need any meditation at all. But I don't think anybody can think like that. One moment we think of him as a human being, the next moment we think of him as less than a human being, and the next moment we think of him as God. So this is just an academic or intellectual way of saying that master is God; but the mind doesn't believe that. If we really believe and really are convinced and really feel he is God, then you don't need any meditation at all. But that's impossible. These are only things to say, but practically, nobody can do that.

79 Master, does the disciple who sees the master frequently in the physical form stand a better chance of seeing you inside than the disciple who is unable to come to the Dera?

No. This has no bearing at all. It depends upon our intensity of love and meditation more than seeing the master physically outside. Physically seeing him also depends on so many factors. Merely seeing him doesn't solve any problem at all. That devotion and depth of meditation naturally can only come when there is devotion and love for the master. If that is there, it is immaterial whether you are here or far away. It doesn't make any difference. If that love is not there, it is immaterial whether you are here or far away. And it also depends upon an individual's load of karma.

80 Master, when does darshan help to clear karma?

You see, mere darshan doesn't clear karmas. The intention, the faith with which you look at the master – that helps you to build your meditation. The faith, the intensity of love which provokes you, pulls you to look at the master – that helps you.

Well, I've been told that a moment's darshan of the master will wipe away twenty-one lives. Is that inner darshan that they're talking about?

But darshan of what intensity? Darshan doesn't mean just looking at the master. Just merely looking at the master is not darshan. The helplessness of a disciple – he cannot help but look at the master, thinking him to be God – that is darshan. Guru Nanak has written somewhere that if you look at your master with faith that he is God – and it is very difficult for us humans to put that faith in anybody, no matter how much we may convince ourselves intellectually – that darshan washes away all your karmas. But it is impossible to be in the flesh and to look at another human and believe him to be God. Intellectually we may be convinced, but the faith which comes from the heart doesn't accept this at all. But darshan helps us to attend to our meditation, to do better dhyan, to hold our attention within; and it strengthens our faith, our love, which is very helpful for meditation.

81 *Maharaj Ji, at satsang in Delhi, before you came on the dais, a gentleman was giving a satsang and in English he mentioned that to have darshan from a satguru wipes away all the karmas of twenty-one lives. He said this in front of 80,000 people.*

Darshan means when you are in love with somebody and you can't help looking at him. You are always happy to look at him and you want to go on looking at him because you are in love with him. Minus love, just looking at a person is no darshan at all. Guru Nanak makes it very clear. He says that when you look at the master, thinking him to be God, believing him to be God, having faith, real faith that he's God, then it is all right, you will have that effect. But if you look at him as a human, then you are just looking at him. It may create that love and devotion someday, but you won't have that effect. So it is your own receptivity, your own approach, your own way of looking at the master that determines darshan's effects.

But is this receptivity due to your inner progress?

Real darshan is when you see the radiant form of the master, because then you get real faith, then you get real devotion, and then that real love develops. Then nobody can pull you back to this creation. There is no question of twenty-one births – even the karmas of a million births can't bring you back to this world.

Generally we don't want to work hard to reach that stage or level of consciousness where real darshan is, but we want to have that advantage outside. Real darshan is inside. As Christ also explained somewhere in the Bible: When I am in the body, you have all sorts of questions, all sorts of doubts, but when I come again and you see me, then you will have no questions, no doubts.[127] That seeing is within. He says, now when you ask me a question, I just put you off with one excuse or another. But when you see me within, I will not put you off – I'll grant what you want, but then you'll want nothing but love and devotion. You will have no worldly desires to ask for. You will just want him. You will be so absorbed, you won't be conscious of anything else in this world.

That is real darshan. And that darshan washes all your sins and makes you one with the Lord. Mystics always refer to that kind of darshan, but we always like to interpret from the outside, for our own advantage.

82   *Master, in regard to darshan, I have a confusion: It seems that two images come to mind when I'm in your presence. One is that the master is the sun and his presence radiates in all directions, so regardless of where you sit before him, or whether he's looking at you or not, you are receiving his darshan. But then there's the other longing that you should feel, and that is to receive the gaze of the master, to have the master look into the eyes of the disciple. Is there a difference between these two feelings of darshan?*

I think that feeling you should be able to gauge. It depends upon you, what you feel when you are in the presence or when you're a little away. It's not for me to tell you what you feel.

Is it important that the master see the disciple?

It is for them to know – whatever they prefer.

I perceive that all disciples prefer to have the gaze of the master, but is it important whether the master looks at us or not?

You see, the lover never calculates what he gains or doesn't gain. He only can express his helplessness to look at the object of his love. He doesn't want any gain. If he's calculating gain out of love, then he's not a lover at all. It is immaterial for him whether the object of his love looks at him or not. He's only interested in looking.

Can you remember times when you were sitting in satsang with Great Master, when he was giving darshan?

Sister, I'm remembering only that. I don't remember this at all. I live only with that, I don't live with this present at all.

SEPARATION AND LONGING

83 *Master, we wait so long to come to the Dera, and then when we're here, we spend a lot of time waiting to see you. And during our meditation we're always waiting to see you, and the master is also always waiting for us at the third eye. Why is there all this waiting?*

Why all this waiting? Because we are separated. We are separated from our focus. We are not at the door of our house, and the master's there at the door of our house, so we are waiting to go to the door. Let us go to the door of the house; then there will be no more waiting.

84 *Maharaj Ji, when you leave this country, we are all going to suffer a devastating loss. Can you give us any type of*

*first aid or comfort to help us through that time when
you leave?*

Brother, as I said yesterday, are you sure I am leaving?
[Laughter]

*I know that you will always be with us, but I mean your
physical presence?*

Brother, the more we miss anyone, the nearer we are to the
one we are missing. We only depart to meet. We are never
separated.

85 *In* Spiritual Letters, *Baba Jaimal Singh tells the Great
Master: "Therefore to settle his worldly account, the
perfect master separates a loving disciple from him physically, but never from the shabd." Does this mean that it
is easier to settle our karmic accounts when we are physically separated from the master?*

You see, you get an opportunity to gauge your love and devotion
when you are engrossed in worldly activities, worldly possessions, worldly love. You know then in that atmosphere whether
one really misses the master or one does not. In the presence
of the master, we always feel that we love him because there is
nothing to pull us aside and we are charged with that love and
devotion. But how much depth does it have? We can only know
when we are separated from him, when we are absolutely occupied with worldly activities and worldly attachments, if we still
miss him, if we still have the same love and devotion for him.
If we are still yearning for his physical form, then we can know
we really love him. If out of sight we forget him, then you can
imagine the depth of our love. That is what Baba Ji is saying to
Maharaj Ji: You will know how much you love me when you
are away from me.

86   When do the yearnings and the longings and the pangs
of loving the master cease? And when does it become
pure joy? Is it also in the third stage?

I think this longing is also a joy. No lover would like to get
rid of it. This pain, the pangs of love, the separation of a lover
from the beloved – he doesn't want to get rid of that at all. Of
course, as long as the separation is there, then this longing is
there. When it becomes a union, then who's to long and who's
to love? Because then 'you' cease to exist. You lose your identity.
You merge into the other being. 'You' are no more. Then who's
to love and who's to long? The longing is only as long as the veil
of separation is there. But in spite of that, no lover would want
to get rid of this pain.

Christ gives a very beautiful example. He says that a
woman, when she delivers a child, has to go through lot of
pain.[127] But if you tell her not to try to have a child because it is so
painful, she will never listen to you. She knows that joy is waiting for her after the pain. After she delivers the child, she's the
happiest person in the world. Before she can get that joy, she has
to go through that pain. And she doesn't mind the pain because
she looks to the joy ahead. So similarly, a lover never minds the
pain at all. He's looking toward the union ahead. A woman is
never frightened of the pain of delivering a child – she's prepared
to face it. Similarly, the lover doesn't mind this pain of separation at all because he's looking forward to the union.

87   Master, what is meant when people say that Sant Mat is
like walking on the edge of a sword?

You always live in agony of separation because you're so filled
with love and devotion. But you love that agony – you don't want
to part with that. But still, it's not a very pleasant feeling.

*88   In 1976 – I believe I have the words close to what you
said – you finished an evening meeting by saying, "I
think the real lovers are those that appreciate the separation more than the union." Could you please comment
on that?*

Mira Bai was in love with her guru. Somebody asked Mira, why
don't you forget him? You are so miserable and so unhappy in
separation. She said: Don't take this love from me. Take anything from me, but don't take my love for my guru. I appreciate
this separation more than giving it up.

There is a pleasure in that love, and at no cost would the
lover like to be out of that pain of separation. He wants to
consume himself in that separation of love. He wants to live in
that separation, he wants to be consumed in that separation.
He does not want to get rid of that. For the lover, separation
and union are the same thing. Lovers are in love with their love.
They are not in love with any personality. They are happy in
their pangs of love.

At least you know when you are separated how much depth
your love has. Is it only when you are looking at your beloved that
you feel love? Or even in separation do you have the same feeling,
or do you forget – out of sight is out of mind? Mira knows there
is a pleasure in her pain; she bases her whole pleasure on the foundation of that pain. So sometimes we also have to feel separation.

Christ said, blessed are those who mourn, for they shall get
comfort.[8] Those who are missing him, those who are yearning
for him, where is the union? They try to go back to the Father,
but at this stage they are separated. He said the blessed ones are
those who are yearning for him, who are in love with him, who
are consumed in his love. When gold is made, the fire burns
out all the residue and gold comes out of it. The metal has to go
through the heat of that fire to become gold. So it's not essential

that there's always a union in love. Separation has its own part to play. No union is complete without separation.

89   Sir, this pain of separation, the pain that drives Mira, was it a real pain or only a way of expressing it in poetry?

This real pain never comes unless love is there. With the mystics, their heart speaks. It is not the tongue that speaks, it is not the pen that writes; it is the heart that speaks, it is the heart that writes. And the mystics just express all that.

Without going through the pain, nobody knows the pain. And that pain can be experienced only with the Lord's grace. When he pulls from within, then this is what happens – what Mira has written. Unless he pulls from within, there is no pain.

90   Maharaj Ji, will you tell us about the value of separation between the disciple and the master?

The idea is that we are in love with the master and we can't live without him. We want to be with him. Since physically we cannot be with him – we have been separated by circumstances – then what is the alternative way to be with him? To find him within. If we turn our attention within to search for him, turn our attention to our meditation to seek him within, then that separation definitely helps. If that separation makes us forget about the master, takes us away to the senses, to the world – worldly ambitions, worldly objects – then that separation doesn't help at all. If the love is intense, and we are detached from everything else, and we cannot find him outside, then we have to seek him within. There's no other way. Then separation is helpful because by following the path we get everlasting association with the master, internal association with the master. If separation makes us forget the teachings, forget the master, and takes us away from the path, then separation doesn't help.

91 *Maharaj Ji, my question is about the inside and the outside master. I understand that your message is to contact the inner master, and that the outside and inside master are ultimately one and the same. My problem is that I start loving you more and more, including your personality. And my reaction to that brings me out of balance because I cannot help longing for personal attention. I'm not ungrateful, but it's still two powers at once that pull, and on the other hand, I'm just trying to be grateful.*

Sister, this love for the body master should ultimately lead us to our inner master. We should channel that love towards meditation and try to reach where we can always be together with our own master. These emotions should not lead us outside; they should lead us inside. This devotion should help us achieve our object within ourselves, not somewhere outside.

92 *Maharaj Ji, there are two quotations from* Spiritual Letters *that I would like to ask about. The first is, "True longing for darshan is the principal means of God-realization," and the next is, "Even after a hundred years of bhajan, one does not get so purified as by intense longing for darshan, provided that longing is real and true." My question is, does this mean inner or outer physical darshan, and how is this true longing engendered?*

If you have longing for the outer darshan, this will lead you ultimately to longing for the inner darshan. Christ said, they are the blessed ones who mourn, for they will be comforted.[8] They are the fortunate ones who mourn, who feel the separation from the Father and who are longing to become one with him. Mourning is when we can't face the separation. Then we mourn and cry. So they are the fortunate ones who have real longing, the urge to go back to the Father. They will be comforted, ultimately; they will be able to reach back to the Father.

And about outer darshan and inner darshan, Christ has referred to that in an indirect way when he says, it is expedient, it is in your interest, that I leave you now, and then I'll be able to send you the Comforter.[126] How can it be in the interest of a disciple for the master to leave him physically? Because by his physical presence he creates love and devotion in the heart of the disciple, but he cannot physically stay here forever. So he separates himself from the disciple. Because of that love and devotion which he has been able to build in the disciple's heart, ultimately the disciple has no option but to find his master within. He will put all his devotion and longing towards finding the master within, and ultimately he will reach the goal.

So it is in the interest of the disciple that the master should leave him because physically the disciple no doubt is in love – he is running about after the master – but how long can he keep hold of the physical form? When he wants to be with the master, he has no option but to turn within and find him there. So this outer form is a means to that end. The purpose of the physical presence is to create that love and devotion in us and ultimately to convert it into the real inner darshan, which is the real love and real devotion. So that is what Baba Ji [Baba Jaimal Singh] was referring to.

93   *Master, you say we can make more progress now, when the master is in the physical form, because he pushes from outside and pulls from within. And somewhere it*

*says that when the master leaves the body, he will be able
to pull us more strongly from within.*

Sister, you are confusing two things. When I said that we can
make the most progress while living in the flesh, I meant that
as a human being we can make more progress now than in the
inner stages after death. Another point that Christ also explains
is when he says, it is expedient for you now that I leave.[126] He
says: My reason for coming into the flesh was to fill you with
love and devotion for the Father through your love for me. I have
told you the way, the path, and now you are so much attached
to my physical form that you are not attending to the holy ghost
within. You are not trying to reach my radiant form within
yourself because you have become so attached to me outside.
So it is in your interest that I leave this flesh now, because if you
can't live without me, naturally you will turn all your attention
inside to reach my radiant form within yourself. Then you will
never be deprived of that.

The physical body of the master has a certain part to play,
a certain function to perform. As Christ said, you know now
where I am going,[118] you know how to reach me; so unless you
turn your energy within, you will never be able to reach your
destination because you will always be running after me outside.
It is in your interest to find me within. That is what he is trying
to explain there.

94   *Master, is the desire and longing for the master the same
as darshan?*

Yes. Even if you don't get the opportunity to see the master but
the real longing and desire is there to see him, you will get the
same effect. Read Baba Jaimal Singh's letter in *Spiritual Letters*,
written to the Great Master. Maharaj Ji [Maharaj Sawan Singh]

had written that he was longing to see Baba Ji [Baba Jaimal Singh]. Baba Ji wrote back that the desire and longing which he was feeling was the same as if he had already seen him.

Ultimately what counts is the love. You may not have that longing even in the presence of the master – the darshan becomes just mechanical, meaningless. And you may have a very deep longing and desire to be with him even when you are a thousand miles away from him – that may have much more value. So it is the love which counts. The Western outlook of calculating everything – calculating the advantage of every-thing – doesn't count in Sant Mat. The lover never calculates the advantage of his love. He knows how to love; he doesn't bother about anything else at all – and that's natural.

So Sant Mat is nothing but love. Meditation creates that love; darshan creates that love. All these things which create love ultimately lead us back to the Father. And what is love? Losing your own identity and merging into another being is love. To lose your own identity, your individuality, to become another being – that is love. 'You' don't exist anymore. Only the beloved exists.

Kabir says very beautifully somewhere, when I existed and you existed, I never knew you. Now only you exist and I don't exist at all. Because you lose your own identity. Guru Nanak has used the words "to die in shabd." When we die, we lose our own identity, we merge into another being and we are no more. In every aspect, physically and in every way, we are no more. That is death. So he says, when you die into the shabd, you have merged yourself completely into the shabd – you don't exist anymore.* That is true love. Many, many mystics have used these same words.

Sabad marai man nirmal santoh. Guru Amardas, Adi Granth, M3, p. 910.

This death is not physical death. It is eliminating your ego, your I-ness. You do what pleases your beloved; you never do what displeases him. You dance to the tune of your beloved. 'You' don't exist anymore at all. And that is why we say, God is love and love is God. Ultimately our love helps us to merge into the Lord and to lose our identity and individuality.

95 *We come here and fall so much in love with the body master, and then we have to go back to our own countries after a while. Is that where we get the longing for the meditation, for the master?*

The object of the body master is to fill us with love and devotion for the Father, to put us on the path, to create that deep longing to become one with the master. Naturally when the physical master is there, we're running about, we feel contented, we feel happy. But this is a means to achieve something much higher. Sometimes it is in our interest that we are away from the master. Since we can't find him outside, we have no other option but to find him within.

As Christ said: You know the path, you know the way, and I'll again come unto you.[118] After a little while I'll come again, but I'm not really going anywhere at all – I am within you. Seek me within, and I'll come unto you again.[121] Sometimes it is in our interest that we are kept away because the body master has performed its function. Now the inner master also has to pull us to its own level. History tells us that many times our Sikh gurus have kept their disciples away from them for many years. It was no fault of theirs, but there was some inner divine design to fill them with more longing, more love, more devotion – to prepare them for something much higher. Bulleh Shah was not allowed to come to his master for I don't know how many years.

96   *Maharaj Ji, should all devotees of the master experience the very painful longing for the master? Will we as disciples all experience this longing in this lifetime, in the physical body?*

I don't know what you mean by longing, sister. The more time we devote to meditation, the more we strengthen our love, grow our love, become rich in devotion. I personally think the more time given to meditation, the more pain of separation you feel. And the more pain of separation you feel, the more progress you make within because ultimately this pain of separation will make you one with the Being, with the Lord. If you are not thirsty, you won't run after the water at all. The more thirsty you feel, the more you will be in search of water to drink. So this meditation also creates that pain, the pain of separation. That is why Christ said, blessed are those who mourn, for they shall get rest.[8] Those who mourn, those who feel the separation of the Father, they are the blessed people, they are the fortunate ones. They will get rest from the transmigration of the soul, from shifting from body to body, from house to house. They are the blessed people, those who feel that pain of separation. And that pain becomes more intense with meditation.

97   *Master, if we cry within, will there be no emotional tears on the outside?*

Our cry for the Father doesn't need tears outside at all. The heart cries. Your eyes may betray you sometimes, but your heart cries tears from the heart.

98   *I've heard somewhere that a genuine tear shed with longing for the master is worth many, many years of longing and meditation. How can we bring that about?*

Well, brother, how do genuine tears come? Not by putting any chemical in the eyes. Those tears come with some longing in the heart, when your heart is full with devotion, full with love. When yearning is there to become one with the beloved, naturally the tears come. Tears don't come without any longing or devotion, and that comes through meditation. That love and devotion definitely brings tears to our eyes sometimes. That's all part of meditation. Without meditation, that much longing doesn't come, that devotion doesn't come. Meditation fills you with that devotion and longing, which ultimately may bring tears – tears of separation, tears of joy even.

99 *Master, sometimes when I look at you – and I don't know if this is true for other people – I find that I'd like to walk up to you and touch your hand and touch your feet, but I won't allow myself to do this. I feel kind of frustrated by it. I don't want it to stand in my way as far as spiritual progress. I was wondering what a person could do to transform that feeling.*

Well, brother, try to channel that desire into meditation. Divert that desire towards meditation, and try to hold master's hand all of the twenty-four hours within yourself. Nobody will disturb you. No sevadar will say anything to you! Just be with him. Then, only you and he should exist within you. You will have him all to yourself. That is the only way, the only solution. You must divert all that love, affection and devotion towards meditation.

100 *Father, is it wrong to be attached to the physical form of the master?*

I don't think you can help having an attachment to the physical form of the master. If you love the teachings, naturally you love

71

the person giving you the teachings. But ultimately, as Christ says in Saint John, it is in your best interest that I leave you.[126] Now you are running after my physical form; you're not trying to give your attention to the holy word within yourself. When you are no longer able to find me physically, the only way to find me will be within yourself. He says, you know the path, you know the way.[118]

So this physical attachment is only meant for one purpose: to create in you a longing to remain with the master. Our real master is within ourselves. So we should try to use this love and devotion within ourselves to find the radiant form of the master. If from that point of view we are attached to the physical form of the master, then of course we gain everything. But if we do not direct this love toward the form within ourselves, then we are not making the best use of our time.

101 *Maharaj Ji, you have often told us to be happy on the path, and yet many of us, particularly here at the Dera, find our-selves so far from the ideal that we are a little discontented, impatient or even feeling a little guilty. What should our attitude be when we find ourselves so faltering, so slow?*

When you are in love with the Father, you are happy even in suf-fering, even in separation. You wouldn't want to get rid of that separation from the Father. Love for the Father doesn't bring happiness from the worldly point of view – it brings suffering, it brings sacrifices. Without sacrifices and suffering, there can be no love at all. But then you are so much in love with that suffering that you wouldn't want to part with it or with the feeling of love and devotion for the Father. There is a certain pleasure in that pain, too. So from that point of view, you can't become happy. But you can be happy in the sense that nothing that happens in the world affects you.

You should have a relaxed mind at the time of your meditation, not be worried about the worldly ups and downs. Attend to meditation with a relaxed mind, forgetting about worldly problems. But the more you grow in love, I think the more you grow in suffering. But then you are happy in that suffering – you wouldn't want to part with it. You read in the history of the mystics that they never deviated from their love for the Lord. They gave their lives. They were hanged, crucified, burned alive, put on hot iron pans, but they never left the devotion and love of the Lord. And they were never bothered by that type of suffering at all. They were happy in that suffering because they wanted to live in the will of the Father. Christ, in the end, said: Thy will be done.[68]

I personally feel that no lover is happy, and no lover is contented with how much love he may get from the beloved. Otherwise he is not a lover. However much the beloved may give to the lover, the lover is never contented, never feels that he has received sufficient love. This is the devotee of the Lord. The more he gives, the more we want. We are never contented with his love and devotion, however much grace he may give us. So this type of discontent will continue for those who are on the path, who are trying to reach him.

102 Why is love sometimes painful? Why can we be happy in the presence of the beloved, but yet there are tears?

Well, sister, love is painful because it has separation in it; it wants to merge. Unless it becomes another being, it is separated, and separation is always painful; so love is painful. When we merge back into the Father, then there's no pain at all. Before that, we have to go through that pain – we can't help it. The more we feel the pull within, the more painful it becomes because we become more anxious, more anxious and more anxious to become one with him.

The more we love him, the more the feeling of becoming one with him is growing. We become more anxious to become one with him, so naturally it will be more painful. Its blessing is also there, peace is also there, happiness is also there in the presence of the beloved. This is a very strange feeling. It is like the example of a lady delivering a child. She has to go through the pain of the delivery, but then she's the happiest woman in the world after the child is born. She can't avoid that pain; that's a part of what she has to go through. Similarly, we have to go through that pain, but it is nothing compared to what we are going to achieve. Even when we feel the pain, would we like to get rid of that love? We would never want to get rid of that love. Separation is painful. If anybody advises you to forget, what is the sense of that? You will never leave it. There is also some satisfaction and pleasure within at the base of that pain. So it is a mixed feeling. The more we grow in love, sometimes the more separation we feel and the more anxious we are to become one with him.

103 *I'd like to discuss the theme of separation. There are many forms of the pain of separation. There's loneliness, lonesomeness, there's even jealousy, or the pain of falling in love. This has been coming to the surface with me for many years. How can we alleviate those pains? Once those pains attack you, there's no way of doing any meditation or having any concentration.*

Brother, definitely there's great pain even in jealousy. In jealousy there's a sense of possession, when we want to possess and do not want another person to possess. So there is selfishness in that love. This is not love. Love is giving, not taking. Love is submission, not making another person submit to your whims. The pleasure lies in giving, in submitting, rather than possessing anything. It is a pleasure to be possessed rather than to possess. So love for the Lord is just submission, giving, merging into him. There's no sense of possessing him, so there's no jealousy in love for the Lord. Rather, fellow beings become closer to us when we love the Lord. When we find somebody loving the Lord, they become much closer to us than our own kith and kin because there is no jealousy in this love, because we are all giving and submitting. We're not trying to possess him, we're trying to be possessed by him. So there's a difference between worldly love and love for the Lord.

Of course, the pain of separation is always there, but there's a certain pleasure in that pain which we would not want to part with at any cost. That is our life – that pain, that pleasure of separation. We exist on that pain of separation and would not want to part with it, though it sometimes looks torturous.

Right now, I'm going through the pains of rejection [for initiation] because of my age, and it's a very, very real pain. It's hard to explain, but there is a definite separation between youth and being a senior, and that separation is brought to the foreground all the time.

Brother, there's no rejection in love for the master or love for the Lord; there's always acceptance in it. Our love is never rejected. Actually, he's the one who is pulling us from inside and he's the one who is making us receptive to that pull. He is the doer. He is the puller. We feel that we love when actually he is the one who is loving us, who is pulling us, who is creating that feeling of separation in us.

104 *Master, when the soul evolves back to the Lord, would he then make clear his reason for sending that soul into the creation?*

These questions only arise as long as we feel separate from the Father. When our individuality is gone, when we don't exist anymore and only he exists, then who's to ask? You see, this love which the Lord gives us burns and consumes all the impurities and make us pure gold. But he gives that love. Nobody else can give you that love, which burns away all our impurities, all our karmas, and makes the soul shine. He gives that love and he gives it from within – that is not in your hands at all. You don't get that with intellect. You can't search for that. You just get it by his grace. And then automatically these impurities are burnt, are consumed. Gold becomes pure when it passes through fire. All impurities are burned. So, similarly, we have to pass through that fire of love which burns all our impurities and makes us pure. He gives that fire of love. We can't get it by our own effort at all. No matter how much credit we may take, it's all his gift, and he has his own ways and means of giving.

105   *Can we work for those wages, Maharaj Ji, for the Lord's love?*

Again you're thinking about wages! A lover is never tired of living in separation from the beloved. Looking at the face of his beloved, he never thinks about any wages. Nor is he worried about any sacrifices he has to make or what torture he has to go through in his love. If anybody would try to deprive the lover of his love, he would react. In spite of his suffering, he would never want to forget his lover. That is love and that should be our attitude towards meditation.

106   *When you feel a great separation, sometimes it's almost unbearable, but yet you don't want to get rid of it. Where does comfort come from? When that comfort comes and*

you feel a sort of a peace, does that mean that the master has withdrawn that pain?

Sister, sometimes separation sharpens our love. And then it creates more and more intensity in us, a more intense desire to become one with the other being. Comfort is always there. It is only in his lap. When we feel the pain of separation, then we appreciate the unity, the union. Without feeling that pain of separation, we do not appreciate the unity.

107 Master, is there anything beyond longing?

Does a seeker need anything else beyond longing? If he has longing, a desire to go back to the Father, love for the Father, longing for the Father, yearning for the Father, is there anything else to be done? But, you see, we only have that longing intellectually. We are actually longing for worldly possessions, worldly things, worldly achievements. Yet we think that we have longing for the Father. We don't have any longing for the Father at all. If we are longing for the Father, then we can't be longing for anything in the world. When we are attached to him, then we are not attached to this creation. If you get that bliss and boon from the Father – the longing to become one with him – then all desires leave you. Your mind is not attached to the creation then. That is why Christ said: Blessed are those who mourn, for they shall get rest.[8] Those who feel the separation from the Father, who have longing and intense desire to become one with him, they are the blessed ones, the fortunate ones, because ultimately they will get rest in his lap.

Longing will eliminate your ego and make you merge into the Father. But this intense longing doesn't come without shabd. The mind refuses to leave the senses unless it has a better taste, and that better taste is that of shabd, that divine melody within. Only when the mind is attached to that does it leave the longing for the world, not otherwise. So without meditation you cannot build that longing for the Father. Intellectually sometimes we feel we are in love with the Father, and other times we feel we are absolutely possessed by the world, obsessed by the world. So real detachment only comes by attachment to the shabd, not otherwise.

108 Maharaj Ji, how can we be cheerful in our separation?

If one is filled with love and devotion for the Father and he wants to become one with the Father, he is the happiest person because it's a special blessing of the Father that he's pulling him from within. Unless we are thirsty, we will never try to search for water. Only a thirsty man is running about to find a well – if you are not thirsty, you don't bother about water. Unless the Father gives us that feeling of separation, that longing, how can we become one with him? So that is a rare blessing. If he is kind enough to give us that separation and that longing, he's also kind enough to make us one with him. It means he has not forgotten us, that he is pulling us from within. And if he is pulling us from within, then he will also make us one with him.

RUNNING AFTER THE MASTER

109 We're told that the more spiritually advanced you become, the more longing you have to see the physical master. And I was wondering, why is this so?

You want to remain disciplined, but that doesn't mean you have no love. Running after the master doesn't show any love at all. Love is always within. When you try to dramatize your love, you lose its depth. You have to digest that love within. You have that love within, but the moment you try to dramatize it, you lose its depth.

110 *Does it displease the master when we run after his physical form instead of letting the inner master run after us?*

If everybody starts running after the master, where will master hide? Where will he go? We have to remain in discipline. This outside running doesn't lead us anywhere at all. We should try to run within and be with the master always, so that he may not be able to hide anywhere. We must search within. Outside, we can get help, we can get strength from each other. But this outside running doesn't lead us anywhere at all.

The real love and devotion should all be diverted within, towards the meditation. That is really loving the master. Running after him is not loving the master at all. We can't control our emotions and we try to copy each other. But we should try to divert all this energy within towards the real form of the master. How long will you go on running outside?

But when I am not physically with you, you will divert your energy within, and once you get to my radiant form, then I will never be able to go away from you; I will always be with you. The purpose of the physical form is to fill us with love and devotion for the Father. But then we have to use that love and devotion to reach the Father, not waste it. And for reaching the Father, we have to search for him within, not anywhere outside. So we should try to run within rather than outside.

111 *When disciples say they want to follow the master everywhere he goes, what do they mean?*

To follow the master means to follow his teachings, to live the Sant Mat way of life, to attend to meditation, to withdraw from the sense pleasures. Following him does not mean running after him physically. That is why Christ said: If you simply claim that you are my disciple and I am your master, but you do not follow my teachings, you will not be able to go back to the Father.[32] To withdraw to the eye centre and be one with the spirit within – that is following the master, not running after him outside.

112 I think this is the only spiritual path that teaches us how to find God within ourselves, rather than emphasizing rituals and ceremonies.

There should be absolutely no rituals and no ceremony. People think that by running after me or by visiting [the Dera] many times or by saying "Radha Soami," they'll get some benefit. This is nothing but their own mental deception. What do they get out of these things – touching my hand or touching my clothes or putting dust on their forehead? Everything we get is from meditation or from seva or satsang. These are the three things that help us in our spiritual development, and we should try to concentrate on only these three things. Either we should be attentive in satsang, or we should be doing some seva or we should be in meditation. These are the means for our spiritual development. But the mind always likes to run outside performing rituals and ceremonies and doing all these things outside. It's just a waste of energy.

PARSHAD

113 I have a question about parshad. To me parshad seems more like a religious ritual rather than pertaining to the science of the soul. So I was wondering if you could explain it a little better to me, please.

Parshad is something personal. It should remind us of the teachings, of the master. It should create love and devotion. It's a link between the disciple and the master. If we eat parshad, we always think of the master, of the teachings. From that point of view, it is very beneficial. But if you just take it as a ritual – that perhaps it will have some medicinal effect or some spiritual effect because you are eating it – then you are deceiving yourself. It depends on with what attitude you take the parshad. Your attitude helps. We often exchange gifts with our friends. You don't value the gifts according to their price. You value them according to the love with which they are given to you because the gift reminds you of the giver, his qualities, his friendship, his love, his concern about your welfare. So that reminder of his love, of his qualities, of his concern about you – that matters, not the gift itself.

114 What is the value of parshad to a satsangi, a seeker or to a relative who is not interested in Sant Mat?

Parshad should remind us of the teachings of the master, the love of the master, the devotion of the master. It should refresh in us the teachings when we eat it. You give a gift to your friends. What is the value of a gift? The value cannot be measured in money. Its value is that it reminds you of your friends, of your relations, of your love. Similarly, when we take parshad as a gift from the Father, as a gift from the master, it should remind us of the master, the teachings, love and devotion for the Father, and it should give us the strength to follow the teachings, live in the teachings and devote ourselves to our meditation. Then parshad has advantages.

If you just take it as a candy or a sweet, then it is just a sweet and nothing else. So you have to take it with faith, and that faith helps you to live in the teachings. And if you give it to relatives, it is meaningless to them because they will not have that faith.

So it will just be candy for them. Actually, parshad is meant for those to whom it is given. It is not given to be distributed to others. It is a personal treasure which we should always try to cherish as personal property.

Master, is parshad communion?

That was the basic concept of communion.

115 *Master, the parshad that you gave us in an interview, are we permitted to give that or share that with our family?*

Actually, it is personal. It is for the individual to decide what he wants to do with it. Generally, it reminds you of the person who gave it to you. It is between the one who takes it and the one who gives it. Its value is in their contact – the parshad reminds us of that contact. You present a flower to your beloved. What is particular in that flower which is not in the rose garden? The whole garden is full of flowers, but why does that flower become precious for you? Because it is between the giver and the one to whom it is given. That contact is beautiful. The contact is more important than the flowers. You can always get flowers from any garden.

116 *What happens when we bring you a shawl or some object to have you bless it?*

Just attend to your meditation. That purifies the mind; that does everything. You can't find any short cut by wearing a blessed shawl or anything, but meditation makes everything blessed. And there cannot be better parshad than the initiation a disciple gets. That is why Christ said that it's like a new birth. Just as a child grows under the care and protection of the parents after its birth, a disciple grows under the care and protection of the master. There's a new birth for the disciple. And that is the real parshad, the real grace. All other things are a means towards that protection, towards the growth of the disciple.

117 Master, could you please tell us about parshad? How should we take it – should we eat it all at once?

Yes, you can eat it all at once if it is sweet; otherwise you can eat it slowly.

Parshad is something which you take with devotion, with faith, with love. Whether you eat it every day, or whether you eat it all in one day, there's no chemical effect in it. The effect is already in you.

118 If you mix parshad with what isn't parshad, does the other food become parshad also?

You mean, if there's a little parshad and then you mix more candy with it, does it all become parshad?

It is personal, you see. Actually when parshad is given, it is not the candy which is the parshad, it is the master and the disciple. It is the master's intention in giving the parshad that makes it parshad for the disciple. It is for the advantage of the disciple. The advantage is given to the disciple, and the master's good wishes are the parshad for the disciple. The candy is just a means. You can't take the good wishes in proxy for someone else. It is just personal for the people to whom it is given. But anything which reminds you of the master and the teachings is good. Nothing is required for the giving of parshad. Parshad doesn't pass through to the disciple by eating it; it passes through by other means.

119 If you have the parshad and you mix it with other food, does that turn everything into parshad?

Not everything. That part which is the parshad remains the parshad.

120 *I have some parshad at home that I asked a friend to ask you to bless and to bring to me, and he did. Now a little of that goes in my salt box and a little of my salt goes in everything that I cook all day, and I've gone on believing that makes everything blessed. But people have told me that the blessing doesn't get carried on into other things, and other people have said that unless the parshad is given by the master without the recipient asking for it, it isn't parshad at all. Could you put me right, please?*

Any moment when we think about the Father, when we think about the master, when we think about the Lord, that is a blessed moment. That makes it worth living in this creation. All others are useless moments. Whatever time we devote to our meditation, whatever thoughts we devote to the Father, they are the blessed moments; that is the blessed time. Only that will be to our credit. All other times and thoughts are pulling you back to this creation. Only this thought and this time will help you to go back to the Father. So that moment becomes blessed, that time becomes blessed, those things become blessed which remind you of the Lord and of your love and devotion for the Father. So if that parshad or anything reminds you of the love and devotion for the Father, then automatically everything is blessed.

121 *Would you please explain to us the purpose and the significance of parshad?*

Parshad generally is very sweet – you must have noticed that. Parshad should remind us of the teachings, the master. Parshad is not something that you eat and then you have some spiritual experiences within. That's a wrong concept. It should remind us about the Father, about our master, about the teachings and provoke us to do our meditation. That is the advantage of parshad.

If you love somebody and that person gives you a present, what is the advantage of that present? If a small handkerchief is given to you, what is the advantage of that? You can buy a hundred and one in the market. Why is that special to you? You love the person who gave it to you. It reminds you of the love of that person, about his good feeling for you, and you're so happy to have it. You can buy the same thing from the market, but you won't be as happy to have it. Why? The base of it is love. One handkerchief was given to you by someone you love, who loves you, so it becomes priceless for you. It's the same with parshad. Otherwise there's no dearth of candy anywhere.

122   *Is there anything spiritual about eating parshad or wearing blessed clothing?*

There is no spirituality in that at all. We generate spirituality only by meditation. By merely eating parshad, you don't become spiritual at all. That is a wrong concept. By wearing certain blessed clothes, you don't become something better. It just reminds you of your master, of his teachings, of his love, which should lead you towards meditation. It can become a strong means to achieve a certain end. But parshad is not an end by itself. The concept that if I eat parshad I'll become very pure, very noble, is wrong. It will remind you of the teachings, of your master, of his love, of that atmosphere. And it should lead you towards meditation, to make you a better human. That advantage will be there. We often have pictures of our beloved in our home, and we keep their gifts with us, but those are not a substitute for the beloved. They just remind us of our beloved.

So these things should remind us of the master, but they cannot substitute for the master.

AWARENESS OF HIS PRESENCE

123   Master, the happiness of feeling the presence of the master when you're back at home or wherever you are, is that just purely his grace and his will, or is it something that we do, maybe some way we act or think that makes that presence come or go?

We can shut everybody out, but we can't shut him out. The Lord is everywhere. We can't deceive him. We can't shut him out. He is always watching us, whether we are conscious of it or not. If we could realize this simple spiritual truth – that here is one Lord; he is within every one of us and the path leading back to him also is within; and whatever we do, we are being watched and have to account for that to him – I think everybody's life would change in a second. We believe in all these things; we say all this, but somehow it doesn't impress us. Still our mind deceives us. If a five-year-old child is standing before us, we wouldn't do anything bad. But what don't we do in his presence? He is not sleeping when nations are fighting with each other and people are cutting each other's throats. He is not hiding anywhere. He is within them. He is seeing, watching, and yet we do all this. We say these things intellectually, but they don't create any impact on our mind.

124   Master, we long to be close to you, but it's impossible for 600,000 satsangis to be close to the master physically.

You see, whenever you are attending to the master within, you are showing your presence to him physically, within. The master is within you. So be in his presence; you are physically present before him.

125 *Sometimes when I am in my office, or when I am doing something else, for some reason or other I want to think seriously about Sant Mat and my relationship with Sant Mat. If I endeavour to concentrate at the eye centre, am I then in contact with the inner form of the master?*

Whatever you do in this world to keep your master within you or keep yourself with the master is meditation, is a part of meditation. Whether you are properly sitting or just sitting quietly, full of love and devotion for the master, or hearing the sound, seeing the light – whatever you are doing, even worldly work – if your master is with you in your mind, in your heart, if all your dealings conform to the teachings, to the commands of the master, then you are with the master. That is why we say that Sant Mat is not only meditation; it is a way of life. We have to mould ourselves to that way of life so that we are always with our master, in all the activities of our life, so that we don't forget him anytime, anywhere.

126 *A question arose in our sangat overseas, where a disciple got up and said how beautiful it is to be around the master and serve the master. All these wonderful people are around the master, getting his darshan every day, getting his help every day. I'm sure they'll evolve very fast and go to Sach Khand. I only hope I could be given that opportunity.*

I think some people, being far away, are maybe nearer to the master than the people who are very close to him physically. They may be farther away from him, but nearness or distance doesn't make any difference at all. It is the pull of the heart, how much love they have in their heart that makes them near or far away. It is not physical nearness which matters; it is longing with real love which matters.

Maharaj Ji used to say there are many people in neighbouring villages who are not satsangis and may not have come to the Dera even once. And there are people who have come a thousand miles from America just to hear satsang. So it is not a question of being near or far; it is a question of love.

127 *Master, there are times when the master seems withdrawn, when he seems very distant. Is he making us run after him, as it were?*

Well, brother, if you're nearer to him within yourself, he will be nearer to you anywhere in the world. If you're far away from him within yourself, he will be far away from you even if he is living next door to you. You see, nearness you will only feel from within if you are attending to your meditation. If you are in love with him within, then wherever you may be living, you'll find him always near you. And if you are not able to build that love and devotion within yourself by meditation, then even if he's living next door to you, he's far away from you.

128 *Master, you've been with us for three days and we've been very happy, and now you're going away and I think we're all feeling very sad. But when you go away, it seems as though you're going very far. I know you've told us that you're within each and every one of us. But I can't seem to be constantly aware of your being within me – you seem so terribly far away when you go back to India. Could you please tell me how I could preserve that awareness?*

Sister, if we find our master outside, then naturally sometimes he's far away. If we find our master within, he's nearest to the nearest. So we should always try to find him within. Nobody is the master; nobody is the disciple. Your real master is shabd and nam within – the spirit within – and the soul is the real disciple. So the soul should try to search for its master within this temple of the living God. And that will give him the constant company of the master, where there's no separation at all.

129 *Maharaj Ji, I have a question that's been bothering me for some time. I really want to know how to properly handle the longing to see the master again while going about our daily lives, other than doing our meditation. After I left the Dera last time, I would start crying in the market all the time, but I think that wasn't the right way to be missing the master. But it lasted for years.*

Well, the only solution that I can suggest is to be with your master always. Don't remain separated from him at all. He's always within you. Try to be at that level of consciousness where you can always be with the master, so that you don't have to pass through this vacuum. That is the only answer. Then there'll be tears of joy rather than of sorrow.

130 *Can you give us a few words of reassurance and explain to us what Christ meant when he said: It's expedient for you that I leave you now?*

Your master is always within you. He is not anywhere outside at all. We should try to reach him, seek him who is our constant companion. He never leaves us, though we may leave him. So we should never feel disheartened at all. We are never alone – our master is always with us.

89

*131 Master, I recently read an article where the author sug-
gested that a good thing to do was to visualize the master
with you in your daily activities on the outside, for instance
driving with you in the car or walking with you down the
street. I was wondering if that's a good practice or if it
would be better to keep the visualization of the master at
the eye focus.*

Well, if you can practice this – that master is always with you
and whatever you do he is the one who is watching you and he
knows what is approved and what is not approved – you will
never do anything wrong in your life. We always try to deceive
and cheat other people when we think we are not being watched
by anybody. Nobody knows what we are doing; we can do anything by closing the door. But if we feel his presence always, all
twenty-four hours, we will never do anything wrong at all.

If a five-year-old child is with us, we would shudder at
stealing even anybody's pencil – we'd tremble. We all say the
Lord is present everywhere, but we mean it just intellectually,
we don't actually feel it. If we did, there would not be so much
chaos in this creation. If this one fundamental thing can be
realized by everybody – that he is within us, he is watching us
and we will have to explain all that we do, all our actions, to
him – this whole creation could change today. There wouldn't
be any bombs or tanks or rifles for killing each other if we could
realize the presence of the Lord within us.

We try not to do anything bad when we are watched. We
try to be good. We are supposed to be good, but the pity is we
are only good when we are being watched. We do everything
and yet we pray to the Lord to forgive us. He was there right
when we were doing whatever we wanted, right under his nose.
And yet we ask him to forgive us. So asking his forgiveness
is just hypocrisy. We just want to feel light by asking for his

forgiveness so that we can repeat the action again. But if it is a weight on my mind that he has seen me and is going to punish me, that he will deal with my actions, then I will never repeat them again.

132 *Master, yesterday you spoke about darshan and the help-lessness of a disciple being pulled towards the master. When we are in his presence or reading a book or even in meditation, feeling some fullness, being filled by the master, is this also darshan?*

If you are feeling him, if you are thinking about him, if your attention is towards him, you are always with him.

133 *When we are initiated, we are told that the master is with us from then on. What I want to know is, does the master know everything that goes on within our mind or within our actions, or is his attention only drawn to us in a spiritual way when we are meditating? He does not really watch all that is going on, does he?*

I think that perhaps it would be better if he did not watch all that we do. Unfortunately, he watches all that we do. Do you not think that God exists everywhere and that he is within each one of us and watches every one of us, what we do?

134 *The time for departure from the Dera is rapidly approach-ing, and I want some reassurance that we can take all this love with us and that this is as easily accessible at home as it is here.*

You see, our master is within every one of us. No matter how much we try to depart from there, we can't. So if we are carrying him with us, the question of departure doesn't arise. Being here at the Dera, if you don't carry him with you, it is the same thing as being away and not carrying him with you. If you are here, he is with you if you are carrying him with you; it is the same even if you are a thousand miles away, if you are carrying him with you. He is within you. So we have to carry him with us always, within us. Then there's no departure at all. A feeling of depression shouldn't come then because we are carrying him with us – he is with us.

135 *What can we do to keep the wonderful atmosphere there is now when you are here, when you are not here?*

Sister, don't send me away. Keep me here! Are you sure that I am not here when I am not here? If we can just know and understand that we are never alone, that our master is always with us, we are never without him, then the atmosphere would always be the same. We try to tell ourselves that he is not here when actually he is here. So we just have to know that he is always with us.

136 *Master, other than learning to love you a little more, is there any specific spiritual gain for disciples visiting Dera? For example, guest house gossip has it that because saints have trodden here for so many years now, even walking around the Dera washes off a whole series of karmas. Is this true?*

Is there any place in the world where the Lord doesn't exist?

No.

Is there any place the Lord doesn't walk? You will get everything from within yourself, not from brick and mortar. You have to build your own atmosphere of meditation within yourself, and you have to live in that. And that is the fold in which you have to live. No brick and mortar can save you from anything, however holy you may think it is. After all, it is only brick and mortar. The real Dera is within you, and you have to reach there within yourself. It is all just gossip. Or an excuse to rush to the Dera.

137 Can you talk about the pain of leaving here?

The Dera is not brick and mortar. You have to build your own Dera around you. You have to live in your own Dera. You have to carry your Dera with you wherever you are, and that is within you. You have to build up that atmosphere, that environment in which you have to live. Everybody has to carry one's own fort with him – that is the Dera. That is all within you, not outside in brick and mortar. It is only the love and devotion which makes you feel sad when you leave. Love and devotion for whom? For the master, who's always within us. So if we try to seek him within, then there will be no separation at all. And that we have to build within ourselves.

138 Master, it's very hard to leave here – the Dera and you. How do we deal with leaving here?

Then you are not taking the Dera with you. We have to do our worldly activities and we have to build our own atmosphere, which is helpful to us for meditation. Because we are part of a very long chain, we have to shift from place to place, country to country. There are so many activities around us which are pulling us to the right and left, so first we have to create our own atmosphere in which we should live, wherever we may be.

You see, our problem is that we always love the company of others; we don't love our own company at all. If you sit in a room for five minutes, you will either switch on the television, call somebody or start reading a newspaper or some magazine because you are not in the habit of living with yourself; and when you try to live with yourself, you think, "I am bored." We don't try to live with ourselves at all. We must learn to live with ourselves, independent of anything in this world. When you get into that habit, then it becomes very easy to build that atmosphere in which we have to live.

Meditation is a great thing, but even to close ourselves in a room, to sit in one place for meditation, is to our great credit. The mind runs out; the mind doesn't want to sit at all. So we must get into the habit of living with ourselves, enjoying our own company, loving our own selves. The minute we are left alone, we say, "I am bored, I have nothing to do." Because we are not in the habit of living with ourselves, we always want to be with others, to enjoy other people's company; we always need something to keep us occupied. So try to build that atmosphere in which you can always be happy.

139 *When Dera guests ask you what they can take back home with them when they leave the Dera, you always say, take the atmosphere that you find here back with you. Could you say more about how we can build that atmosphere of the Dera when we are away from you?*

Brother, Baba Ji Maharaj [Baba Jaimal Singh] and Hazur Maharaj Ji [Maharaj Sawan Singh] have laid the foundation of the Dera on love, humility, seva and meditation. That is the foundation of this Dera. Everybody's equal here, irrespective of country, caste, creed or colour. And if we feel we have not been able to come to that level yet, we try to improve ourselves. That is the atmosphere of the Dera and that is the atmosphere which we take with ourselves wherever we may go. The Dera is not built of mortar and bricks. It is built on seva and love and

devotion and humility and meditation. And we have to build
our whole life on these principles. Only this foundation will
take us back to the Father.

140 *Master, some of us are realizing that we'll have to leave*
you in a few days or a few weeks. I was wondering if you
could make some suggestions about how to prepare for
leave-taking and for re-entry into our normal lives?

You have to leave the same way as you came. You made preparations to come and you have to make preparations to leave.
You see, we have certain obligations, responsibilities in life,
and destiny has placed us at certain places to discharge those
responsibilities and obligations, and we have to attend to them.
And we also have to meditate, which is the main purpose of life.
So we cannot always remain in the presence of the master. We
have to build our own atmosphere of devotion and love within
us in which the master is always there with us. Ultimately we
have to leave this body. Ultimately the master has to leave this
body. It is a relationship of the soul with the inner master, the
divine master, the shabd. And that has to be developed while
being in the body. That relationship of the soul and the shabd
has to be strengthened while we have the privilege of being in
this human form. Then we are always with our master. As Christ
said, you have come unto me and I have come unto you.[122] That
is the merging of the soul into the shabd. So we have to prepare
for that.

141 *Being at the Dera, I tend to realize that the master is*
the ultimate giver. You give food and shelter, you give
medicine to the sick, and you give spiritual medicine to
the spiritually sick.

Brother, I don't do it. The sangat does it. They bring it to give to others.

> But I think the sangat follows the master's lead, and I think it has created a very dynamic atmosphere here at the Dera. And I think in the West, sometimes we get caught up in the opposite energy in which it is better to receive than to give. Can you talk about this giving spirit that is around here at the Dera?

Well, if you have experienced it, then what is there to talk about? Experience is much better than mere talking. We give in order to receive the Lord's love, his grace. We give what he has given to us. And we like to receive because he wants to fill us with his love and devotion, so we have to be receptive to that. In love there is always giving. Love means merging yourself, losing your identity, thinking that everything we have belongs to your beloved. Nothing is yours; everything is the beloved's. And the beloved is never unconscious of our giving. He is the one who is within us, who's helping us to give and then helping us to receive his grace.

> 142 Master, I notice that when I leave India, after I get back to America, it's almost like the time I spent in India was a dream, but while I was in India, it was wonderful – I felt lots of very special feelings toward the master. Then when I get back home, it feels like it's a dream and it kind of fades away, and that's painful. It feels very real while I'm here, and yet when I go home, it feels like a dream. How can I keep all those feelings real?

This whole life is a dream. This may be a dream within a dream. This life is nothing but a dream, and in a dream everything looks real. We feel, we cry, we laugh – we only realize it's a dream when we wake up. So keep on sleeping, don't wake up. It will remain a dream. Live in this atmosphere – it will remain a dream. Always keep yourself in this fort, in this atmosphere, so you'll be happily living in this dream. Don't come out of it.

143 Are you considering an American Dera?

Wherever there is a sangat, there is a Dera. A Dera is not a place made of bricks. It is made up of the devotees, of the lovers of the Lord, of the seekers of the Father. That is a Dera. Where the sangat is, there is a Dera. Without a sangat, there is no Dera at all. So don't think that a few buildings or houses or a colony make a Dera. The Dera is just your love, your harmony, your affection, your understanding and your cooperation with one another. That is a Dera.

PASSING OF THE MASTER

144 Maharaj Ji, I've heard so many versions as to what happens to a satsangi when he passes away: If he attends to his meditation, the master will come and take him by the hand; or if he has not been attending to his meditation, the master will not come; or that regardless of what he has been doing, the master will come. Would you give us a little more information about this, and what happens when the master passes away?

Well, the master never leaves the disciple. For a disciple, the master is always living because the body is not the master. The master is that divine melody which is within every one of us. And the body is not even the disciple. The soul is the disciple, and the shabd is the master. And once the soul is brought in contact with the shabd, the shabd never leaves the soul. Sooner or later it has to take the soul back. That shabd may take another form of a master for the benefit of a particular disciple who has to come back into the physical body. But the master will always remain the shabd, and the disciple will always remain the soul.

And also the master looks after his predecessor's disciples because that task has also been allotted to him. But their own master is within them. Ultimately all masters are the same. Christ has mentioned in the Bible that he is responsible not only for his own sheep but also for the sheep of his predecessor.

145 *Master, if a follower is initiated late in the master's life, and the master then dies, but the initiated pupil has not been able to see the radiant form yet, when he eventually does see a radiant form, whose will he see? Will it be that of the master who initiated him or the master at the present moment who is alive?*

Sister, when master initiates us, his duty does not cease until he takes us back to the Father. Even if he leaves his body the next day, he is always within us to guide us back to the Father. We have only to look to him to guide us, and we will always find our own master within ourselves. But as I said, ultimately all masters are the same because their real form is shabd and nam. Even if master leaves the body the next day after initiating a soul, the master never leaves him because he is responsible for taking that soul back to the Father. That responsibility comes to an end only when the soul merges into the Father. That is why Christ said that ultimately there will be one shepherd and one flock[107] – because the master merges back into his own master, and that master merges back into his own master. Ultimately the Lord will be the shepherd and we will be the sheep around that master, around that Father. There will be one master and one flock, so all become one. But we must look to our own master who has initiated us, and we will only see him within ourselves.

146 What happens if our master dies before we do?

The master never dies. Once a master initiates us, he never dies. He's immortal for us. He always lives within us, and that is our real master. The body is not the master; the shabd is the master. And the body is not the soul, nor is it the disciple of the guru. The soul is the disciple and the shabd is the master, and neither of them dies.

147 Master, what happens to the initiates of a master if he passes on before the initiates do? We won't have a living master?

Brother, as far as the disciple is concerned, his master is always living. Our master's responsibility is not only to initiate us but also to take us back to the Lord. He is there with us. The physical body is not the master. Something else is the master. As you have read in the Bible, Christ said, in effect: For a little while I am with you, then after a little while I will leave you, and again a little while after that you shall see me. And he also said: Now you see me in the flesh and you have no faith in me. Then you will have no doubt, for all your doubts will be resolved.[127]

The master never leaves us. He never leaves a disciple. He is responsible to take him back to the Lord. His guiding hand is always there. He is within us. He remains within us. We should never look to anybody else. We can get help from each other, we can get strength from each other; from his disciples or his successor we can get a sort of strength, we can resolve our doubts, but we should look only to our master as a master. For us, he is forever. And he will remain with us forever. He is our real master; the body is not the master. Our master is within us and he remains within us. He watches us, he guides us, and he takes us back to the Lord. So the initiate should never feel that his master has left the physical form. The master never leaves a disciple.

> *After the master passes on, he is still able to help his disciples who became his disciples while he was here in the flesh? But beyond that he cannot help anybody else?*

He does not. He cannot.

148 *Master, wasn't it difficult when Great Master left the body? It seems that it must be very hard, when the master dies, to switch the love and affection you have for your master to the next master.*

Why? With great difficulty we are able to switch our affection to even one master. And even that is not perfect. There's no necessity to shift it again to another master. Why should we? We are always concerned with our own master who initiated us, who put us on the path. We can get strength from someone, help from someone, and someone can fill us with love and devotion and keep us straight on the path, but we should look only to our own master. Why should we switch to another master?

> *Well, if you were living …?*

Because for us the master never dies. He is always there within us. We should always look to him, not to anybody else.

> *Then how would you describe the position of the master for somebody who was initiated by the Great Master – how would you describe their relationship with the successor?*

They have their relationship of master and disciple with their own master. They can treat the successor any way they feel like. Naturally he commands respect and love and affection because he's also carrying on the same mission and filling them with the same love and devotion for that very master. He helps them to create love for their own master. He doesn't want their love to change to him.

149 What happens when a master dies? How can we develop faith in the successor? Won't we want to keep our love for our own master?

You see, this will be automatic. When you have faith in your own master, your love is not lessened by loving the successor. When you love the successor, love for your own master increases. It will be automatic because you love your own master so much that you are willing to accept whatever he does. Whatever respect, regard and love you give to the successor shows your love and reverence for your own master. But for him, you wouldn't have faith in the successor at all. You are not loving him at a personal level. You are loving him because he has been appointed the successor. Actually you are loving your own master. On the last day they're all the same. On the inside, there is no difference between one master and another master.

150 Maharaj Ji, I notice that the very, very old people around here who perhaps were initiated by another master look at you as devoutly and lovingly as your own disciples. Do they perhaps see their own master in you?

You'll have to ask them. Christ says in the Bible: I have to look after not only my sheep but also the sheep of others.[107] He means the sheep of his predecessor. The master is responsible not only for his own disciples but also for those of his predecessor because he comes into the shoes of that predecessor. He is part of the predecessor, so we strengthen our love and faith in the teachings and the path with the help of the successor. And then, ultimately there will be one shepherd and one fold. They all become one because all masters are one. There is no difference between them.

151   Master, if we do have to come again, will you be there with us, or will there be some other master?

All masters are one. They are all waves of the same ocean. You cannot distinguish one wave from the other. They all have their roots in the ocean. The waves look different from each other, but they are all part of that same ocean. So once a soul is initiated, it will have to be initiated again in the next birth if it comes back. It may be initiated by any wave. The ocean is the same. The shabd is our master, not the body. The body is a means to connect us to that shabd. Ultimately the master also leaves this body here, just like everybody else. It is the soul which goes back to the Father, not the body. So the master's body is not the real master, nor is the disciple's body the real disciple. The soul is the real disciple and the shabd is the real master. And the shabd is one.

∾ 13 ∾

Satsang and Seva

IMPORTANCE OF SATSANG

152 What is the advantage of satsang?

They say the path is simple, but you can only understand the path with the advantage of satsang – when you go to the company of the mystics and saints. Then the path becomes easier for us to understand. There's no secret to satsang.

When you go to the company of the mystics, the teachings become so simple to understand. You think: Why do I remain in delusion at all? Why didn't I realize the simple truth before? But to follow the path is not so simple. To follow a simple thing is very difficult. To live a simple life is very difficult; to live a complicated life is perhaps very easy. To accept simplicity in a simple way is very difficult for us – we always like to be told the truth in an intellectual way. If you tell an intellectual person something in a complicated way, then he tries to think about it; but if you tell him a simple truth in a simple way, he doesn't accept it at all, doesn't understand it at all.

The teachings become very simple to us when we go to the company of the mystics and saints. The Lord has brought us into their company because he wants us to understand the teachings. He is the doer, and he wants us to follow them, so the teachings become simple for us. Of course, to practice the path is very difficult. It is easy to give something in charity; to go to a church or a temple and to pray for two, three minutes and then be absorbed again in worldly affairs. But to sit in meditation for a couple of hours in a closed room – that's a very difficult thing. And to lead a Sant Mat way of life is the greatest struggle for us. To become a worldly-wise man or a slave of the senses is very easy.

So believing in and living the teachings is difficult, but to understand the teachings, in the company of a mystic, is quite simple for us.

153 Maharaj Ji, here in the West we have so little opportunity for darshan.

Well, brother, real darshan is inside. Everyone has to work for that. The outside darshan is good, but then we have to take a practical view. So in the absence of all that, we can hold small group meetings and read literature, and try to devote more time to bhajan and simran.

Group meetings are very useful, provided there is no bickering, no petty jealousies, and provided they bring us nearer to each other. We do not hold meetings to give vent to our differences, or to show our superiority, or to boss over others. That is not the object of the meetings but is rather contrary to the very purpose of the meetings. The object of the meetings is to inculcate humility in us and to bring us together and to encourage each other on the path. Our example should be such that if anybody is in some doubt, it will help him to come back on the path again. That is the object, just to create that atmosphere. Because mere mechanical meditation, say, giving time for two and one-half hours every day and then forgetting about Sant Mat, is not the right answer. We have to live in Sant Mat, so that we are in it the whole day. And that can be done only if we carry Sant Mat in our own atmosphere around us. If we just leave the atmosphere in the house, again try to pick it up the next morning, in that way we are satsangis for only two hours or so and not the whole day. We have to be satsangis for the whole day. We have to build that atmosphere around us so that whoever comes in that is automatically influenced and affected by it. We have to do the same thing in India as well as here in America. There is no difference. For a master and a disciple, this space or distance does not count at all.

154 *The other day, you said there's infinite grace. I've also heard you say we need to come to that level of consciousness where we can really hold him and look deeply into his eyes. When I hear you say that, it's as though you're calling to us to do it right now, tomorrow or next month or next year. It's as though we don't have to wait till the end of our life, or till death, to come to you inside. And yet you also say to try not to resist. Is it true that you're calling to us to come right now?*

Sister, what else are these meetings meant for? When a master initiates a disciple, he's more anxious to pull that disciple to that level of consciousness from where the soul can be pulled upward – inward and upward. What is the purpose of initiation? The soul should come to that level where it can be pulled inward and upward. All these meetings, all these satsangs, all these questions and answers are meant to help us do our best to come to that level from where we can be pulled upward.

155 *Could you talk about the importance of satsang, where the master is not present physically?*

Well, brother, the purpose of satsang, of holding meetings is just to strengthen our faith and meditation, to create the atmosphere of meditation, to create the atmosphere in which we have to build our meditation. If we have any doubt, any question, any obstacle, it gets answered, dissolved, resolved. And we are able to hold that atmosphere in which we have to build our meditation. That is the main purpose of satsang. It is no ritual, no ceremony. You will not get anything by merely attending a satsang. The atmosphere that you carry home from the satsang and attending to your meditation will give you everything. The mind's doubts that are resolved and dissolved in the satsang will give you everything. The faith and devotion which the satsang builds in you will give you everything. Otherwise it is all the same old questions, same old answers – nothing new. But we are a source of strength to one another, and that helps us a lot in meditation.

156 *I believe Great Master said that satsang is the haven of the agonized.*

Yes, it is an anchor. You see, if your boat is caught in a storm and you reach the shore, you feel so relieved. We are all in the storm of our mind, and when we go to the satsang of the mystics, we find we can land on a shore. How relieved we feel. Satsang is a great anchor. We are always influenced by the company we keep. If you can become a drunkard by being with people who drink or a gambler by remaining in their company, why not become a devotee by remaining in the company of mystics and saints? It's the Lord's grace that we seek such company, and that we get such company. Christ said, wherever two or more meet in my name, I'll be there.[59] What does that mean? That is why we have group meetings and discussions, because nothing but the master and the teachings are discussed. In satsang we discuss nothing but the Lord.

Satsang is not for having cookies and parties, not a place for gossiping or recreation. It is meant to influence each other in the right direction so we can be a source of strength to each other, and to build faith in us so that we can attend to our meditation in that atmosphere, build our treasure in heaven in that atmosphere. That is the purpose of satsang. This teaching should not be confined just to the literature and the tapes. Satsang helps us to build an atmosphere of meditation and to live the teachings.

157 *Is it okay to get a group of people together and listen to tapes of you, Maharaj Ji?*

It depends upon your approach to the meeting. If you take it as a ritual, then it is just a ritual. You can listen to tapes at home. Why drive seventy, eighty miles just to hear a tape that you can listen to at home? At meetings we should be a source of strength to each other, a source of help to each other on the path. We should derive inspiration from each other. We should come back filled with love and devotion for meditation, for the master, for the path, for living this way of life. If you go to hear a tape just as a ritual, or if you don't feel inspired or get any strength at the meeting, it's not good. It depends on your approach.

You're not going just to enjoy each other's company but to get inspiration for meditation. Satsang shouldn't become social events. In satsang, generally, we should talk only about the path, about the way of life, rather than any politics, any stories, any miracles.

158 *Is there any special way in which you want us to conduct our meetings?*

Well, it depends upon the individual groups, how they want to conduct their meetings. There are no hard and fast rules. Then the meetings would become just a ceremony. We don't want to lay down any rules and regulations about what people can or cannot say. We should just get together to create an atmosphere of meditation in which we can build our treasure within. That is the purpose of satsang. There should be absolute harmony in satsang. There should be no question of any parties or anybody bossing others or being superior. That concept is wrong. We should be helpful to each other, a source of strength to each other, an example to each other.

Sometimes you get tired, you become sick, so you keep your hand on your friend's shoulder to be able to walk and go home. We do falter here and there, so we need the support of somebody to help us get up and walk again. That is the purpose of satsang. We do need help from one another, and then it's entirely up to the individual group how they want to conduct their meetings. The main thing is that when we leave, we are filled with love and devotion and enjoy that bliss and atmosphere which we build, which should induce us to go back and attend to our meditation. That is the atmosphere we should create in satsang.

159 *Should any special effort be made to attract people?*

No. We should not worry about advertisements or publicity, but the real seekers we should try to help – and we know that there are real seekers. We send so many complimentary books from the Dera, complimentary small pamphlets which you can give to the real seekers for reading. If they are interested, they will naturally ask you more questions and will attend your meetings. You can suggest to them what books to read, help them to get those books; but if one is not a seeker and he does not want to understand it, do not bother about it. However, we should really help those who are honest and sincere in their search for God-realization.

160 Sir, is there any particular format that you would recommend for satsang?

An intellectual format is all right if you are addressing intellectual people. You always have to come to the level of the audience. Otherwise they won't understand. If you try to explain to intellectual people in a simple way – they will never understand anything unless you explain it in an intellectual way. When their intellect is satisfied, then simple things appeal to them. And if you try to explain to simple people in an intellectual way, they won't understand anything at all. So you have to come to the level of the audience to whom you are explaining. The speaker always has to look to whom he is addressing because he has to reach everyone. That is the main thing.

Perhaps for those people who have satisfied their intellect and have been able to build faith and devotion and practice within themselves, a format that is too intellectual may not appeal to them at that stage. But for people who are going through that stage of satisfying their intellect, a simple explanation won't appeal to them at all.

The approach of every mystic is different. But they are all harping on the same tune. They have the same spiritual truths to share with the masses. Every mystic has given us the same teachings, but their approach has been different, depending on the people whom they are trying to reach, to whom they are trying to explain. Their parables will be different. Their way of explaining will be different. Their reasoning will be different. But they have the same thing to share, nothing new.

161 Maharaj Ji, in the Western sangats, we do not sing shabds like they sing here where you are physically present. Is there any reason why we mustn't do that, or is it permissible?

There's no reason why you should do it. Why should you try to adopt Eastern ways? You see, here in India the congregation is in the habit of collecting together and singing. But you have your own way of collecting together and congregating. Why should you try to copy them? The first time I went to America, they were trying to go to the meetings with their hats on and trying to take off their shoes and sit in the same way we sit in India. What is the use of all that? Why should you try to copy them?

Let people sing. But why should they make it a ritual? Here, naturally, it is always better when there are so many people sitting in satsang. If there is no singing, everybody's talking and gossiping and creating noise. Now everybody is absorbed in that devotional music, so people are sitting quietly. But if someday the pathi doesn't sing, just watch – everybody will be talking and there'll be so much confusion. There'll be talks and discussions going on with each other. Now probably a stronger atmosphere is being created for the satsang, for what they're going to hear.

But it's unnecessary for you people. If you want to sing, you can sing in your own language. Why should you sing these songs? You don't understand them.

No, that's what I mean – can we sing our own songs, or would it make satsang seem like a religion?

You can sing if you feel like it. Generally in churches, people sing psalms and hymns – they're very beautiful, very good. I don't mind your singing what you're used to. But why should you try to copy devotional songs from us?

The singing is just to hold people's attention so they don't gossip and talk unnecessarily. I don't want to introduce any Eastern rituals unnecessarily into Sant Mat. The teachings are, of course, the same everywhere, but environments everywhere are different. Why should people take off their shoes? In the East the custom started because people used to travel on dusty roads and there was so much dirt and infection, so people took their shoes off when they entered a temple or someone's home. But now that is not the case. People come in their car and their shoes are so neat and clean that they can sit with their shoes on. Why should they not? There's no ritual.

162 Master, while you're gone at satsang, you said anybody could give satsang. Should we stick only to the philosophy that's in the books or can we discuss other people's philosophy that hasn't been written in the books?

Actually, the spirituality at the base of every religion is the same. There's no difference at all. Every mystic has the same message to give, the same method to tell us. No mystic creates any religion. They come only to show us that particular path which leads us back to the Father. But generally, after the departure of such mystics and adepts, we forget their real teaching and try to arrest it. We form strong organizations and make strong religions. We hold on to the dogmas, rituals and ceremonies and lose the reality.

So if you discuss the philosophy of any mystic, it will lead you to the same place. They have the same thing to say. Everybody believes there's one God. Everybody believes he is within every one of us. Everybody believes in the necessity to go back to him. And everybody believes that we have to search for him within the body. And if he's within every one of us, then naturally the path leading back to him can only be one, it cannot be two or three.

So those mystics and adepts all try to show us that particular path which leads us back to the Father, within the body. Every day we read from so many mystics, so many saints: Dadu, Paltu, Mira Bai, Nanak, Soami Ji, Kabir, Shams-i Tabriz and so many more. We discuss the Bible because we find the same mysticism in that. But they all have the same message. Everybody's harping on the same tune. The main thing is to understand and follow it, to practice it.

163 *Can you give us a little pep talk or something to encourage or inspire us to put in a little more effort in meditation?*

These meetings are held just for that purpose – to encourage seekers and initiates to give more time to meditation and to live in the way of Sant Mat. I don't know what more encouragement you would like me to give. These meetings are just hammering every day, hammering on the same thing every day. Someday they will make a dent. We are hammering practically every day.

164 *We can't ask other satsangis to help us meditate because all the satsangis I know have worse problems meditating than I do. Could you give us any advice?*

You see, this satsang, our group meetings, discussions, seva – they're just means to induce us to attend to meditation. When we are hammering on one thing every day, definitely it leaves some mark. So we can be a source of strength to one another in order to attend to our meditation. The main thing is to give time to meditation.

It is a constant struggle with the mind. And all the time you spend struggling with the mind during the course of your meditation is itself a meditation. Because a child after birth cannot start running at once. He has to pass through so many phases before he learns to walk and run. So the mind has to be disciplined. It has become quite wild for so many ages, so it takes time to discipline it. But as long as we are regular in giving our time, fighting with the mind, disciplining the mind, we are attending to our meditation.

We can only knock at the door. Then it is for the owner of the house to open it from within. We are all beggars at the door of the Lord. Our duty is to go on knocking. It is for him to open it whenever he wants to. We should not hesitate to knock, that is the main thing. We should be knocking constantly. And we get inspiration and help from one another to strengthen our faith in meditation by attending group meetings, by reading the right type of literature, by doing seva for the sangat. These are good means to induce us towards meditation.

165 *Sir, I read somewhere that satsang to a satsangi is like a fence around a crop.*

What's the purpose of a fence? To protect the crop. That is the purpose of satsang. Whatever meditation we build, we have to protect it, so that ego may not come in us and we aren't tempted to perform rituals, miracles and all those things. We are able to build humility and meekness in us in satsang, and we can be a source of strength to each other and help each other rise above our weaknesses. That is the purpose of satsang. If that love and devotion is missing, if that atmosphere is missing, then it is just a fill-in-the-blank, nothing more.

166 *Maharaj Ji, my understanding of the term 'satsang' is where there are two satsangis or more gathered together at a proper place, reading some text bearing on Sant Mat and trying to understand those texts, even though the master may not be physically present there. It is assumed that the master is there, not in person but in spirit. Is that correct?*

Yes. As you know, the real meaning of the word 'satsang' is the company of the truth. *Sat* means everlasting truth, and *sang* means the company of the truth. So wherever we meet in the name of the Father, wherever the Lord is discussed, wherever we fill each other with his love and devotion, strengthen each others' faith to worship him, I think that is satsang, because naturally in our conversation, our master is there, the Lord is there. Without that, satsang means nothing. We always discuss the teachings, whether he is physically present or not, but naturally when he is being discussed, he is very much present. He is very much alive when we are discussing his teachings and the way he has told us to lead our life. Satsang increases our love and devotion for our master, for the Father, and we become an example and give strength to each other in satsang. So as long as the Father is there, the Lord and master is there, that is satsang.

Whether you read from the texts or just have conversations about him – that is satsang. Naturally when there are too many people, you can't personally discuss anything with anybody – that will just create confusion. So we read from some mystic and try to explain the teachings from that. If there are five, ten people, a few people, a reasonable group, even without any book they can discuss the teachings, the master, the Lord. They are creating faith in each other, love and devotion in each other for the Father – that is also satsang. It is not essential that a text be read. But naturally in a multitude, in a crowd, you have no other alternative. Either you can give a lecture on some subject of Sant Mat, or you can take some text to explain the teachings. It comes to the same thing.

But is it essential that the physical presence of the master be there?

No, it is not essential. As long as the master is there in our mind and we are being filled with his love and devotion, our conviction is being strengthened; he is very much there, because he is within every one of us. Christ says, wherever you meet in my name I'll be there.[59] That is what he means. Even if the master is sitting there, and we are not there mentally – being there, we are not there – for us that is not satsang. And even if the master is not there physically but is very much there in our mind, he is there; that is satsang for us. It depends upon us and what mood we are in.

167 Maharaj Ji, is it okay to read the works of mystics outside of the Radha Soami philosophy?

Satsangis can enjoy the works of those mystics much, much more. Now when you read the mystic works of Hafiz, Shams-i Tabriz, Maulana Rum and the other Persian mystics, you will appreciate them much more than before. You will also know where the author has misinterpreted or wrongly translated. So there's no harm in reading any book at all; it can create the atmosphere in which we can build our meditation. The main thing is meditation. These books are just to give us conviction and corroborate what we believe in. The human mind always needs corroboration – that what I'm doing is right – and if a person finds that corroboration from different sources, he gets convinced and then he wants to follow it.

These books are just to create conviction in us. They will give you nothing. But conviction ultimately will give you faith, and faith will give you practice, and practice is the main thing. For an intellectual person, without the books he can never be convinced. Without conviction an intellectual person can never develop faith, and without faith he can never build his meditation. These are essential for us. That is why we have so many meetings, so many books.

Now we have printed about forty, fifty books in English; actually one is enough. After all, they talk about the same thing, in a different way; they all ultimately talk about sound and light and the Father within the body, nothing else. But some people get conviction from this one, others get conviction from another one, for others another book appeals to them. Their purpose is just to create that atmosphere and corroborate our faith, nothing else.

168 *Master, it is said that if two satsangis are together, gathered in your name, that is a satsang. Does the same thing work if there is only one satsangi in a town – if you are alone?*

Naturally, you have no alternative, brother. If you find good satsangis, nothing like it. We always like their company because our object is the same, the pivot is the same, the platform on which we stand is the same. We strengthen each other's faith, each other's love, each other's devotion for the Lord, and our association helps each other to meditate. That is the purpose of collecting in the name of the Father, in the name of the master. But if we have no alternative, then our books should be our companion.

169 *On the subject of health, we have had disagreements at our meetings where most of our members say that we should read only from Radha Soami books. But these books tell us nothing about our health. In order to serve the purpose of a certain cause, we have to be healthy. So I have said many times to our secretary that we should have readings on that subject – how to breathe, how to exercise – and we can learn a lot and improve our health.*

Brother, there are so many schools that will tell you how to breathe and how to exercise and how to keep healthy. You have so many sports clubs and other organizations, and from these you can learn all those things about health. But spirituality is something different. We of course need health for the purpose of spirituality, but in this school [of spirituality] how many things can be taught? There is, so to say, a specialization on all subjects. Here we are only concerned with spirituality. Naturally, a healthy body is a great aid on the path to spirituality. You can keep your body healthy by doing yogic exercises, by running, by walking, and by so many different kinds of exercises.

Master, I want to know if we are allowed to hold lectures on the subject of health – whether it is not against the theory or teachings of Sant Mat?

No. The teachings of Sant Mat do not tell us not to keep or preserve good health. You can lecture, if need be, on how to preserve health; but these things are very unnecessary, elementary things in such meetings. One can learn from books, or one can go to other places to know how to preserve or keep good health. For example, these yogic exercises – all of them tell you how to preserve health. But why waste time in discussing these things in the group meetings? We should talk only about spirituality. Other people already know about these things or they can always learn from books or other teachers or organizations. The main purpose of health is that we should be able to devote our time to meditation. These yogic exercises were just a means to keep healthy. They were not the meditation itself, but simply the means for meditation. Sometimes we confuse these things. We take these yogic exercises as meditation by itself, and that is wrong.

A healthy body is required for meditation, but health alone is not sufficient for meditation. We need so many other things besides health. Proper practice of meditation is what we need. It is good to be healthy, and there are so many exercises which help you. And then exercises differ with different individuals. One exercise which I do for preserving my health may not suit another person who may be a heart patient.

*Well, Master, my point was that though there are quite
a few societies, the average person does not know, is not
enlightened enough to go there. We should hold lectures,
let us say at our satsang every week or so, on that subject.
They do quite a bit of good and give you so much information which I myself learned, and I can assure you that
my health is due mostly to that. And I do not see why
everybody else cannot do that?*

You can just suggest that in these meetings and you can refer
others to these books. We have no objection to that. But the
purpose of our group meetings is not so much to discuss about
health as it is to stress spirituality. Otherwise we may deviate
from the real subject – that is what I fear. For instance, if we
start telling how to cook good food, or how satsangis should
dress, and we start giving demonstrations of all that – well, we
are lost. Where is the time for all this, and where will there be
an end to all these things?

*I do not mean all the time – only occasionally, once in
a while?*

I have no objection. You may discuss anything from the health
point of view. Or you can say that these exercises have helped
you, these books have helped you. Then if anybody else is
interested, he can join those organizations, or he can read those
books from the health point of view. You people meet just once a
month, or once a week, and just for about an hour or so. In this
little time, how can you discuss all these multipurpose activities of our daily needs? It is always good to discuss spirituality,
because the purpose of the group meeting is to build that atmosphere in which we have to live for meditation. We should not
do anything which deviates our attention from that meditation.
We have to build that atmosphere of meditation around us by
reading Sant Mat literature, by giving help to each other. We

should always be helpful to each other. We should try to create in ourselves love and devotion for the Lord and help the new students on the path, so that they too can live in that atmosphere of meditation. That is the object of these group meetings – nothing else. But, if there is disharmony, unpleasantness, or bossing in the group meetings, I do not think that you practically gain anything from such group meetings at all.

Another point to consider is that other people may not feel inclined to hear about health or cooking or other things. They may say that all these other things can be learned in other schools, but what they cannot learn in other schools is about meditation, about spirituality; and that is the purpose for which they come here. We are not against talking about health, or how to breathe, or how to exercise; but there are so many other places where we can learn these things.

If anybody needs help, whether spiritual, mental or physical, and we are able to help, we should always do so. But what I mean is that we should not be lost in so many activities that we forget the real purpose of these meetings. The real purpose is to create love and devotion, because a healthy, good atmosphere of love and devotion is very essential for meditation. There should always be love and harmony in your groups. You should be helpful to each other, and a new seeker coming and entering your hall should automatically realize the difference between other organizations and your organization. You can advise them in health and cooking matters, but we need not waste time in discussing these things in our meetings.

But people have to be informed. Of course, they are not ignorant, but they are misguided. They are not informed about health, and neither was I many years ago.

If the impression in satsang is that we have to ignore health, that is wrong. We have to look after our health, but the purpose of keeping healthy is meditation. The object should be kept in view; that object should not be lost; that destination we should not forget. We have to maintain our health. Everybody needs health. But we cannot teach all these things. We should discuss only spirituality, which is the food for the soul and the mind. Other things automatically come to us when the love of the Lord and devotion come in us. We should not lose time in those discussions; those other things we can always learn elsewhere.

ATMOSPHERE OF SATSANG

170 Master, you tell us time and time again that harmony in our satsangs is what pleases you. From my point of view, it seems that one of the things that gets in our way is the tendency to ascribe weaknesses and negative character traits in ourselves to other people. Christ spoke of this also in the Bible when he said that we see the beam, the splinter in our brother's eye, but we fail to see the beam in our own eye. Can you explain this, please?

Well, you yourself are explaining the point. There should be harmony in satsang. Sometimes I wonder: What is there to differ about in satsang? We get together for what purpose? If there were any elections or any manipulation of funds, or any authority or power, then I could understand disharmony in the masses and the people. But when our goal is the same, and such events are not there in our satsang, then how can there be disharmony in a satsang? I can't understand. We just go there to be a source of strength to each other, to build our faith, to be helpful to one another, to be a support to one another. That should be our attitude in satsang. We don't get together for a cup of coffee or a cup of tea and just exchange greetings or have our dates. That is not the purpose of our meetings at all. Our meetings should just be to help each other, to be a source of strength to each other. And they definitely have that effect on us if we go with that intention.

And especially the leader of a meeting should be very humble. He should never try to project that he is in any way superior to others. We are all struggling souls on the path. We all have our human failings. Some are exposed, some are not exposed. So we don't go there to expose the weaknesses of other people. We go there to help them, to pull them out of their weaknesses, not to expose them or boss over them. That should not be the purpose of our meetings at all.

I remember, Christ gave a very beautiful parable in the Bible. He said: That ground was fertile, seed was good. Then the owner of the field asks: From where these tares, these weeds have come? He says that the enemy has sown them. A servant asks: Should I go and pluck all the weeds? The owner says: No, my fear is that when you pluck all the weeds, you may also uproot the crop with them. Leave the weeds. When the time of the harvest comes, first cut down all the weeds and burn them, and whatever is left – that crop you can bring home.[50]

The idea is that when in the company of the mystics, all sorts of people come. But some people are victims of their human weaknesses. They try to do their best to be on the path, to remain on the path, but still, human failings are there, here and there. And if we go on exposing them, they will shun your company, they will run away from your meetings. And whatever little chance they have to improve themselves by being in the company of good people, we have shut them off from that opportunity. So rather, our approach should be very positive. Our approach should be very loving, helpful. We should give only as much advice as the person is receptive to. Otherwise, we should leave it to him. At least he comes to the meetings, at least he attends to meditation, whatever little he is doing, and he may realize his folly someday and may come back to the path again. But if we all try to expose him, without sitting in judgment on ourselves, we are not helping those people at all. We are depriving them of the opportunity to be better people, better satsangis, better humans. So that approach should not be there. Our approach should be of service, of help. We should be a source of strength to each other. We should have a very loving, kind approach. And that definitely helps to pull people out of their weaknesses.

In meetings, nothing but Sant Mat teachings and love for meditation should be discussed. All aspects of the teachings should be discussed from different angles. We each have our own approaches, own angles, from which to discuss the same thing. Actually, Sant Mat is so simple, but still, if we go on hammering, hammering, hammering, there may be some dent. Otherwise, there are just a few things which we discuss every day. But there is no dearth of our discussions, no dearth of questions, no dearth of books printed. This is just hammering, hammering, hammering. And it has its effect. Even if a drop starts falling on a stone, it makes its own place there. It creates a dent there. Similarly, that is the effect of satsang, of group meetings.

And the people who attend to meditation – good, noble satsangis – even they need that atmosphere, just to retain that humility within themselves, just to escape from unnecessary ego. If you have a good crop, you need a good fence also, lest somebody destroy your crop. So sometimes the satsang and meetings work as a good fence around our meditation. When we go away from the atmosphere of satsang, the mind starts becoming active again and again makes us dance to its own tune and pulls us towards the senses. But if somebody always goes on reminding, reminding, reminding us, someday we may be able to understand, and that moment can change our whole attitude of life. So our approach should be very, very kind and loving in satsang and meetings.

And we don't go 100 miles or 200 miles just to have a cup of coffee, a little recreation, a little cookie here and there, or to gossip or give vent to our temper and show off. If that type of atmosphere is there, it is much better to sit at home and read Sant Mat books and attend to meditation, rather than waste your time.

And you don't need big halls. You can sit even on the roadside and create a good atmosphere. That is more essential in satsang than beautiful buildings, beautiful halls, beautiful places. All that is immaterial. If tranquillity, peace and harmony are not in that beautiful hall, what is the sense of that beautiful hall? If that can be found only on a roadside, a roadside is a much better place to sit and get together. So as the organization has spread, we have given more attention to these beautiful buildings we want to buy, beautiful properties we want to buy. It is all right, as long as you can retain that atmosphere of meditation, of love and helpfulness and kindness. Otherwise, it is just a waste of time, waste of money.

171 *Maharaj Ji, the spiritual literature that I read emphasizes universal brotherhood and universal love – that we are born of the same Father. Are people who do not subscribe to this universal relationship entitled to be admitted into the satsang fold? For example, would a Brahmin in India who clings to the idea of superiority be entitled to be included in the fold?*

We have to change the heart of the people, not to apply rigid rules. You see, Sant Mat is nothing but changing the heart. So when people accept Sant Mat, automatically they accept this equality with each other. But if they are still victims of old traditions, old faiths, or old superstitions, they should try to shed them.

The purpose of holding satsang every day is just to change their heart, to make them feel one with each other – that we are all humans, we belong to the same source, the same Lord is within every one of us, and we are all equals. There's no question of high or low, at least by birth. We are only high and low by our karmas, by our actions. So satsang is nothing but training them to have that outlook on life. But we can't fix rigid rules, that since you believe you are high, we won't admit you, or since you believe you are low, we won't admit you. Sant Mat doesn't enforce things like that. But definitely it changes the heart.

I remember one place in India where there used to be so many prejudices between two different communities. They wouldn't even draw water at the same well. They wouldn't live together or even go near each other. They had separate colonies. Now when I go there for satsang, nobody can say who is from which group. They all cook together, eat together, sit together. Slowly and slowly they are changing, they are realizing they are all the same. But if we had first laid down this condition, that first you change your views and then we will admit you, perhaps we would have had to debar them forever. Now we have reformed them. Now in Dera there are no distinctions at all among people. We never ask what caste you belong to, what religion you are. Everybody is fed in the same langar. Everybody goes and does seva. Everybody cooks. And there's no question of high caste or low caste. We don't believe in those things. But we have to change people's hearts by persuasion, by love, by giving them understanding, not by rigid, militaristic rules. Probably that never works.

172 Back home in our sangats, sometimes seekers and satsangis feel that there's too much emphasis in the discourses on

*the difficulties of the path, how hard meditation is and
how long and hard this path is, and they sometimes feel
discouraged by this. Could you give us some guidance?*

Well, sister, everybody has his own approach. Of course the path
looks so simple, but it is very hard to follow. Nobody can deny
that. But still, if the love and desire are there, the pull is there,
even if one goes through all sorts of hardships, all these obstacles
and hardships become so easy. Actually, it's the love that matters.
Every speaker has his own approach. The main thing is that the
speaker has to fill us with love and devotion for the Father. He
has to create that atmosphere, that haven in which we have to
build our meditation. That is the purpose of our satsang. And
if there are any doubts, they should be dissolved, they should be
cleared, and we should become a source of strength and help to
each other. That is the purpose of these meetings.

*173 What should we do if there's disharmony? How should
we go about solving it?*

Create love, create devotion, create understanding; try to understand another person's point of view. Don't try to enforce your
own point of view and don't always think that you are right,
that the other person must be wrong. You can give way; you
can give in if the other person doesn't give in. And if still there
is a conflict in the sangat, I personally advise you not to go to
that satsang. Because we don't go there for this purpose, we go
for a very different purpose. We go because spiritually, we want
to relax. We don't go there just to become tense or to show our
personality or individuality; we go just to lose our individuality
and personality and forget ourselves, forget the ego which we
have been building the whole week. That is the purpose of going
to a satsang. If that purpose is not there, what is the use of going

to that satsang? And in satsang, we should not talk of anything except the teachings, the Lord, the Father – that should be the foremost thing, and we shouldn't give undue importance to other things.

174 Master I have a question about satsang when it's given by someone other than the master. I have read that the master always uses the speaker as a channel. Is this invariably so, no matter what is said, and no matter if the content perhaps turns away certain seekers, rather than attracts them?

Christ said: Wherever you collect, even two in my name, I'll be there.[59] Wherever we collect in the name of the master, master should be there. If we are discussing the master, if we are coming together for the sake of the master, then master will be there. And then we strengthen each other's love and affection.

Meetings are very useful, but I can't say that whatever the speakers say is 100 percent true. It may be his own view. And you can easily differ with him. You may know more about Sant Mat's teachings than the speaker. But don't look at him from that critical point of view. As long as we are becoming a source of strength to each other on the path in the meetings, that is enough for the satsang. We should be helpful to each other, we should become a source of strength to each other on the path. That should be the purpose of these meetings.

And you can have honest differences with the speaker on certain points. He's doing his best in the name of the master, but he can be wrong somewhere. But don't look very critically at him. The books are full of the teachings; there's no point which is not clearly described or explained in the books. You can refer to the books. We have so many – I wonder if there is any question left which is not answered in the books. And if still you have some honest differences of opinion, you can always write here to clarify them. But one shouldn't be unnecessarily critical of the speaker, though there can be honest differences.

175 Is there anything wrong with discussing?

No. That is what I say.

Even to the point of arguing?

No. There is no harm, but it must be constructive and in an endeavour to understand certain things; not to hurt anybody or for the purpose of asserting your point. The purpose should be to understand or to feel convinced or get convinced, or to convince the other person. It is not a matter of arguing about opinions but of stating facts, and that should be done with a view to help each other. Meetings should be helpful, and especially the old initiates who understand Sant Mat should help the new seekers or new initiates. Naturally they have so many hurdles to cross, they have so many things to understand, so they should be encouraged to understand through these personal discussions, Sant Mat discussions.

Another thing is, if you hold group meetings, you should keep in touch with the centre at Beas. We send you news and writings on different spiritual subjects, which you can read and discuss. Your collective problems that you cannot solve locally may also be sent to us, and we shall reply to you as a group instead of individually. So these group meetings are helpful, especially to the new seekers, but only if there is absolute harmony and love there. This should be so much in evidence that if a person comes from the outside, he should feel that harmony and love, and that there is something different in the group, something other than merely going and chatting, expressing opinions, eating and coming back home.

176 Maharaj Ji, does the atmosphere of satsang help us, as well as what's discussed?

The atmosphere helps us a lot. There should be absolute harmony in satsang. If there are differences, then you will never be able to build an atmosphere for meditation at all. There should be absolute harmony in satsang. If you are always maligning one another and bossing one another, then you can't build that atmosphere, you can't even think about the master during that time. Even if you sit on the roadside and have that harmony and atmosphere of love and devotion, it's much better than sitting in a very luxurious, very decorated hall where there is no harmony, where you are quarrelling and fighting with one another. And there should be no discussion of politics in satsang. There should be no family disputes brought to satsang. Satsang should be just pure satsang. We don't go there just for having a cup of coffee or a cookie and all that. That is the wrong concept of satsang. You don't drive fifty, sixty, a hundred miles just for a cup of coffee. It may be essential, but that's not your purpose for coming. The satsang atmosphere should never be spoiled. If you can't adjust, you can sit at home and meditate. Why create strain on other people's minds by your presence and just punish your own self?

177 When satsangis get together, can that be satsang too?

That is satsang. Satsang is not only hearing a sermon. All the good company which comes together at that time to help each other, to get strength from each other – sometimes they have to lean against one another in a weak moment to get strength – that's also satsang. Anything which is persuading us towards meditation is satsang.

178 Maharaj Ji, sometimes people ask us questions like: I cannot understand why, when a person is initiated, he

*still attends meetings of different societies, other than
our own.*

Sister, we should not pay much attention to these things. I generally tell everybody at the time of initiation that I do not bind you
to any particular thing. I do not want you to withdraw from any
point, from any circle, any organization, any society, as long as
you remain on the principles of Sant Mat and you attend to your
meditation. The meditation automatically withdraws them from
all those things, eventually. When initiates no longer feel interested in them, they do not live in these things, then you do not
have to tell them, for it comes from their own heart. It is much
better not to tell them not to attend that meeting or to leave that
organization. There is no use in telling them. When they feel
the bliss of the elevation in their own heart, they will not feel
at home in those places, they will feel that they do not fit into
those things. Then they themselves will discontinue those things
and will be nearer to you. If, on the other hand, you try to pull
them away and tell them, "Do not go," their mind will always
want to go to that side from where they are being stopped. So
there is no sense in hurting anybody by telling them, "Why do
you attend that meeting, where is the sense in your going to
that group?" and all that. But if you create an atmosphere full of
love and devotion in your own group meetings, they would be
so happy that they would not like to go anywhere else. In that
way, you automatically attract them towards that atmosphere.

*They are initiates who ask those questions, and then we
have to answer them and don't know what to tell them.*

You tell them that we have no organization, that we are not
bound to any particular religion, we are free to go anywhere we
feel like going. We are only concerned with devotion to the Lord,
with our meditation. We are not bound to any particular thing

and we are not stopped from going anywhere. We go where we feel like going, and when we no longer feel we are a part of that activity, we ourselves will no longer wish to go there.

179 *If we are all the same and should love one another, why do only certain of the more well-to-do gain everything and all others are left out in our satsangs?*

I don't know about this problem. But there should be love for everybody. The meeting should be open to everybody, and there should be harmony and love among the satsangis, among the seekers. As you know, Christ has very clearly written about this in the Bible. It is the first commandment he gave. He said: Love the Lord thy God with all thy heart, with all thy soul, and with all thy mind. When you realize the Lord within yourself, naturally you are in love with the Lord with your mind, with your heart and with your soul. Then he said, once you realize the Lord within, love thy neighbour as thyself.⁶⁷ Then you will be able to love your neighbours.

This means that the whole creation is your neighbour and you will find the Lord in every part of the creation – in everyone he has created. Then you will see nothing but the Creator. Then you are not in love with the creation, you are in love with the Creator who has created this creation and who is in every part of this creation. So those who love the Lord naturally love his creation also. They see the Creator in every part of the creation.

It's not practical to love the Lord and hate his creation. If you love the Lord, you also love the creation. So if anybody doesn't love the satsangis or seekers, then I do not think he has the right approach.

180 *Maharaj Ji, in our various satsangs, we do not always have perfect harmony. I think our average is better than*

many of the other institutions, but still it lacks perfec-
tion, and from my limited point of view, it appears the
root of it is jealousy or envy among satsangis. How can
we as satsangis, not me particularly as the representa-
tive, but we generally as satsangis, avoid this difficulty?

This is a very difficult question to answer because sometimes
I too become the object of jealousy among the satsangis, and
I have to experience a lot of difficulty. To me everybody is the
same, but some people, for some reason, which perhaps even
they do not know, think they are nearer to me. Others think
they are a little away from me. We have to analyze what jealousy
is. I have something and the other person cannot get that and
he is jealous. He wants to get what I am possessing. From there
it starts – to possess what the other person is possessing, and
being incapable of possessing it, one starts being jealous of the
other. If we are material-minded – and we are now becoming
more material-minded every day, whether it is conscious or
unconscious – we are quite jealous. All are running this race
of materialism, running after these worldly objects and trying
to achieve these worldly possessions. It is actually making us a
jealous nation, jealous people, whether we realize it or not. We
are every day becoming more jealous in our attitude toward
everything. My neighbour has a good car, I have an old one.
I must have another car. I work. I am jealous. Why can I not
have what he has? Slowly and slowly it becomes a habit to be
jealous of each other.

But in Sant Mat there should be no jealousy. The question
of jealousy does not arise at all. Sometimes one feels that perhaps
the master is giving more attention to a particular disciple or is
no longer attending to other disciples. Then he starts becoming
jealous, but he does not know how much attention he needs and
how much the other person needs. There is a beautiful parable

which I can never forget. I read in the Bible that a shepherd has a hundred sheep and one goes astray. The shepherd leaves the ninety-nine sheep and goes after the hundredth sheep which has gone astray from the flock.[57] He goes after that sheep, and the other ninety-nine think he is ignoring them. He brings back that one sheep to the flock. Now if the ninety-nine sheep start becoming jealous of that other sheep, thinking that the shepherd is giving more attention to that one, how far are they justified? A sheep that has gone astray has to be brought back again to the fold. So the question of jealousy does not arise. The shepherd loves all the sheep, and anybody who goes astray will perhaps get a little more attention from the shepherd.

In a class, some students do not give any attention to their studies and they are displeased with being on the back benches. They do something to the teacher in order to draw his attention so that he will ask them to come to the front row. It is not that the teacher does not like the intelligent or the well-behaved students. Perhaps those students on the back benches needed more attention. So if the other students start getting jealous, demanding to know why those students have been given a front seat and more attention and not they, there is something wrong in their way of thinking.

If we cannot rise above these small differences, petty human jealousies, I think we have not understood the real teachings of Sant Mat at all. You see, there is a difference between physical love and spiritual love. Jealousy comes in physical love, when we are conscious of others. We are jealously possessing certain things, and we fear other people might deprive us of them. So we are jealous. It means that each of us is conscious of the other person, besides the Beloved. But in Sant Mat there is only one Beloved. You become unconscious that anybody else exists in the world for you. Jealousy starts only when you are conscious of anybody else existing besides the Beloved. But when you are in love with the master, when you are in love with the teachings, when you are in love with the Lord, you automatically rise so much higher and forget about the whole world. You are not conscious of anybody else existing in the world at all. You see only the Lord everywhere. Then you get rid of jealousy.

When we try to monopolize, we think that we must have something and that the other person should not have it. As far as the world is concerned, it may be true that one person is getting more attention than another, but as far as the master is concerned, he has equal love for every disciple. They may think he has given certain others more love, but he knows it is not so. I have told you that some students definitely need more attention than other students. So each one gets attention according to his needs at the time. Everybody needs love, some perhaps need a little more to understand what that is. But the master is gracious and gives his love equally to everybody, to every disciple, in the same way. Some people, due to their past sanskaras or past associations, do surround him or come nearer to him, but that does not mean that the master loves them more than those on the back benches, or those who are silent, or those who do not exchange words or exchange letters with him. It is wrong for them to think so; perhaps he loves them much more, and they have his attention more than those who are surrounding him. So there is no room for jealousy in Sant Mat. The question of becoming jealous does not arise at all. We must try to rise above these petty differences.

The nearer we are to the Lord, the nearer we feel to each other. The more we are away from the Lord, the more we are drifting away from each other. So if we have real devotion to the Lord, real devotion and yearning to meet him, we will also be nearer to each other. We will also love each other. We will also be good neighbours and good friends. Harmony and good association among us will also grow. If that real devotion is not in us, we really are not near him, and we will have so many differences among ourselves. So the more we love the Lord, the more that love will bring us nearer to each other. That is loving thy neighbour. Christ also said words to that effect when he said that those who loved him also loved one another.[115] Actually, when one loves the master, love for others is automatically created in him. Automatically such lovers feel that they are nearer to each other. There is a certain understanding between them which is lacking in other people. There is something which brings them together. There is a certain bond which is unknowingly bringing them nearer and nearer to each other.

Jealousy comes when we have organizations, administrations and offices like secretaries and presidents. When we start thinking about these offices, then we sometimes become victims of all these things. We forget that all these offices are for the purpose of rendering service. Service means what we are doing to please the master and to be of utility to the public and to that organization. Service is not for bossing. This presidency or secretaryship is something very different from what exists in outside organizations. This is to eliminate the ego, but we try to weigh all these things on the same scale, in the same way we are used to doing in worldly matters. So actually there should be absolutely no jealousy in any group. There should be no hatred towards anybody. When we hate anybody, actually we are hating ourselves. We have not risen above that, to where we can see the equality in everyone. There should be absolutely no jealousy. We should have harmony, and the more harmony, the nearer we are to each other and to the Lord.

You have read so often in the Bible that if you have any ill feeling, any grievance, anything against anybody, first go and ask for his forgiveness; otherwise, your prayer will not be accepted.[15] The Lord will not forgive you if you have not forgiven everybody else. It means that we have to pray with an open heart, with a clean heart, with a meek and humble heart. Except for the Lord, there should be nothing. The object behind Christ's saying is this: If our heart is full of malice, jealousy or hatred, that is not a pure heart, and our prayer will never be accepted unless we have a pure heart. So in order to make it pure, we have to drive out all sorts of ill-feelings and jealousy we have against anybody. When our heart becomes pure, our prayer is accepted. If we do not forgive anyone, how do we expect the Lord to forgive us? First we must earn it by our own example, that we forgive people. Naturally we can then ask the Lord to forgive us our sins. So you see, every saint has been trying to tell us the same thing, that we should absolutely have no ill feeling toward anybody. But because we are humans and have the instinct of possession, we become the victims of jealousy.

If I have any problem with satsangis, I think I have only this problem: Sometimes they do become jealous of each other. I have had personal experience of many such situations. For example, in India, when I go to a home, they all love me and I of course love them. I ask for a glass of water. Six or seven people run out and each brings me a glass of water. I do not know from whom to take the water. I know that the others will feel jealous, so I just excuse myself, saying that I think I do not need it. These are very petty things, but they go a long way. I know my people. I was not conscious of these things in the beginning, but now I think I am quite trained for these things. Somebody makes a cup of tea for me and somebody else presents it, and they have differences between each other – "He asked me, he meant me, and you have given him the cup of tea," and this and that – and they start quarrelling for no reason at all. Rather, it should make us happy. Does it not make us happy if more people come to the path? It does make us happy. So it should make us happy to see others like us holding to our own ideas, our own principles, our own master, the Lord. It should rather make us happy.

The trouble is that we wish to exclude others, just to possess the master ourselves. This is a wrong conception of love. We should be forgiving to everybody. We can pity people but we should not hate them. That is wrong. We should have absolutely no ill feeling or grudge against anybody, or such thoughts as, "He got a favour and I did not get a favour; he got time to talk and I did not get more time to talk; he was invited to come to India and I was not invited to come to India." These are all petty things. Sometimes I just do not understand. We have to rise above all these small things in order to have the real devotion for the Lord. On the path of love there is no jealousy. Everybody is absorbed in love. Everybody is loving. If there is any jealousy, I can only ask people to rise above it, to rise above such differences. If they do not, sometimes I think I have not been able to do my duty to help them rise above these things; that I have failed, not that they have failed.

There should be absolutely no jealousy at all in satsangis. We should have open feelings for everybody. Everybody wants to do something for the master, something for the Lord, something for the path, and we should have open arms for everybody to do so. It is not a monopoly of anybody. Everybody has a heart. Everybody wants to do the same thing, and we should give a chance to everybody to do the same thing. And naturally everybody's circumstances do not permit it, so no one has reason to be jealous if he cannot do it. He can say that the Lord got it done. He should like those people who are doing it. They should be appreciated. They should be loved because they are doing it, rather than other people being jealous because they are doing it. We should also try to do it; not by becoming jealous, but by becoming more helpful to them, more useful to them.

181 Master, can you speak a little bit about harmony?

I'll just tell you. Everybody loves the Lord. At least everybody *wants* to love the Lord. Are we jealous of each other, that someone loves the Lord more than me? And why does he love the Lord more than me, why does he pray more than me, why does he give more time to meditation than me? We're not jealous about it; we're happy. If anybody is attending more to meditation, loving the Lord more, seeing the Lord in everyone, we are rather happy for him. The problem with the master comes when we don't think he's God. When we bring him to the human level, then there are jealousies. If we keep him at the same level as God, it should rather please us, make us happy if anybody loves him more than we do. Then his love can strengthen our love. Our only problem comes when, being human, we pull him to the human level and we start being jealous of each other. If we keep him at the level of the Father, then there's no question of any jealousy at all.

In a class, there are so many students. Some students need personal attention. Other students are so sharp and intelligent that they grasp everything the teacher is saying and the teacher hardly even looks at them. They always come first in the class; they're at the top of the class. But those who are getting the personal attention of the professor may even be failing. The professor is teaching everybody.

So everybody has his own place. Some need more attention, some need less; some have different types of seva; and some have different ways of coming near the master. They may even get more scolding sometimes. Those who are nearer to the master may perhaps be getting much more scolding than the others who are not that fortunate. So we only see one aspect, not the whole picture.

*182 Maharaj Ji, when we are having satsang, sometimes we
have beginner satsangis who answer another person's
question. When they answer the question, and some
of the older satsangis know that the answer is wrong,
should we just let it go or should the older satsangis give
the correct answer?*

Sister, we can only share with others what we have. If we know
the answer, we should try to help them. If we do not know it, we
can refer to the books. If you cannot find it, you are most welcome to write to me. We have to help each other. Of course, we
can only help with what we know – what we have, we share.

*But if we just know through the books, should we just sit
quietly?*

No, you can quote from the book and very lovingly and gently
point out what seems to be the right answer, as mentioned in
the book. If anybody is in conflict with himself or in doubt,
he can write. As I explained to your group in Detroit, there
must be harmony among satsangis, there must be love among
satsangis. There must be an atmosphere of helping each other,
not an atmosphere of bossing over the new initiates or thinking ourselves superior to others. No, with a very loving and
helpful attitude, we have to help them and to make them
understand the light, the wisdom, the path. You see, we have
to build the atmosphere of love and peace around us in which
we have to live and meditate. If that is not there, there is absolutely no point in holding group meetings. We do not come
there to show our differences. We do not come there to show
our superiority. And such meetings should not be dinners and
parties and this and that. These are not the proper attitudes for
group meetings.

The object of group meetings is just to create a healthy atmosphere for meditation, to build that atmosphere of love in which we have to meditate, in which we have to live – that should become a fort for us to help us live in this world. That is the object of satsang and group meetings – to clear people's doubts, to make the path clearer to them, to create devotion, love and faith in them. If there is wrangling, if there is pushing and there are differences, I do not find any useful purpose in such group meetings at all. In every group meeting we should feel that our love has been strengthened for the master, that there is more devotion in us now for meditation, and we should be filled with a desire to meditate. There should be more peace within us after attending such group meetings.

Seniors have certain responsibilities to the new initiates: to give them a welcome smile, to make them feel welcome in these meetings, and to give them the feeling of equality in the meetings. We have a certain responsibility to be helpful to others, mainly by our attitude and good example. The group meetings serve the proper purpose only if there is absolute harmony and a calm and peaceful atmosphere of service and brotherly love.

183 *Maharaj Ji, along the line of what you were just talking about a while ago, about satsang meetings – is it acceptable to you to have some of us invite groups to come to our homes now and then?*

I cannot fix any set rule as to how you should conduct your meetings or where you should conduct your meetings. If there is affection and harmony among the group, it does not make any difference even if you sit on the roadside and conduct your meeting. It is the love, faith, and the devotion that matter; the place does not matter. It hardly makes any difference whether it is in your home or in a hall, or in some other place. When such questions arise, it indicates that there is no unity at all. You can meet anywhere, but it should be in the right spirit, keeping the purpose of the meeting in view. In that case the heart feels happy in love and devotion, and that meeting, regardless of where it is held, is useful even if it is held by the roadside somewhere. The place really makes no difference, as we have to create our own atmosphere of love and devotion. When others see that we are actually living up to the teachings and are happy and harmonious as a group, they will also feel attracted to the teachings. That is the best publicity.

184 How come we feel so much better when we're in the company of satsangis?

Sister, it's not a question of how we should feel. Automatically one is influenced. You go to a happy person and he will make you happy in two minutes; you go to a miserable man, it doesn't take one minute to make you miserable. We always radiate what we have. One who has been able to obtain peace within radiates peace, so we are automatically influenced by them. People who are attentive to meditation, when we are in their company, it strengthens our belief in meditation, our faith in meditation. We help each other. We have a common goal. We are always influenced by the company we keep.

185 Can you speak about building an atmosphere of meditation?

Well, the meetings we hold, the good company we keep, the books we read – these all help us build an atmosphere of meditation. Because we are always affected by the atmosphere in which we live. If you go to a happy person, he makes you happy. If you go to a miserable person, he makes you miserable. So if there is an atmosphere of meditation and devotion and love for the Lord, naturally you are influenced by that and you start thinking in the same way. The atmosphere always helps us. That is why people go to churches and mosques or temples, just to feel that atmosphere in which we can remember the Father. Otherwise the same books are at home; the same bricks and mortar are at home. We go to these places only for the atmosphere, which reminds us of the Father. So the atmosphere goes a long way – that is why we hold satsang so often, and why we write so many books.

186 In our local group, we often have what we call an all-day love affair with the master. In the morning we'll have a kind of formal satsang, when someone will give a gist of the teachings and then somebody else will give a satsang on some subject. Is that okay?

It depends upon how the group wants to conduct satsang. Maharaj Ji [Maharaj Sawan Singh] used to tell us that even if you don't derive any advantage from the satsang, at least during that time you don't go to bad company. That advantage is always there. If you don't attend the satsang meeting, you might be rushing to some other social gathering, and God knows what you might collect there. If the stone doesn't dissolve in the water, at least it saves itself from the heat of the sun. That's the example Great Master used to give us. If people in the satsang don't attend to meditation, at least they are saving themselves from the vices of the world to a great extent. Even if they don't dissolve in the water, they at least save themselves from the heat of the sun – the bad influence of other people. So that advantage is always there. If one can also take advantage of the satsang, there's nothing like it. If one comes inspired and full of devotion – he's happy and enjoying meditation and wants his battery to be recharged by attending a satsang – then it is all right.

187 *When satsangis get together for satsang, is the master present in a different way than he is present within each satsangi all the time?*

We have to create a holy atmosphere. We should build an atmosphere of satsang there, so that when we go back home we can build our treasure in that atmosphere. Master is within every one of us, but we always get strength and help from one another's company. If you meet another devotee of the Lord and you associate with him, you are automatically filled with love and devotion for the Lord. He strengthens your faith; he strengthens your love and devotion. It is natural.

188 *I would like to ask about the possibility of starting groups. Is it possible to contact other people who believe along these lines, to get together? Groups should be established so that the teachings can expand.*

Brother, we are so few in number that it would be an unnecessary burden on initiates, on satsangis to spend money and to make places and then to collect there. Then there may be some differences in organization. I do not want satsangis to be lost in organizations or in management of those organizations and forget the real objective of initiation. When the number of initiates increases, we may find it necessary, and that time may come. But now [1964] I think there is hardly any need. We have a limited number of satsangis in almost every big city. So we can hold meetings in homes, as we do now, gathering in different houses, in various cities.

WHAT IS SEVA?

*189 Maharaj Ji, today in satsang you spoke a lot about seva.
I was wondering if you could talk to us about what you
said, and also if you could say something about how we
could best do seva so that it's most helpful to our spiritual growth.*

Seva has been so clearly described in the books. Real seva is meditation – withdrawing your consciousness back to the eye centre
and attaching it to the divine light or melody within, attaching
it to the sound within. Other sevas are means to that end.

Seva of the body is when we serve people with our body, so
that we may eliminate ego from within ourselves and be filled
with humility. Then there is seva with money. As Christ has said,
unless we detach ourselves from our worldly possessions, it's very
difficult for us to go back to the Father.[61] So when we give our
money in seva, in service to the masses, we detach ourselves from
that money. And then there is seva of the mind. Living the Sant
Mat way of life and creating a foundation for meditation is seva
of the mind. With the help of simran and dhyan, we withdraw
our consciousness back to the eye centre and hold it there – that
is seva of the mind. These three sevas are to achieve one end – to
be one with that divine melody within. That is the purpose of
real seva. That is a real seva in itself.

So Soami Ji was laying emphasis on that point – that you
should do that seva which pleases the master. And this seva
pleases the master – other sevas are means to that end. So every
seva pleases the master, and all these sevas will lead you to the
real seva. The real seva will help you to go back to the Father. The
purpose of seva is to create humility and meekness within ourselves, not to achieve any leadership, to show our superiority over
others, to boss others. The purpose of seva is to please the person

whom we are serving, not to show that you are superior to him, not to boss him, not to show your authority over him – that is no seva at all. Seva is to please another person. If the person whom you are serving is pleased, then your seva is beneficial. If he feels hurt, if he feels humiliated that you are trying to boss him or show his weaknesses or show your superiority to him, then of course he is not happy. And unless he is happy, the purpose of seva is not achieved. So we have to do seva to please another. If they are pleased with our seva, then our seva is fruitful.

190 Can you say something about the value of seva?

Seva comes from the heart. It is not a compulsion for any-body – it's not that you have to do it, but you want to do it. It must come from within, and there must be love in doing seva. There should be no feeling of obligation that we have to do it.

191 Maharaj Ji, could you tell us the value of seva at home, at our own satsang centres?

The greatest reward in seva is the contentment and happiness that you feel within, that you get an opportunity to serve some-one. That is the greatest happiness one can ever get, to make someone happy. It doesn't make you so happy if anybody makes *you* happy, but it definitely makes you very happy when you are in a position to make someone else happy, and that is the real seva. Seva for any institution, seva for any individual, seva for the masses – in other words, a charitable attitude of helping other people – that is seva. We do seva with our body, we do seva with our mind, we do seva with our money. The base of seva is love and devotion for the Father. Seva is not meant to make one a leader in the community, in the group, or to wield any authority – that is not seva.

Seva should create humility in us, should eliminate ego from within us. The more you feel at the level of the earth, the more your mind will go to meditation, to the Father. So seva always has an advantage. That is why you find this missionary spirit in Christianity. That's the greatest boon Christ taught his disciples – serve one another, help one another, help the needy, serve the needy. That's the real seva.[115]

192 Maharaj Ji, will you please tell us something about seva and the value of doing seva?

The purpose of seva is to create humility in us, to help us become one with our fellow humans, to be humble, meek, to fill ourselves with humility, because the Lord created us all alike. It is the ego which separates us from the Father, and we have to eliminate that ego. When we serve the masses, serve the people, then automatically we become humble. That is the real purpose of seva – just to be humble, just to be meek, just to be one with the masses. When we sit together to eat and work shoulder to shoulder, we are nearer to each other than when we sit on a very high pedestal. At some point we all become one, and that fills us with humility.

The purpose of the guru opening a langar, a common kitchen, was so that his followers could eat together in that kitchen. There is a caste system in India, as you know – so many differences among high caste, low caste, economic classes, social classes. But when people all sit together and eat the same food, naturally they feel for each other. When they all work together for a common cause, they feel for each other, and automatically ego is eliminated.

Seva of wealth is to detach us from our wealth and use it for a good cause, so that it may not tempt us to evils and vices. Christ said that it is easier for a camel to go through the eye of a needle than for a rich man to go to heaven.[61] This means that one who's attached to riches can never go back to the Father. And surplus money generally becomes the cause of vices and bad habits.

193 Maharaj Ji, yesterday you spoke about seva done with love and humility. Love, I can understand a little because there's human love, which gives me some idea of what true love is. But I don't think I can feel a little humility. Either I feel humility or no humility. So my question is, what is true humility?

Well, brother, seva can never be done without love, and if you do seva, humility automatically comes. Seva is always done with love and humility. Humility is a part of love. If there is love, automatically there is humility in it. There can be no love without humility. Love makes you humble. Love makes you meek. Love means you want to do that which pleases the other person, not what pleases yourself. Similarly, seva is done to please another person, not to please yourself. When you please another person, the reaction will be that you'll be happier to do seva. There's more happiness in giving than taking, more happiness in donating than accepting any gift, more happiness in helping somebody than getting help from anybody.

People have a wrong concept that they become happier when they accept something in charity or accept some help. But the pleasure that you get by helping somebody, making somebody happy in life – there is nothing to compare with that pleasure. You have a certain satisfaction within yourself that you have been able to do something good for somebody. So seva is always done with love, otherwise it's not seva. Seva is not mechanically working with your hands. Seva is our intention to please another person, to do something for another person so that the other person is pleased with what I am doing. So it means there's a certain love within us for the institution, for the person for whom we are doing something. Automatically there will be humility. Humility is part of love. Love is part of seva.

194   If we are trying to do seva for our sangat, and we notice that we are so full of pride that even our attempt at seva has a lot of ego attached to the result or to the satsang we give, should we give up that seva until we can be more detached?

We should give up that ego rather than the seva. Seva will help you to create humility sooner or later. But give up the ego which you think is attached to your type of seva. By running away from the situation, we don't solve any problem. We have to tackle the situation.

195   If you're cleaning your house for satsang because satsang is in your house, is that seva?

Well, if you are calculating that by this you will get some merit, then you don't get anything at all. In seva we never calculate what gain we are going to get out of it. Seva is spontaneous – the desire to do it comes from within. We never think about any gain. We are filled with love and devotion for other people and we would like to serve them, help them, do something for them. We never think about what gain we are going to get out of it. If your mind calculates how much you have gained, then you gain nothing. Love forces you to do something for another. If you love somebody, you always want to do something that pleases the other person. A lover never tries to think what he gains by loving the other person. The lover never calculates, never thinks. He is happy that he gets the opportunity to love the other person. So we should be happy that we get the opportunity to serve the masses because we love them, because they belong to the Lord. Gain is in his hand, but we should never calculate such things.

196 Would you talk about selfless service and how to generate more of that?

Well, sister, service always comes out of love. Whom you love, you want to serve, to please. Service is not to show your superiority or authority over anybody but to create humility in yourself. You do it to please another person, not to exert your authority over another person – that is no service. So the people you love, you always want to serve, to please. You don't want them to dance to your tune, you want to dance to their tune. If we love the Lord, we love his creation, and we also want to serve his creation because we see the Lord in everyone that he has created. We don't want to hurt them. We want to do that which pleases the Lord and avoid what displeases him because we don't want to offend him by our omissions and commissions – and that is service. One can expand it in any direction, to any extent. There can be no service without love.

197 Maharaj Ji, in the West, away from the Dera, is there a way that our worldly work can be a form of seva? Is there some approach to our worldly work that you can take to make it like seva?

If you keep the Lord and the master in your mind for all twenty-four hours, whatever you do is seva. You don't bring your ego into whatever you do, you do everything as a duty towards your Father. If the Lord is always in your mind, whatever you do is seva.

198 Master, sometimes a certain sevadar in my area acts a little bossy.

If someone is spiritually advanced and he's trying to give strength and faith to other disciples, he should not feel that he's a boss over them. He should feel that he's their servant. He has been given this seva and opportunity by the master, and he should be happy to be their servant and not try to boss over or act as if he is superior to them. He must be humble and meek. Only then can he be perfect in his seva. Only then can he do his duty. If he starts thinking that he's a boss, that he's superior to the others, then the ego comes in and he loses the opportunity of that seva.

199 Master, if meditation is the highest form of seva, is any other form of seva – the external forms of seva – really necessary for inner progress, and if so, how much external seva should we be doing?

External seva definitely helps us in every way. It helps to eliminate ego from us. We are so conscious of our rank, our wealth, our status, our achievements. These things make us so egoistic, and seva helps to eliminate all that. It brings us to the human level. It definitely helps us.

How much seva should we do?

It depends upon the individual and the opportunity. It is entirely by his grace that we get an opportunity to do seva and that we are capable. Everybody doesn't get the opportunity. Many people may be wanting it, may be anxious to do it, but they never get an opportunity. Their circumstances don't permit them, their environment doesn't permit them, their family commitments don't permit them. It's by his grace that we get this opportunity, I would say. So we should be grateful to those people also who give us the opportunity to serve them.

TYPES OF SEVA

200 Maharaj Ji, you've written in one of the books – I believe it was Divine Light *– something to the effect that Sach Khand can be reached through either simran and bhajan or seva.*

No. Seva is of four types. Rather, seva is actually one. The other three sevas are means to achieve that one seva: seva with the body, seva with the mind and seva with money. All these sevas are done so that we may be able to bring our consciousness to the level of the shabd.

We do seva with the body to eliminate our ego, to create humility within ourselves, to be one with the masses and to free our mind of distinctions like rich people, poor people, this caste, that caste, black and white. We mix with everybody, so whether I'm the employer or the employee, we all become one in seva. Another seva is of wealth. This is a source of evil at a certain point. Attachment to it pulls us back to the world and leads us to the senses. Its exploitation leads us to the senses and to worldly pleasures, so we try to detach ourselves from it by using our wealth for the welfare of human beings. Then there is seva with the mind, which is running to the senses and spread into the whole creation. We try to bring the mind back to the eye centre by means of simran.

All these sevas are done to achieve one seva, which is also the biggest seva – to bring our consciousness in touch with the shabd by means of our meditation. Every saint has used the word 'seva', by which they mean meditation. Other sevas are just to clean our cup so that we may be able to fill it with that nectar within. If our cup is dirty, it's not worthy to be filled. If humility is not within us, if we are attached to wealth, if our consciousness is spread into the whole creation, we cannot taste that nectar within us – as Christ calls it, the living water which gives us everlasting life.[82] When we are able to achieve all those three sevas, only then are we fortunate enough to taste that nectar within. Then our cup is full.

201 Master, does seva burn up our sinchit karmas?

I don't know what your concept of seva is. Seva is of four types. The first three are with the mind, the body and wealth. These sevas help us to clean our mind. When you want to fill a utensil with milk or anything, you clean it first, otherwise whatever you put in it will just get spoiled. You wash it, then whatever you put in it is always preserved. So the purpose of seva is to clean our mind so that we can withdraw our consciousness to the eye centre and attach it to the shabd and nam. That is the real seva. The other three sevas are just the means to clean the utensil so that it can be filled with nectar, with shabd.

The whole of meditation is seva. The purpose of meditation is to prepare us to accept what the Lord gives, to prepare us not to expect. In prayer we always expect, but in meditation we always accept. That is the difference between meditation and prayer. We pray because we're expecting something; we do meditation because we are preparing to accept what he wants to give us. In prayer we speak to the Lord; in meditation we hear him. So meditation itself is a seva. First we have to clean the utensil, then we have to fill it. This is also known by mystics as seva. So whenever a disciple can get an opportunity for seva, most welcome.

202 Is seva always serving someone else?

Seva means service to the Father. Actually, it is our own service. Seva means to serve someone. So we are serving ourselves. It's a service of the soul. We can purify our soul with the help of our body, mind and wealth. You see, now we do not realize that our real self is the soul. We think our real self is the ego, the body, the mind. To begin to realize that the reality is the soul, not the body or the ego, is also service. To eliminate that I-ness, we have to devote our time to meditation. Actually, it is a service to the soul. We are taking pity on ourselves, so to say – taking pity on the soul.

Since the soul ultimately has to become the Father, this service is known as service to the Father. Every soul is potentially God. We have to not only realize that, but also actually become God, by becoming perfect like him. We do that by releasing our soul from the mind, by eliminating the ego and purifying the soul. Once the soul is purified, automatically it merges back into the Father. So it's a service to the Father, so to say, because ultimately the soul becomes the Father. That is why it is known as seva or service.

203 *Maharaj Ji, could you elaborate a little bit on how we go about dedicating our mind, our body, our wealth to the master?*

Dedicating all these things is simply meant for the purification of our mind, to detach ourselves from our body and from our wealth and to attach our mind to the shabd. What you are referring to is the three types of service. Service with the body is to subdue our ego, our self-importance. When we do some social service, under the instructions of the master, and move shoulder to shoulder with the common man, much of our pride and I-ness is eliminated, and we feel on the same level as any other man. Too much wealth, and attachment to it, leads to many unhealthy desires and habits. The master does not want our wealth, but when we spend it under his instructions – in acts of charity and so forth – we are detached from it to a great extent. Service with the mind is to do our meditation and live in the teachings of Sant Mat.

204 Master, giving the master one's wealth, body and mind seems an almost impossible thing, at certain levels. How can we really accomplish this?

Brother, the master never accepts a single penny from any disciple. If he accepts money, he's not a master. Giving our wealth, body and mind to the master means thinking that everything belongs to him and nothing belongs to us in this world. We are only puppets. Whatever he wants us to do in this world, we will do. Our wealth belongs to him. Just as a clerk pays the bills with his employer's wealth and buys whatever his employer wants, our wealth does not belong to us. So don't think that this wealth which we have acquired is ours. It has been given to us by our master, and we are only spending it on his behalf, so that we may detach from it. But he doesn't accept it from us.

And giving our mind to the master means keeping our mind within the commandments which have been told to us at the time of initiation. Not compromising with those principles is giving our mind to the master. Giving our body to the master means serving the creation of the Creator with our body. That will create humility in you because this body is not yours. When you think it is yours, you want people to praise you, to give you glory. So ego comes into it. Think humbly: This body doesn't belong to me – even this belongs to the Father, even this belongs to the master. Do not use your body as your own. Use it as if it belongs to your master, and then you won't ever do evil deeds, because it doesn't belong to you at all. So be of service to his devotees, to his creation. That is using our body as if it belonged to the master. Master needs neither our body, our mind, nor our wealth. These are for our own spiritual progress.

CHARITY AND DESIRELESS ACTION

205   I have always been interested in helping handicapped children, from a teaching point of view. Not as a teacher, but as a helper.

Sister, we should try our best to help them. We must help people in the world. We are born for that purpose. Only humans can be helpful to humans. But we should not be involved so much that we do not have time for our own selves. Keeping our other duties in view, we should try to be helpful to others, according to our means. When sometimes, even with our best intentions, we are not able to help them, that is their karma. Their karma will automatically take care of them. But we must help them as much as we can, according to our means and the time at our disposal, so as not to interfere with our other duties. We should always be kind and helpful to each other. Yet, when we are not able to help them as much as we want to, then we can say that it is their karma that we cannot help them to a greater extent.

206   If we are all a part of all that lives and moves and has its being in this world, then should we not feel so close to all other things that we should help wherever we can, or even go out of our way to try to help and not consider that it is karma, and if we help, will it bring us back again into another life in this world?

We should definitely help others, and we are meant to help others, but not at our own cost. First we must help ourselves in order to be able to help others. If we are not living with ourselves, actually we are not in a position to help others. We must come to that level to be able to help others, to feel affinity with them, oneness with them. There is no harm in helping anybody; in fact, we should help others – not only human beings, but even the lower creation. We should help them and will help them by not killing them and by being merciful to them, by not eating them, and in so many other ways we can help.

When the devotion of the Lord comes in us, we find that same devotion of the Lord in everyone. Then we actually want to help everybody. We feel like helping because we find the Lord within everyone. The Lord is our object of love, he is our beloved. So we want to do everything for others, just for the love of the Lord and not the personality. But that is possible only if we develop that devotion and love of the Lord within ourselves. As long as we do not succeed in doing that, I do not see how we can help others. If there is kindness in my heart, naturally I will feel a little tender about things and want to help others. But if my own heart is rough and hard, and not at all mild, I am not in a position to help others. I must therefore first improve myself, help myself, so that I will be in a position to help others.

207 *Maharaj Ji, sometimes we have been asked, what about people who feel that they have a job to do in the world for other people – to be of help – not necessarily in their profession, but just to be helpful? How does this fit into Sant Mat?*

Sister, we should always try to be helpful to others. We should not help from the point of view that someday they will also help us. We should help without any intention of getting a reward. Generally, we think of the missionary spirit as being helpful to other people now, so that later in this life or in the next life they will be helpful to us. That attitude is not correct, for then we are sowing the seed to return to this world in order to get the reward of what we have done for them. We should be helpful to the public, helpful to society, helpful to everybody in whatever way we can. All this should be done with a detached mind.

It should be remembered that we need also to help ourselves in order to be in a position to help others. Actually, if we do not help ourselves but try to help others, we are deceiving ourselves and we are deceiving others. So first we must help ourselves and then we should help others.

208 Master, could you please say something about charity. Should we do it? To whom should we give it and how much?

Brother, charity should come from the heart. There is no tax which you have to pay. It only concerns your heart, what pleases you to give in charity. That is the first thing. Then it should never be done to blow your own trumpet, as Christ says – just to gain public appreciation and impress people.[19] We should never bargain with the Father – that if I give you one thousand dollars, you will give me twenty thousand dollars in the next birth or thirty thousand dollars in the next birth. That is not charity. That's bargaining with him, trying to make a business deal with him. We do charity for our own good. He has given us so much surplus, and we want to use it in the service of his creation so that we may get detached from it. Whatever we have earned, we should become worthy of what the Lord has given us. In gratitude we'd like to share with his creation. Charity is not to impress other people, to build our ego, to boost our ego.

People have a wrong concept of charity. They try to blow their trumpets in the newspaper, on billboards so that everybody knows what they have given in charity. And even if they go to a temple or a church, they try to bargain with the Father: I am giving to you today because I have a surplus, but when I need it, you should then give to me. Since they can't take their wealth with them after death, they want to invest now, so that maybe they can get it after death. We're trying to be very clever. Otherwise we know we have to leave it here. So we try to bribe the Father, cheat him – we'll donate money to you now, and after our death you help us. This is no charity. It's just self-deception. It is your motive and intention with which you give things in charity that matters.

209 *I was wondering if it is right to give money to people; how should we give, and to whom?*

There's no harm in giving money in charity to deserving institutions, to deserving people, helping people who are really in need. But giving to those people who will use it for drugs or alcohol or who will just waste the money in sensual pleasures is no good at all.

210 *Maharaj Ji, is it consistent with Sant Mat that satsangis should adopt an attitude of complete indifference to the suffering world? That is, should a satsangi say to people: You are suffering, but you are suffering the results of your past actions, so I needn't do anything to bring you succour or help you in any way?*

If that had been our attitude, I would not have opened the eye camp at the Dera every year or taken on the very big hospital project. We are very much concerned with the suffering of humanity, and we want to do whatever we can. Our attitude should always be to help and to be a source of strength to people, and to be loving and kind to everybody. But in spite of all that, we know that we cannot change their karma.

We cannot have the attitude that I am not going to help you because it is in your karma to suffer. It may be in my karma to help that person. How can I deny him help? If it is written in my karmas that I will be a source of strength to somebody, if my loving regards or kindness can help somebody to pull out of a certain misery, how can I deprive myself of discharging my duty? That may be in my karma to do it.

So that attitude is wrong. Our attitude should be one of help, cooperation and kindness to people. But the philosophy is right in that everybody has to go through their own karmas. We do not know what is in their karmas or what role we have to play in their karmas, so we should do our best.

∼ 14 ∼

A Balanced Life

*211   You ask us to lead a normal, natural life on this path.
       Could you please clarify for us all the aspects that a nor-
       mal, natural life may consist of?*

I don't know what this question means. But I generally mean
that we are to live in this world; we are not to escape from this
world or run away from our responsibilities as a wife, a husband,
a child or a citizen; or hide ourselves somewhere in the Himalayas or somewhere in synagogues or churches and not shoulder
our responsibilities. We have to live in this world but not be of
this world, not be attached to this world.

Guru Nanak and other mystics have given us a very beautiful example. A married girl lives with her parents, but she's in
love with her husband, though he's far away. Similarly, we have
to live in this world, but our real husband is the Father. Our
love, our devotion is in the Father, and at the same time we are
living in this world, fulfilling all our responsibilities and duties.
I generally give the example of a duck. It remains in the water,
but whenever it flies, it flies with dry feathers. It's the same as
the water lily, whose flowers always remain above the water.

Actually, these examples mean that we should try to keep ourselves attached to that holy spirit, the shabd or nam within, while we perform our worldly duties and responsibilities. So even while living in this world, we'll be out of this world.

212 *Master, I find that bhajan makes the daily living very difficult for me, because when the bhajan is truly concentrated, I find that my mind, my spirit, or my soul, whatever it is, is reluctant to once again re-enter the swirl of daily living.*

We have to do both things. We have to live in the world, but we have to meditate also. We have to keep the balance, because a certain load of karma can be cleared only by facing life, not just by attending to meditation. When we become too absorbed in meditation, sometimes the master withdraws the grace so that we work in the world also. You are not to leave your worldly work. Rather you may even be pushed to the world, to face the world.

It's a very strange thing. I can tell you a little from my personal experience also. First we have no love for the path, we have no love for the master. Master forces us to love him, creates love for the Lord in us. He holds satsangs, he makes us work, he makes us do seva. All these things he does just to fill us with love and devotion for the Father. And when that love arises in us, when we become victims of that love, then he conceals himself. Then it is a game of hide-and-seek. He does not want us to be so absorbed that we leave our worldly duties and worldly work.

As a child, I got my education in the colony here – probably I was just five or six when I was brought here by the master. Naturally as a child everybody is fond of play and friends, so we used to play a lot here and run about on the river banks and here and there. But a man would always be sent to bring us from where we were, and we would be made to hear the satsang. We were made to sit at the front, and if we were noisy, we would have to sit at the back, but we could not leave the satsang. We had to be present in satsang. Slowly and slowly, slowly and slowly, things started making their way in us, and we realized what we were getting. Then we were pushed out of the Dera and told to go and practice law here and do jobs there, and don't come to Beas for six months and then don't come every month. I used to come from Sirsa every month, and hardly a day would pass that Great Master would not call me and say: "Haven't you gone back yet? So go tomorrow." Sometimes I had to bring a written note from the magistrate that court really was closed for holiday. Then I'd be sent packing before even four days had passed.

This is a very strange game of hide-and-seek. As children we were all right – we were very much used to playing with our friends. We never thought about the path and the master and love and God and all that. So first the master created all that in us. When he succeeded in that, then he pushed us into the world to face the world. So this happens; there's nothing new to it. The master would like us to keep the balance.

213 *How do you achieve a balance between a materialistic attitude and a spiritual attitude?*

Christ said that you can't have two masters.[24] Either mammon is your master or God is your master. When you are below the eye centre, your mind is your master; when you are above the eye centre, God is your master. To keep a balance in the world, you should hold your attention at the eye centre. If you do this and if you're attached to the spirit within, you will be able to keep your balance in this world; you will be able to discharge your worldly duties and achieve that goal for which you have taken this human form. That is keeping your balance.

We have to go through the karmic accounts which we have collected in past lives; that is why we have taken this birth. But we should not forget why we have been given the opportunity of being born in this human form. It is to go back to the Father. So he says, if you withdraw your consciousness to the eye centre and become one with that spirit, that holy light within yourself, you will be able to discharge your worldly duties better. Also, you will be able to go back to the Father. That is keeping a balance in this world.

214 *I have got to know whether one should meet a problem head-on, or whether one knows inside what is right or not?*

We should not feel disturbed inside. We should not lose our balance. We know these things do happen and everybody has to pay for his own karma. People are just dancing to the tune of their mind, so we have to adjust. If we try to solve the problems of the world, we can never succeed. We can only rise above these problems. If we start picking up the thorns of the world, we can never succeed, but if we have strong shoes on our feet, these pricks do not bother us. We should rise above these things by means of our spiritual practice and not feel much disturbed about them.

215 *How can you keep up your interest in daily life after studying and hearing about spiritual things? For me, it is sometimes a problem. Sometimes I am feeling a little bit paralyzed after studying or hearing spiritual things.*

Brother, the main thing is, what is our interest in life? We have to keep our goal in view and we have to follow the path which leads us back to our destination. And, keeping that goal in view, we have to do our worldly duty. We should not get so much involved in our worldly responsibilities and duties that we forget the purpose for which we have taken this birth. But, keeping that purpose in view, we have to do our worldly duties also in order to attain that goal.

216 *Should we shut ourselves off from worldly news and that sort of thing, or would that tend to make us less efficient in performing our worldly duties?*

We have never advocated that we have to leave the world. We are a part of a chain, and we have to remain part of that chain. You can't run away from the world. You have certain obligations, certain duties towards some people, towards your country, towards your family, towards your children. You have to discharge all those duties and responsibilities, but then, above all, you have a duty towards the Father and you also have to discharge that – not one at the cost of the other. As you work to support your wife and children, similarly you work to support your soul.

Our main object is to escape and also to discharge our responsibilities and our obligations in life. You can't escape from that. Even if we try to escape, there's no place to go. We will still be in the world. We will still need food, shelter, clothes. So we have merely become a parasite on society. Our needs are the same. It's just self-deception to think that I've left my children, my wife, my house, and I've gone to a forest, to the Himalayas and I'm meditating there. What have you left? Your mind is still with your family and you still need food, shelter, clothing. What have you left? Even the Himalayas are part of the world.

It is the mind which is to be withdrawn from these attachments. Being with them you're not to be attached to them. But even being away from them you can be attached to them –

running away from the situation doesn't solve any problem at all. Rather, that creates suppression, obsession. Slowly and slowly this obsession and suppression builds up, and then there's a reaction – sometimes a horrible reaction. So we have to live in the world like everyone else and yet not forget our goal, our object in life – the path which leads us back to our destination.

We try to escape from situations because we think we're weak. We can't face them. But that's cowardice. We think we're influenced by the people and that they pull us down. But if we are strong, we won't be frightened. We will be able to influence them. Why should they be able to influence us? So we must build that strength within ourselves. It has to come from within, not from running away from life. Why should we run away from situations? Face them.

217   *So it's a matter of clearing away everything in life that is unnecessary, of making that choice?*

No, it's a matter of changing the attitude of your mind. You have to do your worldly work; you have to discharge your responsibilities, your obligations. But your attitude of mind can be one-pointed, focused within. Then you don't forget your goal, your destination. You are not so lost in outside activity that you forget your destination and goal. You are not to leave the world, your obligations or responsibilities. You have to discharge them. But an actor is conscious that he's acting.

One more question. I find that my mind becomes obsessed with things that have nothing to do with my life – for example, wanting to change the world. Really silly things. It takes up all my meditation time.

Sister, it depends upon the individual, how much we can give to the world and how much we have to give to ourselves. There's no do's or don'ts. Everybody individually has to plan and to think how much wealth we can give to others and how much we have to give to ourselves. We shouldn't give to others so much that we forget what we have to give to ourselves.

218 *Maharaj Ji, we're told, particularly as satsangis, to do our work particularly well. How would you advise us to avoid becoming too involved?*

Well, sister, if you are tied to a strong chain, you can move only within a limited area. So if we are tied to our meditation every day, no matter how much we're involved in other things, we will always remain within the circle – we will not be able to get out of the circle. If the chain is broken, then of course you are absolutely gone, you're involved. So the chain of meditation should not be broken. Meditation must be attended to every day, and then no matter how much you try to involve yourself in other activities, you'll never be allowed to go astray at all. You'll never be allowed to get involved so much that you forget your real path, because your chain is very strong – you are just tied down to that bulldozer and it will not let you go anywhere. So if we don't compromise with that, then everything will be all right.

219 *Master, you say that people who meditate get more will-power to go through their fate karmas. I've heard someone say that people who meditate can also get more violent, more angry than people who don't meditate. Is this true? Is that the other side of the coin?*

It can be. Sometimes people just try to close themselves off in a room and don't want to lead a natural, normal adult life. They try to meditate all day and the mind reacts, and they lose their balance. They behave quite abnormally. Meditation is a slow process. That is why it is known as *sahaj marg* [the natural way]. You have to be part of the world and also attend to meditation. You cannot fight with your mind day and night. You also have to divert it into worldly affairs, and then bring it back to meditation. Otherwise, sometimes you build too much suppression, and the mind can react, sometimes violently. That is not a healthy approach. So we are never advised to cut off all our worldly activities and just attend to meditation. We have to lead a normal human life. We have to be a part of normal society and then also attend to our meditation. Meditation is a way of life, it's not just closing yourself in a room and cutting yourself off from everybody and sitting in meditation. That's not meditation. Meditation should reflect in your whole life, your whole day. It becomes a part of your life, your way of life. That way your whole day is spent in meditation.

220 *In following the material life in whatever our ambitions or worldly job is, in differentiating between how much we should pursue our career or profession or whatever and our spiritual efforts, should we not try hard to see that our material life does not affect our spiritual attempts?*

We shall have to try our best for our living in this world, and then if we do not achieve it, we should leave it to the will of the Lord. The results should be left to him. That does not mean that we should not try to do our best for our promotion and work hard to earn all that. We have certain responsibilities and duties which we must do in this world. At the same time, we should not get so involved in these things that we forget their real purpose. These are just a means to a certain end. We should not be so involved in the means that we forget the end. The end should always be kept in view, and we should try to achieve that end.

221 *There are only so many hours in a day. Is there a certain*
number of hours we should work?

We are to consider so many factors in our life. You cannot draw
a line about how many hours we should work for our living – it
depends on so many factors.

Well, supposing I work only six hours a day and spend all
the other time in meditation, or trying to?

I personally feel that if we are regular and punctual in our meditation and we are living in Sant Mat and for Sant Mat, then
two hours and thirty minutes or three hours daily are sufficient
for meditation.

I have worked eighteen hours a day for two years straight
without any time off.

I am just telling you, since you have asked me the question. It
is not the mechanical meditation which brings about better
results. It is the living of Sant Mat. By meditation we have to
build that atmosphere around us in which we have to live, in
which we have to imbibe Sant Mat. It is not the time that matters. It is living the life of Sant Mat, that life of devotion, that
life of meditation that matters. We do not live in it only for that
two- or three-hour period. We live in it the whole day. That does
not mean that we give three hours to meditation and the rest of
the day we forget what Sant Mat is. We have to live in Sant Mat
daily, for twenty-four hours. Out of that, two or three hours of
meditation is sufficient, if thereby we can build that atmosphere
in which we have to live the whole day.

222 *I find it very difficult on this path to balance a house-*
holder's life, which is what you suggest for most of us,

167

versus living alone. I have such a desire for time alone to put in my meditation, with your grace – to be alone and think of you and to be in nature, and when I'm in a relationship or a householder's life, it seems that that takes me out into the world. I'd like to know if it's at all possible to balance that – to be in a marriage that's harmonious, toward the light, toward you, and make as much progress as one could possibly make alone. I find it almost impossible to reconcile the lower desires with the higher desires.

Well, sister, definitely we have to balance our life, balance our worldly activities with our spiritual activities. We definitely have to keep the balance. We have to discharge our family responsibilities and also to attend to meditation. Meditation will help you to discharge your obligations with a detached mind. Slowly and slowly you will automatically feel detached from all that, even while discharging your responsibilities.

How will I know when it's the right time for me to marry?

Well, sister, marriage solves lots of problems. It may create many problems, but it also solves many problems. Probably it is a necessity – somehow we can't help it. These are natural urges we have to satisfy to some extent – to be a mother, to be a father, to have a family, to have a house, to have a partner. Human beings have these natural urges, so we have to satisfy them. Otherwise there'll be a lot of suppression and we may not be able to resist those urges. You will always be fighting with them and may not be attending to meditation at all.

223 *Is there no advantage then in cloisters, where people keep to themselves and are not distracted by the world?*

Sister, there are two sides to that. Some people may be in a room, yet they are not there, because their mind is always running out. And there are other people who are moving about with everybody, yet their mind is not moving; it is somewhere else. So it is a question of the development of your mind. It does not make any difference whether you are in a cloister or outside, for you have to control the mind and not the body. If you have to imprison the body, then it may be a different proposition to avoid people physically. But you have to avoid them mentally. For example, if you are in a house but you are always suppressing the desire to go out with friends and all that, there is no sense in confining yourself in the house.

We have to train and develop our mind so that in whatever situation we may be, we are not affected by anything, because our attention is somewhere else. Naturally we have mental stress, so we have to avoid those situations where we think we cannot stand them because we are weak and we may become a slave of an undesirable habit due to falling prey to temptations and attachments. We naturally try to avoid those situations. But that is not a permanent escape. We have to develop our mind so that wherever we may be thrown, we remain on our path, on our way, with our own self. Otherwise that would be a suppression and suppression is never good, for the more you try to suppress the mind, the more it reacts.

Sometimes the mind deceives you and violently reacts if it is suppressed too much. We should not have too much suppression as an escape, but gradually develop the mind to such an extent that no situation affects us at all. That will be a much better state of mind. For example, if we put a snake in a basket, we save ourselves from its bite or poison only as long as it is in the basket. The moment it comes out, it is going to bite. On the other hand, if you take out its poison sac, you can put that snake around your neck and it becomes your friend. So we have to develop our mind in that way; not by escaping from the situation, as that is only a temporary relief, I would say. The moment our mind gets a chance again, it will create a hell for us, if it has been only temporarily subdued. Too much suppression does not let us remain even a normal human being. But if we develop our mind by spiritual practice, that is just like taking the poison sac out of the snake. It then becomes absolutely harmless, and no situation affects us. Our main object should be to train our mind from that point of view.

224 What do you think about life in a monastery?

It's a very good idea to live in a monastery, but it is very difficult to find a monastery outside. Your body is the monastery in which you have to live. You cannot find a better temple, a better monastery than your own self, your own body. Try to live within it! This is the best fort you can find – the Lord has given it to every one of us. We must take a shield within ourselves. You can never find a monastery which can detach your mind from everywhere else. Your mind will run to people; your mind will run to the world, no matter where you live. That is why Christ said, this body is a temple of the living God.[132] You can't find a better temple than this body. So attach yourself within to that divine melody. You are already living in that monastery where nobody can harm you, nobody can reach you, where you can save yourself from the senses and all the enemies of the world who are pulling you in different directions.

You will never be able to conquer your mind by austerities, by willpower, by fighting with it. There's only one way to get rid of the evil tendencies of the mind, and that is to attach it to the divine shabd within. And that helps. We have not to arrest our

body, we have to arrest our mind. In a monastery you can succeed in confining your body to four walls, but you can't detach
from outside. The mind is running wild.

A monastery is restful in the sense that you don't have to
go to a job, you don't have to work for your living, you live on
the charity of other people. You may call that rest, but it is no
rest at all. Being in your home and surrounded by your family
members, you may be detached from them. And being a thousand miles away from them, you can be attached to them. It is
the mind which is to be detached, not the body.

But isn't our environment important?

Of course our environment is very important. With the help of
our environment, we have to withdraw within. We have to build
our own environment. We have to build our own fort around us.
You have to carry your own atmosphere within you, in which
you have to build your meditation. We have to select the right
environment for meditation, but by running to monasteries and
caves and the Himalayas you don't solve the problem at all.

*225 Master, what is the advantage in living a detached life
while in this world, rather than renouncing the world?*

With renunciation, we try to run away from situations and
there's likely to be suppression; and with detachment, the mind
is attached to something else and so automatically you become
detached. In renunciation, we run away to the forests; we leave our
children and family, the comforts of home and our responsibilities and hide in remote corners of the jungles and all that, just to
avoid those situations. Detachment comes when we are attached
to something much better. Mere renunciation does not create
detachment at all. Your mind may still be in all those things; there

may be suppression. Real detachment from the world can come only when we are attached within to something higher. That is the difference between renunciation and detachment.

Will we automatically then find a way to make our lives simpler, as we go on meditating?

With meditation we have a detached outlook on life, on everything. We do our duty, but with a detached mind. We are not affected by the ups and downs.

In renunciation we're running away from the situation, trying to avoid it, and there is likely to be suppression. Then sometimes the mind reacts. In detachment there is no reaction at all, because we're already attached to something.

Does it depend on the individual, as that detachment comes, whether he'll be able to simplify his needs?

It comes automatically. I'll give you a crude example. If a river is flowing and you try to build a dam to hold the water in the catchment area, you'll be able to hold the water for some time. But when too much water flows into the catchment area, it will not only break the dam but also overflow the banks and there'll be floods.

Renunciation is just building a dam and not letting the water flow anywhere. Detachment is building a dam and then digging another channel to allow the water to flow in a different direction. You are not keeping all that water in the catchment area. You're digging another canal, an outlet for the water to flow in a different direction so that the water doesn't break the dam. Without that, there's a danger of breaking the dam.

When renunciation and attachment go together, we are not just suppressing the mind; we are withdrawing it and channelling it into the inner journey, attaching it to the sound and light within. It's only the direction of the mind that is changed. From downward it goes upward, and when it becomes attached to the inner sound and light, it starts detaching from the senses. The senses don't pull it anymore because it's getting a better pleasure than the sensual pleasures. But without getting a better pleasure within, how long will you be able to hold your mind? It will pull you back again, with more vigour, more force, downward. So that is the difference between renunciation and attachment.

226 *I seem to have a conflict between my responsibilities and my desires. Could you give me some guidance? To attempt a path such as this, decisions are sometimes difficult between two seemingly like alternatives.*

This depends upon the individual – what type of problem he's facing in his life. It's very difficult to generalize this question. We have to bear some responsibilities, and we should bear them, and we must bear them. Other responsibilities we ourselves just throw on our own shoulders, and then we find we are slaves to those responsibilities. But it's very difficult to say what types of responsibilities hinder us in our spiritual progress.

227 *If our worldly work reinforces our ego, should we steer away from that type of worldly work, or is it strictly meditation that will eliminate our ego?*

By leaving that work and getting a different job, you will not be able to eliminate your ego. It will project in another form somewhere else. If the ego is within us, it can project anywhere, in any form. We have to eliminate the ego rather than eliminate the job. Ego must leave us. We have to do some job. If you don't take that job, you will have to take some other job. You can't solve the problem that way. We can only solve the problem by eliminating the ego.

How do we do that, Master?

Well, we're harping on the same tune every day. Meditation, meditation. I wish I could tell you some short cut. If there is so much rust on a knife, there is no other way but to rub it against the sandstone. Go on rubbing, go on rubbing, go on rubbing, and someday it will shine. That is the only way to get rid of the rust from the soul, from the mind. There's no other way.

228 *In a situation where one has to work very closely with people who are aggressively hostile, and where the more love you give them the more hostile they seem to be – and if you try to ignore them as the other way out, they aggress upon you with even more hostility – soon it becomes a situation where one of you has to leave this job and find something else. Or should you put up with it some-how or another?*

Well, brother, choose the lesser evil.

What is the lesser evil?

You should not torture yourself by hating anybody. You must live within yourself, with yourself. You should just give love, do your duty in the best way possible, and be kind and helpful and good to the other person. It is impossible to reform another person by trying to set him right according to your way of think-ing. But you can always adjust to his way of thinking. You can always reform yourself. You can always improve yourself. You cannot improve another, so you will always be happy if you are able to adapt yourself to the situation, and you may not be happy if the other person tries to adapt himself to your situation. It is always better that we adapt ourselves.

The world is full of problems and we cannot solve all of them. But by meditation, by spiritual advancement, we can always rise above these problems. Then they do not affect us at all – whether people think about us in a slanderous way, or they do not like us, or disregard us, or are indifferent to us. These things do not bother us anymore because we have risen above their ways of thinking.

Many times I have explained that we cannot pick up the thorns of the world, but we can always wear strong shoes so that the thorns do not affect us at all.

That is the purpose of meditation. That is the purpose of Sant Mat. We develop ourselves to that level that these petty things do not bother us. Then these problems are no longer problems to us. Not that we are able to solve them, but we can always rise above them.

So do the best you can in that situation, in all sincerity, and then leave it to the Lord. Do not torture yourself unnecessarily by letting it bother you. If you are living with your meditation, these small things will not bother you at all.

Does this imply, then, that we should turn our backs?

Do whatever you can under the circumstances. You can avoid the situation and you can be indifferent to their attitude. I mean, do whatever is practical. One should always take a practical, objective view of the circumstances.

Well, we have noticed that the people who handled them best are those who have aggressed right back at them. But is that the best way of doing it?

That is not the right way. For example, I will tell you about an actual experience of the Great Master [Maharaj Sawan Singh]. When he started preaching Sant Mat openly, when he started extensive tours in the country, he had a lot of opposition, especially from bigoted religious people. Perhaps they thought that he was misinterpreting the holy book, the Granth Sahib, and trying to spoil and corrupt the masses. Of course, his teachings were pure spirituality and devoid of commercialism. They appealed to seekers of truth and he attracted large crowds. Those opposing the Great Master became very nervous, thinking that their membership might dwindle and perhaps it might affect their income also. In those early days, they opposed him in devious ways, even attempting physical violence, as you have read in *With a Great Master in India*, by Dr Johnson. In India, we usually hold satsang in the open because no hall can accommodate us. We have gatherings of ten thousand to twenty thousand and sometimes over two hundred thousand.

So wherever the Great Master went to hold satsang, those opposing him set up their own camp next to it and put up their own loudspeakers so that whatever the Great Master said should not be heard by the seekers. When the Great Master had a program to go anywhere, they would be there the day before, parading and announcing with the beat of drums to the whole public that he was coming to corrupt the people and they should not attend the satsang. The result was that more and more people came to hear him and more and more began to follow him, so much so that the people who opposed him attended out of curiosity and ended up becoming his most devoted followers. I know many who are living in the Dera now who, in the beginning, opposed him tooth and nail on the religious platform until they realized what he was really teaching. They are very sincere and devoted satsangis, and some of them are writing books for us now.

Throughout all that, the Great Master never changed his attitude. He never argued with anybody. He simply said, "I am just doing my duty. If the teachings appeal to you, you are most welcome. If they do not appeal to you, I cannot help it. I have to do my duty." He treated everyone with love and kindness, and now the very people who opposed him take pride in being his followers. At first, they had thought that they would attend his satsangs just to expose him, as well as out of curiosity. But in the end they were convinced of the greatness and truth of his teachings.

When you are strong in your convictions and you have no malice or hatred toward anybody, when you do your duty and let others do what they like, they will change and you will remain strong within yourself. At least you are happy with yourself. You do not make yourself miserable by hating them. So we have to make the best use of a situation, without having any malice against anybody.

229 *Master, the philosophy of nonviolence has pretty much escaped us. It's a very beautiful philosophy, but in the world in which we live, where many people take advantage of the nonviolent person or the person who turns the other cheek, what responsibility do we have to protect ourselves when someone tries to take advantage of us?*

Well, brother, this philosophy is not meant for the world at all. This philosophy is meant only for the lovers of the Lord who want to go back to the Father. The world will never understand this philosophy. This philosophy taught by Christ is not meant for everybody. His teachings are meant for the seekers, those who are filled with love and devotion for the Father, who are hungry to become one with the Father. This philosophy is only for them. And even if you teach this philosophy, most people will never follow it. Perhaps the majority of the people of the world are Christians and they all read the Bible, they all read what Christ has said, and you know what is happening. So it doesn't mean that they are going to follow this philosophy. It is only for those people who are destined to go back to the Father. His teaching is meant only for those souls.

Are you saying that if someone is aggressive or not friendly, we should not resist them?

Well, you can save yourself from the situation. Christ has also told us: Be wise like a serpent and harmless like a dove.[34] The moment a serpent hears any noise, he at once leaves. And he says, be harmless like a dove. Don't harm anybody at all. But, he says, be wise like a serpent, not harmful like a serpent. A serpent can harm or even kill you with his poison. So he says, learn from the serpent. Avoid the situation. Why meet trouble unnecessarily, if you can avoid that situation? Be wise. And, having all the power with you, be harmless like a dove.

230 *Master, is it dangerous to the spiritual path to be ambitious in the world?*

Well, brother, there is nothing dangerous about it. But definitely if we have certain desires to be fulfilled, certain ambitions to achieve, to some extent they come in the way of our internal progress. But if you are destined to achieve those ambitions, fulfil those ambitions, you can't help it. So at the time of meditation we should forget the whole world and just relax our mind and sit in meditation. We should not use our meditation to achieve those ambitions, achieve those desires. We have to use our meditation only for our spiritual progress within, just to seek the Lord's grace within. We shouldn't use it to fulfil our worldly desires or ambitions; if we do, our ambition becomes a block.

231 *Maharaj Ji, should we deliberately avoid ambitious projects in our professions, in our work, in order to try and lead a simple life?*

Well, brother, you must have job satisfaction. If it is boiling within you to take some project and to make a success of it, then do it. If it doesn't bother you and you don't have that ambition at all, then forget about it. It has to come from you, from within. And then whatever the Lord wants will happen.

232 *If some fame or fortune comes to one by the grace of God*
     or by one's karma, would that necessarily be a problem?

Don't feel egoistic about it. It depends upon your attitude. A thing which is with you doesn't build ego; it's your attitude towards it that counts. You may be a multimillionaire but yet you may not be attached to any riches at all. You may be a pauper, yet you may be attached to riches; you're craving to become rich. You are attached to that. It depends upon your attitude, not on what you have. It depends on how attached to your riches you are, how obsessed you are. Even a beggar who is always counting his own pennies and obsessed with how much money he has collected is attached to that money. It may be worth nothing. Another man who is a multimillionaire may not be attached to his wealth at all. So it depends upon one's attitude, how attached we are to things, how obsessed we are with them, by them.

233 *We have some satsangis, Maharaj Ji, who want to try*
     and sit for their two and a half hours, but some of them
     can't do it, because they've got trouble in their house and
     so on, and they get absolutely frustrated.

We have created all these activities around us and then we become slaves to them and can't get rid of them. Life is very simple, but we have made it so complicated and now we find it difficult to live in it. Actually, what are our requirements in this life? Our normal, natural requirements are very, very few – just food, clothing and shelter. But we have increased these demands, so now we are their slave and thus have no time for ourselves. We have created so many other problems by satisfying our natural instincts that we find it very difficult to cope with them now.

234 *We are American citizens, and my husband is very interested in politics. We are a powerful country, and so many people are involved in a lot of intrigue and murder, and as a member of a democracy in which citizens are supposed to help direct the government, we bear a certain guilt for the things that our government does, and we live with that daily. I just wondered what our responsibility is because it is something that my husband speaks about continually.*

Sister, just be a good citizen but do not get so involved in these things that you do not live with yourself. The main thing is that we must live with ourselves. We must live with our meditation, and not get so involved in these outside things that they pull us down and make us forget the real purpose of this human life. It depends on individual circumstances as to how much we should get involved and how much we have to withdraw. We cannot have any hard and fast rule about these things. We have to live in some country and we have to be good citizens of that country. But as to how far we have to get involved in these things, I think our circumstances and our own feelings will tell us.

It is awfully difficult.

Yes, these are chains around us to which we have become slaves. We are a slave of a family, we are a slave of a tribe, we are a slave of a city, we are a slave of a country, and then we find that we are a slave of this world and the whole universe. We have small rings around us, which we have formed into a huge chain and have bound ourselves with them. Gradually we have to get out of all these things, and when we get to the Lord, we will find that the whole universe belongs to us.

You have nothing to hate and nothing to feel frustrated about any nation, about any country, about anybody. All that is going on is the Lord's creation, and when we become part of him, the whole creation becomes ours, whether we are in the U.S.A., Russia, India, or any other country. We feel that it is all ours then. But since we now have that narrow outlook, we have to do our best, as circumstances permit. By meditation we get rid of this narrow outlook, attain a much broader view eventually, and go about our own work without letting any of these things bother us.

235 *Maharaj Ji, what is the duty of a satsangi if he finds that his government is persecuting some minority community in a very unjust manner?*

We should not mingle in politics at all. We should try to live without becoming involved in all that, because otherwise the very purpose of our life stands defeated. We should do our duty, whatever little we can to help, but we should remain sufficiently aloof so as not to get too much involved in these things. There are so many other people here in this world just for that purpose, and their main function is to deal with these things.

236 *What about giving gifts to people?*

You may give gifts to people and you may accept them. The thing is that we shouldn't be a burden on anybody. There's no harm in accepting gifts or giving gifts. These are the ways of the world in which we live. But we shouldn't be a burden on anybody. That is the main thing.

Does a true master ever accept any gifts?

The master also has personal relations with people, so he will get gifts from them. But as a master he doesn't accept gifts from anybody at all. He won't. But he lives in the world – he has a wife, children, friends and associates, and so on that level, he gives and takes. That is different. But as a master to his disciples, he doesn't accept anything from anybody.

237 *There have been discussions among ourselves about receiving and giving gifts. Can you explain this?*

I have been receiving many letters about that and I have written many replies. You people put too much emphasis on and unnecessarily analyze very small, minor things. Probably the real teachings do not reach you in the right aspect.

There is no harm in accepting and giving gifts. The object is that we should not be a burden on anybody. We have to earn our own living honestly and live according to our means. We should not be a burden on society or on anybody – that is the object. While living in the world, we give things and we accept things. Practical arrangements with our relations, with our friends naturally will have to be there – I visit people, I dine with them, they come and dine with me, but I should not be a burden on them without doing anything for them.

In friendship, in relationship, nothing should weigh on your heart. You should not worry that he has given you something and now you are bound to give something to him, or that he has not given anything to you but you have given him so much. If that is the attitude, it is better not to give a gift. We should give and forget, and we should accept and forget.

These small things make no difference. We should not try to analyze or give too much importance to these things. We have to live in this world, and this is a world of give and take. There is no harm in these things. The only thing is that we should not be a burden on anybody, nor should we expect people to do for us without our realizing that we should also do something for them.

This principle of not accepting anything generally comes from our Indian point of view, because we have certain classes of mendicants in the garb of sadhus, as well as other beggars, even professional beggars. They will never give or do anything for you, but they always expect you to give something to them. This is wrong. One should not become a burden on society or on any individual family or individual person. But in our relations, in our daily dealings, we accept things – that does not make any difference.

So many say that if you accept gifts, you may have to come back here the next life.

If you give from the point of view that you are giving to him today and in the next birth you will take from him, then you will have to come back. But if you have no ulterior purpose or motive in giving a gift and in accepting a gift, it is just quits – finished. I do not know about your country, but in India people give in charity from the point of view that in the next birth they will get the reward. They think if they give one dollar today to a beggar, they have sown a seed to get at least twenty dollars in the next birth. From that point of view, it is bad to give, because then you also expect to come back to receive. That is not right.

Maharaj Ji, going back to the gifts again, giving should always be in the spirit of love and in the name of the master?

Why bring the master in? Bring yourself in. Give and take. Do not worry about these minor things.

238 Everybody has in his society a special relationship to the state. Is one allowed to get help from the state, perhaps directly in the form of money, if one wants to study? In Europe and Germany, for example, a person can get money from the state for studying.

Well, we shouldn't be a burden on anybody, but there's no harm in accepting help from the state, because we are part and parcel of the state. You have to contribute to the state, and you have to take help from the state, too. But we shouldn't unnecessarily be a burden on anybody.

239 I understand that if someone comes to you and asks for anything or if they want a loan, if you can give it to them, you should not give them a loan but give it to them free, just outright?

We give loans, we take loans, we borrow money, we pay it back. I do not know why we should analyze these small things in such a big way. There is no sense in it. The whole world would stand still with your way of thinking. In the world we take loans from the banks, from business concerns, from individuals; we give loans to the banks, to businesses, to individuals. That is purely a matter of business.

When we give things in charity, we help people, we serve them, but we should never expect a reward. We should not do it with a view to giving one thousand dollars in this life and then expecting it back in the next birth. That is a wrong attitude. In India some people think that if they give you something in charity, they will get much more in heaven. Probably people at the helm of affairs of those sects put that idea into their minds just to induce them to give charity. I do not know why the professionals have done this, for it is wrong.

A very interesting letter was written to me about an American satsangi. The man wrote, "I am in love with ___ and she is in love with me. She is my fiancée and I am going to marry her. I want to give her a watch and she refuses that, saying that she does not accept anything from a noninitiate, though she has been going out with me for the last six or seven months and I intend to marry her as soon as my business is set up. I think within six months I may marry her. She has promised to marry me and I have promised to marry her but she will not even accept a watch. I do not understand this philosophy." Now this is stretching things too far – when she can go out with him, when she can dine with him, when she wants to play wife to him, to not accept a watch from him really hurts. I explained to him that probably she did not understand the basic idea, which is that usually we should not accept gifts indiscriminately when we cannot give in return. Ultimately, they got married. They are both satsangis now. When we stretch things too far or analyze them too minutely, we lose sight of the real significance and purpose behind all this.

There seems to be an aversion to eating in people's houses, or if I talk to somebody, is there a personal karmic debt incurred by the soul?

You should not try to analyze these karmas too minutely. You will get nowhere. The main thing to remember is not to be a burden on anybody. There is no harm in eating in people's houses and no harm in inviting people to your house. We have to live in the world like normal human beings. There is no harm in accepting presents and giving presents. We can also do something for the other person if he does something for us. Naturally, this is the way of the world. The thing that we should try to remember is that we should not be a burden on anybody. We should just try to meet people on an equal basis. That is the main thing.

There is no harm in going to visit people and dining there, provided we can stand that atmosphere. If we are happy within ourselves, we are not going to feel guilty about what atmosphere we have come into. If that atmosphere is pulling us out of our way, if it is pulling us to the senses, then it is wrong and we should try to avoid it. Otherwise, I would never lay any restrictions on satsangis or initiates regarding mixing with their relations or friends who are not on the path. We have to mix with others as normal human beings, as this world requires, but we should be strictly firm in our own principles. We should not be drawn towards worldly people; they should be drawn towards us.

240 *In the past I have received gifts of alcohol from people who don't know that I don't drink, and I just pass these on to other people who do drink. Is there any harm in doing this, rather than just throwing the liquor away?*

It depends on how you feel about it.

I don't want it, but I feel that someone else might.

You see, if you feel guilty about it, then of course you are carrying a weight on your conscience – that you have passed on the drinks to somebody else.

It hadn't troubled me at all until your remarks earlier about charity being misused.

Naturally it is being misused. After all, poison is poison. Whether you take it knowingly or unknowingly, it has its own effect. Whether you give it lovingly to somebody or whether you just want to avoid keeping it in your own home and you just pass it on to somebody else, that alcohol will have the same effect on the other person.

It doesn't have any effect on the giver?

Naturally, he also plays his part. When you don't drink yourself, you are never happy to give alcohol to others. You can't live with yourself. There is always some weight on your conscience that is pricking you. Why have that load at all?

So is it better to refuse to accept it?

Well, it depends upon you. If you have the guts to refuse it, then why not? If the other person is really your friend, he won't mind your refusal. He will respect your principles. And if he's not your friend, you won't mind refusing him. If he's really interested in you, he will want to respect your principles. And if he's not interested in you, then you won't mind refusing such gifts from him.

241 *Obedience very frequently takes the form of blind submission, so that there is no awareness there. It is just a blind submission. How do you relate that to the submission the saints refer to?*

I do not think there is any blind submission. Love does not create blind submission.

But there are many job conditions where the employee is just required to give blind submission.

That is something different from what I am talking about. That is from the worldly point of view. That is our duty. We are being paid for it and we have to be obedient. But on this path we are not paid at all for obedience. Love is the only payment; the devotion, the understanding – that is the reward. There people buy our loyalty, our sincerity and our obedience with money. And here, we buy it with love.

> *The real nub of my question is, what does one do to his own spiritual advancement if he is obedient to orders that have in them some characteristic below his standards of morality or ethics?*

He can escape from the situation. He should try to escape from the situation if he is not able to live with his job, if he is not happy there.

242 *Maharaj Ji, I practice as a doctor and I am sure there are others here who are lawyers. How far are we to go in our efforts in our work? In many cases you can extend yourself beyond treatment. How far should we go?*

You should treat the patient according to the best of your ability, with the knowledge and skill that you have acquired. Still, with your best efforts, you can never get all the results that you want. If people could be saved by doctors and by medicines, nobody would have died. We have no cures for certain diseases, though we do our best. We find that some medicine has cured some people, but others are not affected at all by the same medicine. We know all this, so we should try to use our knowledge to the best of our ability and then leave the rest to the Lord.

MAKING DECISIONS

243 *We live on this level of mind, and we have to make all kinds of decisions all day. Sometimes we face situations*

that tear us apart. What do we do? It seems we always do the wrong thing, never the right thing. Is there any help on this mind level?

Life doesn't run smooth at all – at every step there are obstacles, and we have to make decisions. We stumble, we cannot decide rightly, we decide wrongly, we repent, we cry, and again we stumble and again we repent; again we come back to the same point. That is life.

244 *When you say things like "do what you think is best" in response to our questions, is it because the disciple just wants confirmation of what he wants or is it that the disciple has to struggle along and make mistakes by himself, learn himself?*

Mostly if you have any spiritual problem, the master will never put you off, put off your question; he will answer your question. But in worldly day-to-day problems, how can you involve the master? And then, we have already decided how we are going to deal with them. What is the sense of asking the master? He has laid out very straight fundamental principles on which we have to build our meditation. If we keep straight on those principles, I wonder if there are any questions left at all. When we go astray from those principles, then all sorts of problems arise in our life. Then we want to involve the master along with those problems. Even if we involve him, I'm sure we will never obey him. We still will do what we want to do. We're just trying to take a little burden from our own heart and tell ourselves that we are doing what the master has instructed, nothing else. Otherwise we always do what we want to do.

We have to face our daily problems and we have to solve them. The master is only meant for spiritual problems. I wonder if I've ever refused to answer any spiritual question or letter. There are so many worldly, mostly domestic, family problems. And what can you write to people? So much has already been written. If that has had no effect, then writing more about it won't have any effect. I think most of my letters are on divorces, family disputes, family separations, or adultery – 90 percent. It's not the job of the master to answer such questions. We know it's wrong and we should try to do what is best. You will find that hardly 10 percent of the letters are on spiritual matters. But in the time of the Great Master, as you read in *Spiritual Gems,* I think it was just the reverse. It was 90 percent spiritual letters and maybe 10 percent on worldly problems.

You should analyze what you think is best. If there's any question on the teachings, on the philosophy, anything which is not clear, then we should not hesitate to ask. In our worldly life, we have problems at every step and we have to deal with them in the light of what we know, what we practice. What is there to ask about? Even Christ has said in the Bible: Now you ask so many questions and I put you off. But when you come unto me, then I will not put you off, I'll answer all your questions.[127] Because at that level, they're all spiritual problems – there are no worldly problems.

245 *Master, I'd like to ask you a question about guidance in everyday life. If you have to make a difficult decision, do we get guidance from the master if we keep a question in mind and do simran? Will an answer be just from the mind, or will it be on a spiritual level?*

Brother, at every step we have questions in life. We have so many problems at every step. We have to take decisions at every step in our life. So we should make the decision with our best intentions. Weighing all the consequences or ups and downs, we should make a decision with a dispassionate mind and then leave the result to the Father.

Decisions are always made by the mind, but it is the higher mind. It depends upon the development of your own mind. Decisions are not spiritual. Our problems are worldly. And our decisions are always made by the mind because mind deals with the world. Soul doesn't deal with the world. The soul is always attracted towards its own origin. The inclination of the soul is always towards the Father. It doesn't try to get involved in the creation at all. It is the mind which is pulling the soul to its own level. So the mind has created the problems in this creation. The mind creates all the complications and it is the mind that tries to solve all these complications, all these problems. So decisions have to be made by the mind, but by the higher mind, the better mind.

246 *When we have a choice of two ways to go in our life – let's say we have to live in one place and all of a sudden there's a chance we can live somewhere else – we sometimes experience a turmoil. You're not sure which way to go, whether you want to go – to move to the other place – or stay where you are. Yet you always tell us not to worry. It seems like in order not to worry about that, we should just surrender that problem, but how do we do that?*

Brother, instead of worrying about the situation, one should try to do one's best. With your best available intellect or reasoning or thinking or intuition – whatever you may have – do your best, then leave it to the Lord. Still you can be wrong, but then, you see, you have no other option. What else can you do? You have done your best. Then leave it to the Lord.

If he doesn't want us to do the right thing, we will never do the right thing. If he wants us to do that right thing, he will also give us that understanding to do the right thing. If he doesn't want us to do the right thing, he will not give us that understanding to do the right thing. And it doesn't mean that if you know the right thing, you will definitely be able to do the right thing. Sometimes we know the right thing, but we never are able to do the right thing because we become a victim of certain weaknesses. Even knowing what is right, we can't do the right thing. Or sometimes we don't get that understanding to do the right thing. Things happen in whatever way it suits him, however he wants them to happen. So if he wants us to behave in that way, he will give us the right understanding to behave in that way. If he wants to keep us in the dark, we will remain in the dark.

247 *Master, we are told to apply the test of simran when we go inside, to test whether or not the mind is playing tricks. Is there any test we can use outside, when we are making decisions, to stop the mind from leading us astray?*

On this plane, there is a certain destiny we have to go through. But if we are attending to meditation, then our willpower becomes strong enough so that we can go through that destiny. And naturally, the decision has already been made. You are not making any decision at all. Whatever has to happen has already happened. You have to go through that, but you are now better equipped to face the situation, to face the events of life. You don't lose your balance in going through those events of life, but you can't change those events of life. So meditation definitely helps us. We should do our best and leave the result to the Father.

248 *Are there any of these "I's" I can trust to lead me back to the Father?*

What do you mean by many "I's"?

Well, if I go to work, I'm the boss, and when I come home, I'm a husband or a father. Can we trust any of these "I's" to lead us back?

Trust your own self, not anybody else. You must develop your consciousness to that level where you are facing yourself, where you can stand in any situation, stand on the path and nobody can shake you. You must develop and build that trust within yourself. We have a karmic relationship with people and we can't trust anyone. Everybody is selfish, everybody has their own way of dealing with us and there is always a string behind it. So we should know what we want, where we stand and how to be. We must build that confidence within ourselves and develop that confidence by meditation. It's not their fault. The world is such, the creation is such, because we have karmic relationships. People come and go out of our life. We can't hold them; they can't hold us. Many actors come on the stage and after playing their part, they walk off the stage. So we can't blame them. We must build faith within ourselves.

249 *Every day we find ourselves faced with different situations. Should we just accept them as part of our karmic debt from past lives? And should we pay that debt now?*

Well, sister, if you can know whether you have sown a seed, then you will be prepared to bear its fruit. But you do not know whether you are sowing a seed or whether you are going through what you have done in the past. You don't know at all. So do your best, thinking of every action as a sowing of a seed. Because at this stage you do not know – you cannot say whether you are sowing a seed or whether you have sown the seed in the past and are reaping the harvest now. So you do your best.

250 What must be our attitude towards ourselves? Should we try to be positive or just plain honest or …

Your attitude towards yourself should always be loving. Have a loving attitude towards yourselves. It depends on the situation, what you are discussing. We have so many situations to go through every day. And our attitude changes every time. But our thoughts should be very loving and helpful to ourselves. In the light of the teachings, we have to make such decisions.

WORRY

251 Master, last night you said that all souls are miserable because they're separated from the Father. Why then do some people, some souls, radiate joy and love and positivity, and others are very depressed and negative?

There is always fear of losing whatever the Lord may give us in this creation. If you have a lot of wealth, there's always a fear in your mind that the Lord has given me so much wealth in this world and I may lose it. Banks may fail, companies may fail, shares may fall, dacoits may rob me – there's a fear of losing it. You have a beautiful wife and you're very happy, but there's always a fear she may leave you, she may deceive you, she may become sick, she may die in an accident. There is always a fear of losing even the best things we have of this life. As long as fear is at the base of our happiness, we can never be happy.

252 Maharaj Ji, you say we are always to be happy, friendly and smiling, but sometimes when we're feeling a lot of longing to see the master, we don't smile and we don't appear to be happy, but actually, those are the moments

*when we're the happiest – it's just that people can't tell
that we're happy.*

When are we happy? When are we relaxed? When there is no
worry on our mind; when we throw our worry on somebody
else, then we are less unhappy. If we throw our worry on the
Lord, live in his will, accept what comes and think that whatever comes is best for me, naturally we are happy and relaxed.
When we take all the worries on our shoulder, we will never be
able to solve those worries. Worries will not solve any problem
at all, so naturally we become unhappy. Only when the mind
relaxes can we become happy. And the mind will relax only
when it is attached to the shabd and nam and when we learn
to live in the will of the Lord – then in every situation you are
happy. But when you take all that burden on yourself, then you
are crushed under that burden of worry. Then you can never be
happy, howsoever you may try to smile.

253 *Radha Soami, Master. You say you've been giving the same
      message for thirty-five years. One part of your message is
      "don't worry," and I think it's quite interesting that there's
      a hit song throughout the world called "Don't Worry, Be
      Happy." I wish I could sing it to you, but I can't.*

You can't try to be happy. If you stop worrying, you automatically become happy – it is a positive approach, not a negative
approach. If you have nothing to worry about, you're automatically happy. By nature, man is happy and contented. What
makes us miserable is our wishes, our demands, our ambitions,
our desires. When they are not fulfilled, we become miserable.
But if we don't have any desires, automatically we are happy. It is
our desires which make us miserable, and all our desires can't be
fulfilled. Whatever is in your destiny will be fulfilled; what is not

in your destiny – your worry will not be able to fulfil that desire. So having this attitude is living in the will of the Father.

254 Master, you say one must not worry about anything. How do you stop yourself from worrying?

What makes you worry? Uncertainty about the future and repentance for the past. So if everything is destined, then why worry? Whatever we have done in the past, we're not going to solve the problem by worrying about it. We'll be able to get rid of our worries with a practical approach. So attend to meditation. When your mind is attached to the shabd and nam within, then you don't think about the past or worry about the future. It is all the mind, whether it is coming down to the senses and worrying about worldly problems or attached to the shabd and going up. So when you positively put your mind in touch with the light and sound within, automatically you cease worrying. You get that bliss and peace and happiness within yourself.

And you are training yourself. Meditation trains you to accept what is in your destiny, if not cheerfully then at least with a smile. That is the purpose of meditation. Unnecessarily brooding over the past and worrying about the future is not going to solve any problem at all. So we must live in the present. Every day has to be lived. So we should plan for a day and then live it thoroughly and happily, and attend to our meditation. That is the only way one can get out of these worldly worries and worldly problems. And learn to accept rather than to demand.

255 Maharaj Ji, my question is about worry. When satsangis indulge in worry, it shows a lack of faith. Do we incur any karmas by worrying?

Well, sister, worry never helps anybody at all. It never solves any problem. Definitely, when we worry, we don't have much faith in ourselves and we also show lack of faith in the master. If we have faith, we leave the problem to him and will face what comes and let him deal with it. If we have faith that he's dealing with it, let him deal with it. And anyway, worry won't help you, worry won't solve your problem. If it's not going to solve your problem, then why worry? If an actor has been given a certain part to play, then why should he worry? He has to play that part. He has no option – he's helpless. The part has already been written, so we have to play it. So worry is not going to solve any problem at all.

256 *Master, I have finally stopped worrying, but I'm afraid that when I return home I'll start worrying again. Could you tell me why a satsangi has nothing to worry about?*

It is a very simple thing. If something is destined and we have to go through the destiny, will this worry solve any problem? If this worry is not solving any problem, then why punish ourselves?

Worry can be of many kinds and it depends upon the individual, what problems they have. But our general attitude should be that since things are destined and I have to go through it, good or bad, then why worry? Why not solve those problems, face those problems, live through those problems instead of unnecessarily worrying about them?

I think I spend most of my time worrying about things that haven't happened yet. I just worry for the sake of worrying. I think it's a habit that I had, and I got rid of it while I was here, but I'm afraid that I'll start worrying again.

You see, we worry so much that ultimately it becomes our habit. So if you want to leave the habit, start leaving the worry.

The other problem is that my whole family worries, and I'm around them all the time, so I think that might be a problem, too.

Well, brother, it is not only your family – I think everybody worries. Either we're worrying about the past or we're worrying about the future, but we hardly live in the present. It is the same for everyone, so try to rise above it.

257 *Is it okay to lean fully on the Lord to solve any problems in life?*

Sister, if you have given yourself to the Lord, then you have no problem at all. All your problems belong to the Lord and you don't exist anymore. If you have given yourself to the Lord, then you have no problem at all. Problems only exist when you feel separated from the Father. When you think that you don't exist and only he exists, you have no problems at all.

Swim along with the waves

258 *Master, isn't it best for a satsangi to develop an attitude of cheerfulness and not take life too seriously? I think that's the problem some of us have.*

Well, brother, we have to see what keeps us tense. What is there to feel tense about in life? Why not relax? Whatever has to happen, will happen. Why create tension in our mind? Meditation always relaxes you. The more the mind is scattered towards the senses, the more tense you are. The more you are able to withdraw the mind to the eye centre, the more you will feel relaxed within yourself. When you are relaxed within, automatically you relax others also. If you are able to build happiness within, you will radiate happiness wherever you go.

Your life is fifty, sixty, seventy years long. What is there to feel tense about? After all, how much do we need in this life? We may have the whole world at our disposal, but what do we actually need? How much food can you eat in a day? How many clothes can you wear? How much space do you need for sleep? These are the basic requirements of every human. So why feel tense about all that? What difference does it make if we have one room in which to sleep rather than twenty rooms in our house? What difference does it make if you have two dishes instead of twenty on your table? What difference does it make whether you have two changes of clothes or a wardrobe full of clothes?

It is only your attitude which makes you tense, which makes you want to possess those things. You think: "My neighbour has more and I am left far behind." These things make us unnecessarily tense, which we can easily avoid. We should take these things easy. It is only our attitude which keeps us tense and our attitude which makes us relax. We must accept the events of life. You cannot change the course of the events of life, but you can always adjust to them. Adjusting to the events of life will always make you happy and relaxed. If you swim against the waves, you will drown. If you swim along with the waves, you will get to the shore easily.

Summer has to come. If you refuse to prepare for the summer, you will be miserable. Winter has to come. If you refuse to adjust to the winter, you will be miserable. If we go on adjusting to situations, we will be happy. We have to go through a combination of good and bad karmas during this span of life. So we have to go on adjusting to every situation.

So we need to change our attitude. Then we will be relaxed and happy. If we refuse to adjust to these situations, then we will be miserable. Our relatives have to die, for example. If we accept that as his will, then it is all right. If we refuse to accept it, we will be miserable. Sickness has to come, but we accept it – we try to do our best. If we refuse to accept it, if we go on crying about it, then what? We are not going to change the course of events. You will be miserable unnecessarily.

So if we go on adjusting to the events of life, we will definitely lead a relaxed life. If we try to swim against the waves, naturally we will be miserable. Instead of cursing the darkness, we must light a candle. Why should we curse our destiny or anything? We should try to light a candle. We must have a positive, objective approach in life.

259 Can we ever change our destiny?

We always want the events of life to adjust to our liking, which is impossible. Waves have to come. If you swim along with the waves, it will be easy. If you swim against the waves, it will be difficult. We have to go along with the waves of destiny. We can't change them because our destiny is interconnected with that of others. It's not that one man's destiny is an individual item; he is connected to so many people in this creation. Changing one man's destiny means changing the destiny of the whole chain, which is impossible. Maybe he will not have to feel the effect of what he is going through, but he cannot break the chain. He should accept everything smilingly.

260 How much capacity do we have to plan our future, Master? Is it set for us when we're born?

We have only one future: to go back to the Father. There's no other future.

But we have to live in this world also.

Yes, we have to live. Whether you plan it or not, you will live. If you leave the planning in better hands, you will live much better. If you keep the planning in your own hands, you will live miserably. If you leave it to him to plan your life and go on accepting what comes to you, you will be happy. Because planning is in his hands, and you just have to adjust to the events of life. You are just adjusting, going along with the waves. You can never change the events of life, no matter how much you plan, no matter how much you pray. But you can always adjust to the events of life. Adjusting to the events of life will give you happiness; events will never adjust to your liking.

So it's our attitude that makes it easier?

Yes. Summer has to come, winter has to come. You can never change the course of the weather. If you go on adjusting to the summer, you'll be happy; if you go on adjusting to the winter, you'll be happy. Nobody can change the events of life – we have to go through all that. Planning has already been done; we have to go through it. So it's up to you to go through it miserably or happily. If you go on adjusting, you will go through life happily. If you want to fight with events, to change them, you will go through them miserably.

And then, the Lord makes much better plans than we do. We don't know what is good for us. He knows what is good for us. We spend years on our knees praying to get many things, and when we get them, we probably have to pray ten times more to get rid of them. We are blind; we don't know what is best for us. So it's better to leave it to him to give us whatever he thinks best for us. That is why Christ said: O ye of little faith.[25] You are praying to the Father, making long lists of demands and requests to him to give you this and this and this. That is just showing lack of faith in the Lord, that you believe he won't give you anything unless you ask him.

If a son is loving to his father, the father is always anxious to give to the son. But if the son is disobedient, unloving and demanding, the father hesitates to give him anything. So we have to be loving to our Father, obedient to our Father. He's more anxious to give us what we need. We don't know what to ask him for, but he knows what to give us. We are asking for pebbles and stones – he wants to give us diamonds and rubies. We are happy just sticking to these worldly things, but he wants to give us something much better, much more, much higher. We are very poor beggars, but he's a very good giver. We are asking for solutions to our problems day and night from the Father. But he wants to give us something much higher – if we leave it to him.

So it's all planned already anyhow?

But we have to do our duty. We have to be loving and obedient. We have to live in his discipline. If your maid is working diligently in your house and is very attentive to her duty and very faithful, you always want to give her one present or another. You like to humour her, to give her more and more. But if she's always grumbling and doesn't attend to her work, you want to get rid of her. When we behave like this, just imagine the Father. And Christ gave the very beautiful example: If you are so generous to your children that you give them whatever they want, do you think your Father is less generous than even you? That he won't give you what you need?[30]

261 *Master, when we are working daily with our colleagues, and criticism comes and others join in against us, should we accept this strictly as due to us, or should we ever attempt to hold our own?*

Brother, if we think we will be able to solve the problems of the world, of the people around us, not one whole lifetime or even a hundred lives would be sufficient. We just have to rise above these things, these problems, and not be affected by them at all. What is to happen, let it happen around us. That is why the saints often give us the example of the lotus flower. Its roots are always in the water, but the flower itself is above the water. With the help of meditation and the sound, we have to rise above these things. We cannot solve the problems of the world. History records that so many saints and social reformers as well have come to this world, but it has not improved in any way. Rather, there is more evil, in spite of the best efforts of the saints and the reformers. But saints do not come for that purpose. No saint comes to reform this world. He comes just to collect his own sheep and take them back to the Lord, as Christ also did in his time. He, too, said that he did not come to bring peace into this world.[39] Saints always advise us to remain in the will of the Lord, to submit ourselves to him. That means that we should face both the happy and unhappy situations, which are our good and our bad karmas, boldly and cheerfully. We should neither be so much affected by the bad that we forget the Lord, nor should we be too elated over the good karmas lest we forget the Lord and turn to the worldly pleasures. Whether good or bad, in both conditions we are always to remember the Lord. So the atmosphere around us will never change; it is we who have to change.

262 Are we compelled by predestination as a result of our past karma?

Whatever seeds we have sown in the past, they have become our fate karma which we have to go through during this span of life. That is destiny. It is something with which we are born, which we are going to face during the span of our life. This is predestined. We have committed all these karmas and we are facing the result of them now. They have become our destiny. That we have to go through. But if you attach yourself to the holy spirit within, you will get strength to go through those karmas. You will not lose your balance so easily. You will cheerfully go through them, realizing it is the will of the Lord. Happily you will be able to clear all those karmas.

263 If someone was tired of life and asked the master for a release, could the master release him with death?

Well, sister, one should never be tired of life at all. We should try to make the best use of this life. Whatever life span the Lord has given us, we should try to live by the best possible means, in the best way possible, and always keep our path and our goal, our objective, in view. We have to travel to reach that destination, but we generally become tired because, due to certain circumstances, things are not happening according to our desires. But if we get rid of this body, we do not know what type of body we will get, whether we would be better off – it could be still worse. So we should always try to make the best use of the present and never wish such a thing at all.

264 Are there any satsangis who have had a happy life?

Well, we discuss this every day. It is due to our good and bad karmas that we get this human birth. Hot and cold winds both blow here. When the hot wind blows and we protect ourselves, we are happy; when the cold wind blows and we protect ourselves, we are happy. Hot and cold winds will blow; winter will come, summer will come; the fact of good karmas will come, the fact of bad karmas will come. But if you adjust to those events, you become happy and you remain happy. If you refuse to adjust, you become miserable. You have to change according to the events because they have already taken shape, they have already happened. You can't change the course of your karmas, but you have to change yourself according to those karmas now in order to become happy.

When winter comes, if we have prepared for it with centrally heating our houses and woollen clothes, we're happy. It doesn't bother us. When summer comes we have air-conditioned rooms, fans, cooling drinks, so we're happy. We have adjusted according to the climate; so then we are happy. We can't stop the winter or the summer – that is the wrong attitude.

We get a human birth due to our good and bad karmas. If we had only good karmas, we'd be in heaven, and if we had only bad karmas, we'd be in hell. We have to go through the effects of the combination of good and bad karma. The wind of happiness comes and so does the wind of misery, but by adjusting accordingly we remain happy. This is the correct mental attitude. If some dear and near one dies, it's all right – it's the will of the Lord – we just accept it. But another person wants to commit suicide because he can't bear the loss. For both of them the loss is the same, but their whole attitude is different. We have to adjust our attitude to events in order to become happy.

In whatever way, in whatever circumstances the Lord keeps us, we should try to be happy. Take it as his grace, whatever he gives us. That is why Christ said: Be like a little babe.[56] You give him a stone to play with, he's happy; you give him a diamond to play with, he's happy. He doesn't discriminate between the stone and diamond. So we shouldn't try to discriminate among these events of life, whether a cold wind is blowing or a hot wind is blowing. We are happy in whatever circumstances the Lord keeps us.

And we can have that attitude only if we attend to meditation. Only with the help of meditation will we be able to build peace within ourselves, and then we share that peace with others. You go to a miserable person and he will make you miserable in two minutes. If you go to a happy person, however miserable you may be, you will just come out laughing and smiling – because we give what we have, we radiate what we have.

265 *When a strong desire to service awakens in a disciple's heart, should he think only of turning that service to simran and bhajan?*

No, whatever service he's capable of doing he can do. Of course the best service is bhajan, but there are other services also which are strong means leading to bhajan. To train the mind to live in the will of the Father is also a service.

How do you do that day by day?

We have to face situations at every step in this life, and at every step in this life we have to explain to our mind to accept whatever comes in our fate smilingly, cheerfully – why grumble? It's a constant training of the mind.

This is also doing service, because that will help us in meditation. If we always feel perturbed with every little thing, then how can we concentrate, how can we meditate? If we make every little thing an issue the size of the Himalayas, then how can we concentrate? We have to forget; we have to forgive; we have to train our mind to take things easily, lightly, to laugh them away, ignore them. This is all training the mind.

266 *Maharaj Ji, I'm a first timer. Listening to satsangis, surprisingly I very often hear expressions like, "Master has directed my life in this way," or "he is solving my problems." As people formulate it, this seems to concern the*

body master. Could you please tell me something about the way in which the outer or perhaps the inner master is guiding us?

Brother, we have to go through our destiny. We have a set destiny which we have to go through. Master can help us to go through that destiny cheerfully without losing our balance. If we attend to our meditation, if we live within the principles of Sant Mat, it becomes easier for us to go through that destiny. You can say that the master is guiding you to go through that destiny or that with the grace of the master you're going through your destiny cheerfully. These are just terms to explain certain things, but you cannot change your destiny. You have to go through it. You have to be prepared to go through the events of your life because you can't change them. But if you adjust to them, then there's no problem.

When we refuse to adjust to the events of life, then we become miserable. When somebody has died, if we refuse to accept the fact that he is gone, we are the ones to suffer, because that soul is not going to come back. He has gone. Winter has to come. Summer has to come. You cannot change the cycle of weather. If you refuse to adjust to the weather, you are the one to shiver, or to sweat in warm weather. But if you adjust to the summer and to the winter, winter will pass, summer will pass. There's no problem.

So similarly, we have to face the effects of good and bad karmas. Sometimes we're happy, sometimes we are unhappy, because we all have both good and bad karmas. A combination of good and bad karmas has given us this birth. Sometimes we're weeping, sometimes we are smiling. But meditation definitely helps us to go through the events of our life. You can give credit to the master. You can give credit to anybody. But we have to prepare ourselves to face our destiny.

267 *Maharaj Ji, would you comment on the aphorism directed
to the supreme Father: "If you send me hunger, I shall
be filled with thy name; if you send me miseries, I shall
accept them as pleasures; if you send me happiness, I
shall try to propitiate thee."*

The idea behind this is that in whatever condition or state the
Lord keeps us, we should always remain in his devotion. If we
are rich, we should not forget him, we should give our time to
meditation. That is a part of the karma that has been given us
to pay for in this life. If we happen to be poor, we should not
be frustrated, we should not be unhappy; still, we should strive
to devote our time to meditation, in his memory. The idea is,
in whatever position he places us, we should make the best use
of this opportunity of being in a human body to reach our
destination, to follow that way, to follow that path and merge
back into the Lord.

As I explained yesterday, this whole world is filled with
rich and poor, happy and unhappy people, according to each
individual's karma. We get this human body due to both good
and bad karmas. We have sown good seeds and bad seeds.
While being in this body, we have to reap the fruit of those
good seeds and also of the bad seeds. So naturally we will have
happy moments in life and we will have sad moments in life.
If we have more good karmas and less bad karmas, we will be
more happy and less unhappy in this world. If we have more
bad karmas and less good karmas, we will be more miserable
and have fewer happy moments in life. But good and bad – this
combination gives us the human form. If we had only good karmas, we would have been in heaven. If we had only bad karmas,
we would have been in hell.

If while reaping the fruit of good karmas we are given
to enjoyment and luxuries and sensual pleasures, and forget

the Lord; and if when reaping the fruit of bad karmas we are so frustrated, so unhappy that we cannot even think of the Lord – we are always miserable, even then we do not remember the Lord – when are we going to remember him? We have to experience both, happiness and unhappiness, and remember the Lord under all circumstances. Being in this world, we have to reap the fruit of good and bad karmas.

That saying means that we should remain in his will. In whatever position he places us, whatever we have to account for – whether our good or bad karmas – under every circumstance, in every condition, we should not forget the Lord. We should always keep him in view, keep our destination in view, try to give account of both the good and bad karmas, being in this body but not forgetting the destination that we have to achieve. That path we should never forget. That is why that mystic said, in effect: O Lord! In whatever position you place me, I will never forget you, because I have got this human birth just to remember you, and I can achieve the purpose of this human birth only if I give my devotion to you. If I do not do that, I am not making proper use of the human form.

268 *Master, being that we are all actors on the stage of life, how do we become better at it?*

We can be better actors on the stage of life by playing our part well. Whatever destiny has been allotted to us, we should accept it cheerfully as the will of the Lord. And that you can do only if you attend to your meditation. There is no other way. Otherwise we align ourselves with the acting and take that as the reality, forgetting that we are acting. So we should always keep in mind that it is acting. There's no reality in it. We must have that realization, and that can come only by meditation. There is no other way. Otherwise we get involved with the other actors in the play.

269 What does it mean to come back as a spectator rather than an actor?

Coming as a spectator means that whatever destiny we have brought with us, we just go through it smilingly, without being involved in it or affected by it. You are given a certain part to play on the stage. As a spectator, you play your part on the stage. You do not become involved; otherwise, you start thinking that it's not acting – it's actually my wife, actually my child. If you play your part knowing it's a part, then you are a spectator of the part which you are playing. Otherwise you get involved in it. We are all playing the part given to us by our karmas. But we are not playing it as spectators. We are getting involved in playing the part. We are becoming one with the part.

270 Does the master sometimes turn a disaster in our life into a pinprick?

It's not a question of a pinprick. You are not affected by those karmas – your mental attitude becomes such that you accept your destiny as the will of the Father.

Say for example that somebody's child dies. Naturally everybody is attached to their child. For one person the death of that child is a catastrophe; another person, with strong will-power or with the Lord's grace, accepts the situation and says to himself: "I have to adjust, to live my life." He takes it a little lightly. In both cases, the child has died. So it all depends upon your attitude – how much you want to suffer or how much you want to escape from suffering. With the help of meditation our attitude towards life changes. We start taking the events of life as the will of the Father and we are not affected by them as much. We don't lose our balance so easily. But our destiny, the course of our life doesn't change.

271 Master, I have a question about happiness. I have heard you say many times that as satsangis we should be happy. Many times I feel unhappy because of my separation from you. You also say: Blessed are they who mourn, for they shall be comforted. Those two things seem very different. I was wondering if you could speak a little about being happy in this world.

We are unhappy, but when we are on the path, then we are on our way, we are in the process of going back to the Father. That very concept should make us happy – that now we have realized we have the Father, we have a destination, we have some objective to achieve. We realize our separation and that we have to get rid of the separation and go back to the Father. We know the path, we know what to do, and if we practice that, automatically we will have a feeling of bliss and peace within. If you are in a jungle and somebody points out the direction of your house, it makes you happy. Now at least you know in which direction you have to go. You're not looking in the dark. You will get real happiness when you reach your home, but just knowing the direction and the road which leads you back to your house makes you happy. The nearer you are to your destination, the happier you become.

And then we realize that nothing is in our hands, that what has to happen has already happened at a different level, at a different stage. We are only to go through it, so we should not unnecessarily worry about the events of life because we are not in a position to change them. We cannot change the cycle of our life, the cycle of our karmas. We have to swim along with the waves; we cannot swim across the waves. So we have to accept the facts of life as they come. The very fact that we have to go along with the waves automatically makes us happy – there is no other way. We have to accept the facts.

272 *Actually, Maharaj Ji, truthfully speaking, if a person refers a problem to the master in meditation or within, that amounts to prayer. You're seeking advice really.*

Well, brother, meditation is the solution to all our problems. Instead of putting up your list of demands, put up your meditation. Then you will rise above those problems and they won't affect your mind at all. You will never be able to solve the problems of the world. But we can always rise above those problems so that they don't affect us, they don't bother us, they become meaningless to us. Meditation helps; that is the real solution to those problems. The solution doesn't mean that those problems are going to be solved according to our liking – destiny has to play its part – but you will be happy to go through your destiny. You'll be a willing spectator witnessing your destiny. That should be our approach to problems. Events will never change according to our wishes; we have to adjust to the events. Happiness lies in adjusting to the events, not making the events adjust to your liking. That will never happen. Destiny has to play its own part.

273 *Does sorrow do us any good? Does it detach us or purify our minds?*

Sorrow means repentance. If by sorrow you mean repentance – and repentance is really genuinely resolving not to repeat the same mistake again – it definitely helps us.

Unnecessarily making yourself miserable is not solving any problem. That is not trying to adjust to your destiny. Why not adjust to it smilingly? Why have a sorrowful face when it is not going to change your destiny? When you cannot change the events of life – you have to face them, you have to swim along with the waves – then why not accept them smilingly? Why howl and cry, why have a sorrowful face? There's nothing much to weep about, because the events of our life are not going to change. If they are not going to change, then why worry? Take them as the will of the Lord.

274 *If I have a very heavy problem in my life, and the weight of it seems too much to bear, can I give this burden to the master, or is it my role to carry it alone?*

You can throw your burden away from your mind. Let it go on anybody's shoulder. Don't worry. Just throw it from your shoulder. Let anybody take it. Because one thing we know – our life is predestined. We have come with a certain destiny to go through. So then why should we carry that burden on our mind? If we cannot change anything, let us face it. Why should we worry about it?

275 *Maharaj Ji, we're told that meditation is the panacea for all our ills. But on a daily basis, what is the best way to receive the master's guidance in our everyday problems, when we want to know the right course to take?*

Brother, our whole life is full of problems. It depends upon our attitude. 'Problem' is a relative word. Something may look to us like a problem, but if we look at it from a different angle, it may not be a problem at all. It's a very relative term. If we attend to our meditation and are able to concentrate at the eye centre, and we live according to the principles of the mystics, our willpower becomes very, very strong. Then we will be able to meet all the ups and downs of life. The bliss and peace and happiness that we build in meditation helps us a long way to live with these so-called problems. We can spend our time without losing our balance. We can face them smilingly.

You see, there are many things which we cannot change. We cannot change our destiny. We cannot change the events of our life, but we definitely can adjust to them. Happiness lies in adjusting to the events of life, because they're not going to change according to our wishes, according to our likings. We have to change according to the events of our life.

SURRENDER

276 How do we surrender to the will of the master?

Well, sister, what is surrendering to the will of the master? What is the master's will? If we don't know what the will of the master is, how can we surrender to it? Surrendering to the will of the master means helping ourselves to rise above the realm of mind and maya, helping our soul to leave the mind. When we make the soul whole and pure, then we are surrendering to the will of the Father, the will of the master.

Before that, we are still living in the will of the mind. We are not living in the will of the master at all. You can say, I am living in the will of the master because I am steadfast on the principles of Sant Mat – I am attending to my meditation and living the way of life as taught to me. So, in a broad sense, you are living in the will of the master.

Actually, you live in the will of the master only when you are able to release your soul from the clutches of the mind. You have to go beyond the realm of mind and maya for your soul to be absolutely pure. Then there is no covering on the soul and it lives in the will of the Father. Otherwise, the soul is always enveloped by and under the sway of the mind.

277 Can you talk to us about the unconditional surrender to the master?

First, what is surrender? Surrender is when we take our ego and I-ness out of us. As long as the mind dominates the soul, there can be no surrender. When the soul dominates the mind, then you can say that we are in a position to surrender to somebody. We feel that we have surrendered, even in physical love, when we submerge our will into the will of the other person. We try to merge our happiness into the happiness of the other person. We always try to do what pleases the other person, and never try to assert ourselves or to adjust the other person to us. We always adjust ourselves to the other person's will. That is what we always like to do in love, even in this world. We always try to cooperate and to submit ourselves to the other person. Spiritual love is the same. We have to surrender ourselves to the master. It means that we have to take our ego out of us and blend our whole heart with his heart. He is already merged into the Lord, and by merging ourselves into him we are automatically merged into the Lord. That can be done only by meditation. The more we meditate, the more we are driving out ego. By doing so, we will be drawn towards the master, and we are automatically surrendering to him; and through him, we are surrendering to the Lord himself.

So we can surrender unconditionally only when we go inside, see the radiant form of the master, merge ourselves in him and then go ahead. That is the real unconditional surrender. But we have to work for that while living in this world. To attain that real surrender, which we call *sharan,* we have to remain within the dictates and principles that were told to us at the time of initiation. We have to put forth our honest efforts to remain on the path, to give time to meditation. That, in a way, is surrender to the master, and this surrender will lead to the internal surrender, the real or unconditional surrender. That will be when we see the master inside, forget our self and merge in his will, in his love. We will feel that we are the master there – 'we' do not exist.

278 *It is said the saints teach us two things, but they seem*
to be contradictory. On one hand, they say that every-
thing belongs to the guru. Nothing is our own. We are
nothing but marionettes. On the other hand, we should
live within the principles of Sant Mat and do our best.
Where is our own responsibility if everything is due to the
master and to our karma?

Well, brother, if you really submit to the Lord, really surrender
to the Lord, give yourself to the Lord, surrender your mind to
the Lord, then you don't have to do anything at all. You have no
responsibilities in whatever you may do. What is meant by the
statement that everything belongs to the guru or to the Lord is
that we should think that it belongs to the Lord, belongs to the
guru. We should not think that anything is mine. We should not
get attached to things. We should use them thinking they are a
gift from the Lord, that they are not mine – they belong to the
Lord. And if he takes something away, well, it was his property, he
has taken it away – how can I grumble? If it belongs to someone
else and he takes it away, I have no reason to grumble. That is what
it means to think that everything belongs to the guru, that everything belongs to the Lord and doesn't belong to you. Don't get
attached to those things. If you really surrender everything to the
Lord, then you have no responsibility, whatever you may do.

279 *Master, would you please talk about sharan?*

Sharan means surrender. Surrender of what and to whom? Surrender your ego, surrender your mind to something higher than
you – the Lord. We live in his will. We do not let our mind pull
us to the senses. We have to pull our mind, our consciousness,
up to the eye centre, and with the help of shabd and light, we

have to reach that level within where we control the mind. We can only surrender what belongs to us. We cannot surrender that which doesn't belong to us at all. Now mind is dominating us. We don't dominate the mind at all. You see, the soul, no doubt, is the essence of the Lord. But it has been dominated by the mind, so the mind has become the master and the soul has become the slave. But the mind itself is not independent and has also become a slave of the senses. So actually, the senses are the master of the mind and the mind is the master of the soul.

Unless the whole process is reversed, what can we surrender? First the mind has to be pulled from the senses, then the soul has to be pulled away from the mind. When the mind becomes pure, then it becomes yours; then the soul is the master and the mind is the slave. Then you can surrender the mind to the Lord because you can surrender only what belongs to you – you cannot surrender what doesn't belong to you. When the mind belongs to you, you have absolute full control over it. Then you're in a position to surrender to the Father.

In other words, just knowing yourself, becoming whole, getting release from the clutches of the mind is real surrender, and we can do that only by meditation. We cannot do that by the intellect, by austerities, by running away from situations or by strong willpower. It happens only by meditation. The mind refuses to leave the senses unless it gets some better pleasure than the sensual pleasures, and that better pleasure the Lord has kept within every one of us. Unless the mind gets into the taste of that, it refuses to withdraw from the senses. By devoting time to meditation – by tasting that nectar within – we are just training ourselves to surrender. All effort is being made to surrender. Whatever time we are giving to meditation, we are putting in effort to surrender. We are trying to surrender to the Father, and that is the only real surrender.

Strong willpower and intellectual surrender don't lead us very far. One moment we think we have given our mind to the master, and another moment we start revolting. That is no surrender. Only meditation helps us to surrender. When we merge back into that shabd and nam within, when we lose our own identity, when we lose our individuality and become the shabd – that is real surrender.

280 *Would you discuss obedience and the part it plays in our spiritual teachings? Many people have job conditions that require obedience of many types in their varied duties at work.*

Obedience is another word for submission. And submission is another word for driving out the ego. When we are proud or full of ego, we do not like to submit to anybody, we do not like to be obedient to anybody. In other words, obedience means merging your will in the will of the other person. Driving your 'self' out of yourself and merging your will with the will of another, that is obedience.

This is the first lesson which is given to our children in our Indian homes. They must be obedient to their parents and do what the parents tell them. There is no question or reason why. They must learn to understand in life how to drive out their ego, how to respect the elders and be obedient to their wishes. Then it is for the parents to come up to that standard to demand obedience. But children are always taught to be respectful and obedient to their elders. When we go to school, we must be obedient to our teacher. We must submit our will to the teacher's will. And we have to practice the same thing when we come on the path, which is obedience to the master. But obedience will come only when there is love within us, for without love obedience can never come.

Love always helps us in merging our will with the other person's will. We take our self out of ourselves and become the other person. Love helps in that. Without love there can be absolutely no obedience. So, when love comes, all these qualities rise in us like cream on the milk. We do not have to fight for these qualities in ourselves. When that love for the master, for the Lord, comes within us, all other qualities just come automatically within us. If these qualities have not come within us, we can presume that we have absolutely no love for the master and the Lord. When that love takes its place within us, all other things are driven out. Then there is obedience, there is submission, there is understanding. All good qualities automatically take shape.

281 *If the soul is, as we say, responding to God, responding to spiritual vibrations, then that overcomes this overexcessive I-ness?*

Then we begin to think that everything belongs to the Lord: "I am only playing my part. Nothing is mine. Everything is his." It is not the language; it is the feeling within – it is our attitude. We are mentally detached from those things. Our attachment is with the Lord. That is the main thing required, not the words. Words are just a means to express our thoughts.

282 *Maharaj Ji, Christ said that unless we become like little children, we will not enter the kingdom of heaven. Can you tell us how we can become like little children?*

You see, you give a diamond to a child, he will play with it. You give him a little pebble or a stone, he will play with it. He doesn't make much distinction between the diamond and the pebble. He's happy; and he just gives himself to the mother and he's happy in the lap of the mother. He has no desires; he absolutely, completely surrenders to the mother – he only wants to surrender to her.

So when we are able to eliminate our ego, our individuality from within ourselves, then we become just like a little child. Then in whatever condition the Lord keeps us we are happy, we have no desire of our own at all. We unconditionally surrender ourselves to the Father. In whatever way he keeps us, we are happy in his love, in his devotion. Whether he keeps us rich or keeps us poor – we don't even discriminate whether we are rich or poor, whether we are happy or miserable. We don't even know if we are happy or we are miserable. We have eliminated even our thinking, our feelings, just to become a little child.

283 Master, would you say that ego is really the basis of attachment?

Well, sister, ego covers everything. Ego is attachment. You're always egoistic due to your attachments in this creation. All five perversions are covered by ego, and it is because of ego that we are part of this creation. In submission, there is no ego at all. Submission means elimination of ego. As long as 'I' is there, the Lord is not there. And when you are not there, he's there. This I-ness and my-ness – our individuality – creates duality. Otherwise, if you just eliminate yourself, it is only he and he, him and him. In love, there's no expectation; actually it is giving, giving, giving. If we want some reward, that is no love at all. There are no wages for love – nobody loves for the sake of wages. There is no such thing as conditional love. There can only be unconditional love, otherwise it's not love at all. There's no expectation in love, just submission, resignation.

So before the Father, there's nothing but submission and resignation because he's everywhere. Only he exists. We feel that we exist, but actually we don't exist at all. This feeling that we exist is what separates us from him, and we have to eliminate this feeling, so that only he exists. But it's very difficult – submission is very difficult, because in submission there are no questions; questions don't arise in submission.

We always say, "I love my master; I've submitted myself to master." But when he gives you advice, you judge whether you should accept it or not. You judge whether what he has told you is good for you or bad for you. So if *you* are there, where is the submission? In submission, you don't exist. If you still want to exist, there's no submission at all. So intellectually we say, "I have submitted myself to the master; I've committed myself to the Father; I don't exist anymore." But we always sit on judgment on every little thing, whether I should do it or not do it, whether it is good for me, whether it is bad for me. I'm judging him, so I exist, and that is responsible for bringing me back to this creation.

In love, there is nothing but submission, resignation. That is why Christ said, those who live in the will of my Father, they are my real brother, real mother and sister.[47] Those who live in the will of the Father don't exist at all. For them, only the Father exists. Their mind doesn't exist, their ego doesn't exist – they don't exist at all. For them, only the Father exists, so they're living in the will of the Father. When you are there to think, you are not living in the will of the Father at all. When you think that you exist, and you are judging yourself – whether you are living in the will of the Father or not – you are not living in the will of the Father. Who's judging? You are judging! As long as you are there, the Father is not there. Then you're not living in the will of the Father at all. You want your will to judge the will of the Father, so you very much exist – your ego is there.

LIVING IN THE LORD'S WILL

*284 Master, yesterday we heard from Professor Bhatnagar
about being devotional and submitting to the master's
will – that sometimes it's necessary to use the intellect to
apply the master's teachings to one's own situation. Will
you speak to us about this?*

What is the master's will? Just to be firm on the principles on
which we have to build our meditation and attend to our meditation – that is his will, that is his teaching, those are his instructions. That is the base on which we have to start. The real will of
the master we can know only when we go beyond the realm of
mind and maya. Now, as long as the mind exists, we are in the
realm of the mind, in the will of the mind. So naturally we have
to follow the master's instructions with our intellect, our strong
willpower, obedience and submission in order to reach to that
stage. These things are essential to begin with. But ultimately
we have to reach to that stage where we live in the will of the
Lord, the will of the master – they are the same thing.

*285 If we have our destiny to go through and we want to live
in the will of the master, is that one and the same?*

What is your concept of the will of the master?

> *I can't describe that. I hope what I'm doing is the will of
> the master. I want what I'm doing to be the will of the
> master, but I have a destiny too.*

When you go beyond the realm of mind and maya and merge
yourself in the master, then you are living in the will of the
master. Attending to our meditation helps us to discharge our
karmic debts here in this world and also helps us to get rid of

our mind. Then the soul becomes light, it shines, it goes back to the Father. Then we can say that we live in the will of the Father, not before that.

But it's good to think that I am living in the will of the master in the sense that I am not compromising with the principles of Sant Mat. I am living the Sant Mat way of life. I have moulded my life accordingly, so intellectually I can say that I am living in the will of the master because he has laid down certain principles which I have to follow, on which I have to lay my foundation and build my meditation. So I can say that I'm living in the will of the master, but still my mind can deceive me.

So really we live in the will of the master when we become free. Now we are slaves. Unless we become free, we cannot have free will, and unless we have free will, how can we live in the will of the master? A slave can have no free will. We are a slave of the mind and the mind is a slave of the passions, the senses. So we can't say we live in the will of the master. We try to live in his will. We are trying not to compromise with the principles. We are trying to give our full time to meditation. We are trying to mould our life according to the way of Sant Mat. So we are trying to live in the will of the master. That helps us.

286 *When you talk about living in the will of the Father, I like to think that if we are receptive, we can understand why we go through some of the experiences that we do. Is it possible that it's not just the will of the Father but something that we can understand if we're receptive to what's going on at the time – not just blind occurrences?*

You see, we can only live in the will of the Father when we don't live in the will of our mind. There are only two powers – positive and negative, Dayal and Kal. When we are under the domain of mind, we are dominated by the mind. When we go beyond the mind, then we have associations with the Father. Then we can say we live in his will. Now we cannot say we live in his will because we don't know his will. It is the mind that tells you that you're living in the will of the Father. It may be that the mind is just trying to justify our own weaknesses. Only when we become free can we say we live in the will of the Father. Now we are not free; now we are slaves of the mind.

287 Is it the philosophy of the path to accept suffering?

You have read in the teachings of the mystics that we have to live in the will of the Lord. What is the will of the Lord? Whatever karmas we are born with, whether they are good or bad karmas, we have to go through them without losing our mental balance, taking them as the will of the Father. We should not weep and cry and lament unnecessarily if we have to face the effect of bad karmas, nor should we become so happy and elated as to forget the Lord when we are facing the effect of our good karmas. So every mystic tells us that we have to live in the will of the Father.

You have read: Whatever you sow, so shall you reap.[133] Whatever we have sown in past births, whether it is good karma or bad karma, we have taken this birth now to reap the results of those karmas. So we have to live in the will of the Lord and pay for all those karmas without losing our balance. We can do this only if we are filled with love and devotion for the Father. Without this love and devotion, it is not possible for us to live in the will of the Lord or to face the good and bad karmas patiently in this world.

Every mystic advises us to face all our karmas calmly. When we are filled with love and devotion for the Father, then we do not feel the effect of the good and bad karmas. And all these karmas have association with the mind. When we are able to withdraw our soul current to the eye centre and are attached to the melody or divine music within, only then are we filled with love and devotion, which enables us to go through all these karmas cheerfully, without losing our balance.

Due to our actions in previous lives, we have a certain debt to pay to the prince of this world – Kal, the negative power. So whatever is cleared, we should be happy about it, whether it is good or bad karma. As Christ said, we must pay to Caesar what is his due.[66]

288 *I should like your comment on the beneficence of adversity, such as pain, sorrow, sickness, suffering.*

This whole world is full of misery, sorrow, sickness. That is why we can never get everlasting happiness in this world. In fact, this human body – the top of the creation, the temple of the living God – was bestowed on us due to both our bad karmas and our good karmas. If we had only bad karmas, we would have been in hell. If we had only good karmas, we would have been in heaven. It is the combination of good and bad karmas which gives us the opportunity to be in a human body in this world. So the combination of good and bad has brought us here. And while being in the body we have to face the results of both the bad and the good karmas.

Some people are fortunate in having more good karma and less bad karma; so, due to that, they have more happy days and fewer unhappy days. Others have more bad karma and less good karma, so they face more unhappy days and have fewer happy ones. But every human being in this world has moments of happiness and also moments of sorrow. We will not find anyone in this world who has nothing but happiness and has not faced any sorrow; nor will we find anybody who has nothing but sorrow and never got relief or had some happy moments in his life. This world is the field of good and bad karmas, where both good and bad are harvested. Therefore, because we are in this world, we have to pay for our bad karmas, and that is adversity.

I have tried to explain that saints never come into this world to make it a paradise or a heaven. They come only to take us from this place of adversity, to take us away from this place of good and bad, which is full of ups and downs, rich and poor and the like. Their only purpose in coming is to take us back to the Lord. If we try to solve our problems in the world, we can never succeed; but the saints give us certain handles or levers, a way of meditation, through which we can always rise above these problems. If we try to pick up all the splinters of the world, we cannot succeed. But if we have strong shoes on our feet, they do not bother us at all. The saints arm us with that meditation – the strong shoes – so that the ups and downs of the world do not bother us. We rise to that stage, that level, where our worldly situation makes us neither happy nor unhappy. The real happiness we can get only when we merge back into the Lord. As long as we are in this world, we have to face ups and downs; sometimes we are rich, sometimes we are poor, sometimes we are happy, sometimes we are unhappy. But we should not lose our balance. We should always try to keep our thoughts in meditation. That is why saints advise us to remain in his will.

What is his will? To face these karmas gracefully and boldly, by keeping our attention in meditation – that is living in his will. Why is it essential to remain in his will? If, due to our good karmas, we give ourselves to sensual pleasures and worldly achievements, we forget the Lord. If, due to our adversities, our bad karmas, we worry, we weep, we cry and are full of self-pity, our thoughts again get scattered in the world, so we can never meditate. Since good and bad will always be here as long as we are in this body, when are we going to meditate? So the saints advise us that whether are we reaping the fruits of good karmas or of bad karmas, we should always keep our attention in the Lord. We have to remain in his will. We have to be resigned unconditionally to his will.

Whatever our store of karma is, good or bad, we have to go through it. But I can assure you that by meditation our will becomes so strong that these good and bad karmas do not affect us at all. We rise above the effects of good and bad karmas, and we easily and happily account for all these karmic debts with the help of meditation. And sometimes the Lord, out of his love and with his grace, helps to reduce this load of karmas, or rather to clear our karmas without taking full account of those karmas. So we should not lose our balance when we have to face some adversities, when we have to face the effects of some bad karmas. Rather, that is the occasion when we should give more time to meditation. We should give more time to devotion, our spiritual practice, so that the effect of that karma passes off and we are again on our feet.

289 What is the Lord's will?

Well, brother, when we say that we have to live in the will of the Lord, actually it means we have to live with our destiny, smilingly taking it as assigned to us by the Father, though it is our own actions, our own seeds which we have sown. That is what we call living in the will of the Lord. Actually, they're our seeds, they're our actions, and we are facing the effect of those actions now, as our destiny. But to live with our destiny happily and to accept our destiny cheerfully is to live in the will of the Father. That doesn't mean the Father has written anything for us to go through. They're still our own actions. We are the maker of our destiny. So we accept our destiny cheerfully and we attend to meditation – that is living in the will of the Father.

290 Master, I have heard the word 'grace' used in various contexts. Would you please tell us what it means – the Lord's grace, the master's grace?

It's difficult to describe the grace of the Father. Without his grace, we would not get this human birth. Without his grace we would not get the opportunity to know about the path. Without his grace we would not get an opportunity to meet a living guide who can help us on the path. Without his grace we wouldn't get the environment and facility to attend to meditation and to make the best use of this opportunity. Everything happens by his grace. Now, what that grace is you can define for yourself. Without his grace nobody can go back to the Father.

Is it the same, Master, as the Lord's will, the Lord's wish, the Lord's desire – or is it something extra that he does for us?

You see, the Lord's will is a little different. To go through our own destiny, to collect the crop which we have sown in a previous birth – we can take it as the will of the Father. It is our own creation; it is our own destiny. We are the maker of our destiny. The Lord has not indiscriminately written anything in our destiny. We ourselves have shaped our future in this present life, but we console ourselves by telling ourselves that we are living in the will of the Father – whatever karmas he has given me, whatever destiny he has given me to go through, I am taking it as his will.

But actually the will of the Father is only when we go to the Father, when we go beyond the realm of mind and maya, beyond the realm of karma and then merge into the shabd. That is the real will of the Father, and that is the real fruit of his grace. I won't call it the only grace, but to become one with the Father, to become one with the shabd, to merge into the shabd, to lose your own identity and to become another being – that is the fruit of his grace.

291 *Maharaj Ji, would you discuss contentment and its role on the path?*

What is contentment? To be happy to go through our destiny; not to have any desire and not to pray to the Lord for anything in the world. We are happy with whatever he gives us; we are contented to go through our life. We just see the drama of our life as a spectator in this creation. So we are contented with whatever he gives us. In other words, we live in the will of the Father – that is also contentment. The Father doesn't write anything in your destiny which you have to go through. You have created your own destiny; you have sown your own seeds; your own seeds have created your destiny, what you have to go through. They're our own actions – we can't hold the Father responsible. He has written only what we have sown. But to go through that cheerfully is contentment.

292 *What you said to the young lady about everything that is to happen has already happened has rankled my mind. Is it a trick of my mind to think that I can let go of trying to plan the future or try to take care of future things and just accept what comes on a day-to-day basis?*

Well, if it is in your destiny not to let it go, how would you let it go? If it is not destined that you will accept your destiny, how will you accept it? You think something is in your hands and another thing is not in your hands? Your thinking is not in your hands; to accept your destiny is not in your hands; not to accept your destiny also is not in your hands. Your thinking will be conditioned in that way which has already been destined.

What more could we want, if we can trust ourselves to the Lord? What more do we want? We think we know more than the Lord? What else could we want – that he will take care of us, he will absolve us from all our planning, all our thinking, that he takes our destiny in his own hands – what more could we want in life? These are the most fortunate people.

293 *Master, a lot of times when we're meditating we get a feeling that we should do a particular thing, and then we think it's the master's will, so we do that and it turns out bad. How do you know when something is the master's will and not our mind?*

Sister, you can never know the will of the Lord, unless you become free. How can a slave know the will of the master? We are slaves of the mind, and the mind is a slave of the senses. Because the soul is a slave of the mind, you can never know the will of the Lord at all. We can live in his will only when the soul is separated from the mind. So with our best intention, we should do what we think is the best and try not to deceive ourselves. We should be honest with ourselves and then leave whatever happens to the Father.

294 *Master, what do you mean when you talk about turning the cup right-side up?*

To be receptive to the Father's love in our everyday lives, to accept whatever he gives us unconditionally – without hesitation, without sitting in judgment over it. To accept with gratitude what he gives, because he never does any wrong. When you are not there, then who's to judge what is wrong and what is right? The realization will come to us that we don't exist – only he exists. Whatever comes from him, we accept with cheerfulness, with gratitude. We don't even differentiate between what is good and what is bad because the one who differentiates doesn't exist anymore. We have merged into the Father.

BECOMING HUMBLE

295 *In* Spiritual Letters, *the master [Maharaj Jaimal Singh] tells his disciple [Baba Sawan Singh] to say, "I am nothing." How can this be interjected into meditation? Is it a process of thinking? Is it to be used consciously? What is the idea behind that?*

You will get the feeling that you are nothing when you merge in the love of the master. You are not mentally or symbolically to feel that you are nothing, or say, "I am nothing," nor to feel that you are everything. You will just forget what you are. When you absolutely blend yourself into the love of another person, then you forget what you are. Then you know that you are nothing. Everything is 'he' or 'she'. Similarly, we have to forget by meditation that we are anything and know that everything is the master. That will only be, as I have just explained, when we drive our ego out of us by meditation.

296 *What did Christ mean when he said: The meek shall inherit the earth?*

The meek means those people who are humbly patient, submissive and are filled with love and devotion for the Father. Only they will inherit the earth, meaning where the Father lives – not this physical earth,[9] that earth where the Lord lives, where the Father lives. They will be able to go back to the Father. Meek refers to those who are humble.

When we are able to eliminate the ego, when we are filled with love and devotion for the Father, then we are humble. The Father is indescribably great and mighty. When we realize this, we also realize how insignificant we are before the Father. Then we do not see anybody else in the world but him, and this creation doesn't exist for us. Only we exist and the Father exists. Then we'll realize that we are really humble. He is superior and we are inferior before him. Then real humility comes, real love, and the desire to become one with him grows. These are the meek. They will inherit the earth. They will inherit that earth, that heaven where the Father lives.

297   One of the most important marks of the saint is humility. Could you please speak to us about this quality?

Without love and devotion for the Lord, there can be no humility. You are humble when you think everybody is superior to you. And when you think everybody is superior to you, it means that you find the Lord in everybody. The Lord is superior to all. He is the king of kings, the most powerful. So, when you find the Lord in everybody, naturally you'll be humble before everybody.

When you consider yourself superior, naturally you cannot be humble at all. So long as the ego is there, we can never be humble; we can never be meek. When we are able to eliminate our ego and see the Lord within ourselves and in the whole creation, naturally we will be humble. That is real humility.

298   How can I kill the ego in me?

Well, brother, that is a very important question. Ego comes with the mind. This is the instinct of the mind. As long as ego is there, the soul can never go back to the Lord. We can drive that ego from within us only when we see that light, when we hear that sound, the word of God, the holy ghost. You may give it any name. Every saint has tried to explain the same thing. Guru Nanak described it as *bani, gurbani;* Muslim saints as *kalma, ism-i-a'zam, kalam-i-ilahi;* Chinese philosophers call it *tao;* Greeks have given it the name of *logos;* in the English Bible it is called the word. The same thing has been described by different names. That power, that audible life stream, is within every one of us here at the eye centre. We have to withdraw up to that eye centre to merge into that sound, to merge into that light. Attachment to that automatically detaches us from the senses.

The more we travel on the path, the more humble we become. The more we get the devotion and love of the Lord within us, the more humble we become. The more we are in love with the Lord, the more we realize his greatness, and the more insignificant we are in our daily life – the more humble we become. The more we are away from him, the more the ego increases and we think "I am doing it, I am supreme." When we find the real supreme One, we know how humble we are at his feet. Then the real humility comes. That is why Christ referred to the meek and humble of heart. Every saint has tried to tell us that we have to develop that humility. Guru Nanak said, I am a slave of the slaves. My actions are very, very low. Such is the humility of the saints, which comes only by devotion and love of the Lord within us. When our whole body is filled with love, the ego is gone and only humility and meekness remain. When that love and devotion is not in us, the whole body is full of ego. We have to detach ourselves from the world and attach ourselves to him. Only by the spiritual practice, only by that meditation, can we kill the ego.

299 Master, I wanted to ask you about ego. The Westerners
seem to have a much greater problem with ego than the
Indians do. They're much more humble.

Sister, the word ego is not rightly understood. Ego is nothing
but an attachment to this creation. And who's not attached to
this creation? But for that, nobody would be here. Ego is nothing but attachment, whether to faces or objects. Calculated
humility is okay, but doesn't lead you too far. It is like cosmetic
jewellery. There is nothing wrong with calculated humility,
but real humility is when we are filled with love and devotion
for the Father. It automatically drives out ego from us because
then our whole attention is one-pointed. We are only conscious
of the One and become unconscious of others. Then our whole
attention pivots to one particular point.

When we are filled with that love and devotion, attachment to the creation automatically starts fading out and automatically ego will go. When we see someone greater than us,
we automatically become humble before him. When we see his
radiance within, his refulgence within, when we are filled with
his love and devotion within, automatically we become humble.
The lover has no ego when he comes before the Beloved. He
always likes to do that which pleases the Beloved and tries to
avoid that which displeases the Beloved. He lives in his will, in
her will. He just wants to merge into another being and lose his
own identity, his own individuality. That is eliminating ego.

Just by mere talk, by not referring to the word 'I', people
try to avoid it. By saying things like "this self is doing it," "this
body is doing it," "I am not doing it," you don't avoid ego. It is
how much you are attached that matters, not your language.
You have to refer to your body or to other things one way or
another. How you do that neither increases ego nor decreases it.
We have to detach from the creation – that is eliminating ego.

Shabd and nam automatically detach us from this creation. All those objects and faces which are so important to us now – their importance automatically fades out. They hardly mean anything to us. They hardly exist for us. That is eliminating ego.

300 Maharaj Ji, where is the line drawn between humility and being a doormat?

Only you can know. Only you can know whether you are humble and how much you let people take advantage of you. How can people take advantage of your humility?

Well, it depends on what humility is.

Humility is not to be proud of anything, but then how does this give the impression that other people will take advantage of you?

When somebody higher than us, greater than us, more powerful than us comes before us, we automatically become humble. We automatically bow our heads in reverence. To men in authority, men in power – it may be spiritual power or worldly power – to anybody higher, better than us, automatically we bow our head in humility. So when we see the Lord within everyone, we automatically bow before them because then we see the Creator in them – we don't see them. We are humble before the Creator who has created them. We don't judge their actions. We don't try to boss over them or feel superior over their weaknesses. We become modest. We know the divine spark is there in them. It shines, but it is covered with the dirt of the mind, or they are slaves of their karmas. Humility actually comes from within. Calculated humility is all right, but doesn't lead you very far. But real humility comes automatically in you.

When you love someone you always feel humble before your love. You never feel superior because you always want to give to your love. You never want to take. You never love for advantage. You never love to bargain. You never love for wages. And that love gives you submission. And where submission comes, humility comes. Without love for the Lord there can be no humility at all. If you submit to him, his will, his creation, humility comes in you. So calculated humility is all right for dealing with people, but real humility only comes with love, when we submit ourselves to him. In submission, when you love somebody, you never expect anything in return. You always like to do that which pleases the other person, and you never do anything which displeases the other person. Even if sometimes you feel you are right, you always like to justify with yourself that you must have done something wrong, because you are so in love. We say that love is blind, and that helps you to submit, to merge into another being, and then automatically you become humble. When love comes or humility comes, all other qualities come like cream on milk.

301 How does seva and simran during the day clean the vessel?

Simran, as you know, helps us to eliminate all the worldly thoughts which we are worried about. We don't become superior by following the path. If you follow the path, actually you are filled with more humility. Then we go on realizing our insignificance before the Father. Then we don't look to the creation for comparison. Then we look to the Father for our comparison. Ego only comes when we look to the creation for comparison – "I'm better than him, I have much more than him." Then we feel ego. But when we compare ourselves with the Father, with the help of meditation we realize our insignificance, so naturally we are filled with humility. Then there is no question of ego. Ego is only there when we don't make much progress within and, just by being initiated, we start feeling that perhaps we have become superior to others. The real devotee, the real lover of the Lord will never have any ego at all. There is no question of spiritual ego. When we read the teachings of the great mystics and saints, and they call themselves slaves of the slave, worst of the worst, they are looking to the Father, comparing themselves to him.

302 Master, after we get initiated, sometimes it becomes very difficult to continue living with our families and friends who are not initiated.

You see, sometimes satsangis start feeling superior to the people they live with, thinking that they have become superhuman and that other people are inferior because they're not following the path. That hurts the ego of the other person, which creates discontentment and disharmony. Why should we feel superior or superhuman? We only have to do our duty in meditation. We should rather be an example to the people we live with and win them by more love and affection rather than acting superior. When we try to show that we have become something better, it hurts the other person's ego and it's very difficult for them to bear that. So slowly and slowly, conflict starts. We ourselves have a certain responsibility to behave as satsangis. We're all struggling souls. We're not born satsangis. After all, we have come to this by passing through so many stages, and the people we associate with may be passing through the same stages. So we should be helpful and useful to others rather than show our superiority.

303 Maharaj Ji, sometimes when one tries one's best to live within the teachings of the master, a terrible thing happens. Your ego takes over and one becomes proud. Master, how can we guard against this fruitless attitude?

Spiritual ego? That is the worst. There should be no spiritual ego. We know our reality, where we stand. I don't know what we are proud of. So there should be no spiritual ego at all. That is also ego, and unless we are able to eliminate all types of ego, it is very difficult to make proper progress. To think that we are superior and other people are inferior, that we are on the path and they are brooding about in the dark, is the wrong attitude. We can only thank the Lord for his grace, that's all. We can't put on airs or feel superior about it. Other people may be much better than we are and they may not know anything about the path – yet they may be very disciplined, good people. Everybody has their own destiny to go through, but there's nothing to feel proud of. We can be happy for the bliss and atmosphere we enjoy within, but that's nothing to feel proud of. This is a wrong attitude.

304 *Master, in our approach to meditation, should we have an attitude of total resignation to the Lord's will, or an attitude of limited free will in which we still think we are doing something in meditation?*

You see, we have limited free will, but we should attend to meditation without thinking that I am doing it, I am achieving it. Then there is always a danger of building ego. That ego, even spiritual ego, will be in our way. If you have the idea that I am doing it, I am doing seva, I am doing meditation, I have given so much money in seva, you are inflating your ego. You have to eliminate it. You have to do all these things without bringing your 'I' into it. Ego will be there, of course, up to the second region, but with I-ness you won't be able to reach even there. That gives you ego, that gives you *ahankar* [pride], and that is the only thing which is in our way.

Just by thinking that I am doing it – I attend satsang every day, I sit in meditation every day, I go to seva every day, I am much better than people who don't do all these things – you are building spiritual ego. These things rather should bring humility, should help you to eliminate the I-ness. As long as 'I' is there, you want everybody to see it. You want people to appreciate what you are doing, so you get the appreciation, but that's all.

We are so much in the habit of buying things, and we always want to make a cheap bargain – to pay less to get more. That is what we try to do when we give money in charity. We want to pay the minimum to get the maximum. If we give one dollar, we want a thousand dollars back. We want to invest the least amount possible in order to get the maximum possible. As long as that attitude is there – people should honour me and the Lord should pay me back for whatever I am giving – you will not get anything. There's no use in it, there's no charity.

So you have to eliminate I-ness from all these things – if I sit in meditation, the Lord should honour me, should appreciate that I am sitting in love for him. If you bring I-ness into it, then you will not get anything out of it. We are too fond of calculating: how much time I have given, how much advantage I am going to get from darshan if I have seen the master for five minutes. When calculation is there, we get nothing. At every step, we try to calculate: I have heard three satsangs, I have seen the master for so many hours today – how many karmas have I washed today? When you try to calculate in these ways, you get nothing. You are building your ego. A lover never calculates, he just gives.

305 *Master, how may we safeguard against the intrusion of unexpected or unrecognized ego when we attempt to judge ourselves, like if we are attempting to make certain improvements in our character, in our life, in our efforts? How may we reach some sort of balance, so we do not give ourselves too much credit and yet do not chop ourselves too low?*

Brother, it is a lifelong struggle; it is very difficult to know when ego is there and when it is not there. Sometimes, when we make a research of our humility, we find it is another form of ego. So when we think that we have no ego, actually we have it.

That is the tricky thing about it and I have been wondering, are we supposed to judge ourselves at any time?

We just have to try and then his grace is always there.

306 *Master, we satsangis are often inclined, when we have done something and we are praised for it, to say that it's not we who have done it, it is the master. When we give a satsang, for instance, and somebody praises it, we may say that it was the master. But are we correct in saying that, while we are still operating below the eye centre?*

One can say it's the grace of the Lord or the grace of the master. All what we have is just by his grace. So it's just a question of remembering the Lord with one excuse or another. At every step we want to remember him, we want to thank him. That is why we say that all I have is by his grace.

So it is all right to say it? You feel a little dishonest sometimes because you don't actually feel it.

You can be honest. You can say that I have done it. The idea is that we don't want to feel egoistic about anything that we do. We want to give credit to the Lord for our good qualities. Anything that people appreciate in us, we think it is just his grace that we could do it. We are no one. We're just trying to give credit to the Father and not be egoistic about our own achievements. That is the main purpose. There's nothing dishonest about it.

We want to appreciate his grace at every step. We want to remember him with any excuse. That is the main purpose of bringing in the master or Lord at every step. We say we are following the path. It doesn't mean that we follow the path. By his grace we follow the path. But for his grace we would never even know about the path. We would never have the atmosphere in which to live the path. Without his grace, nothing can happen. So we're just showing our appreciation by saying all these things.

Master, are our failures also his grace?

Yes, if we can learn from them. Our failures are actually a step towards our victory, if we can learn from them. If we don't try to learn from them, then they're just failures. If a child is always frightened of falling, he will never learn to walk. Those who take the risk of falling will ultimately learn how to walk and run, but those who are afraid of falling will never be able to learn to walk. So failures help us to learn to walk and run. Pitfalls will be there, failures will be there, but we should get up again and again try to run.

Can we thank you for our failures?

Yes, you can give him credit for that also. But if without doing your best you knowingly become a victim of the senses, and then you give the credit to the master, that may not be honest and fair. If we are honest, then of course you can give credit to the master for the failures too.

You see, when do we bring things to the master? When we take ourselves out of it. Elimination of ego is submission to the master. As long as the ego is there, we are not submitting at all. The mind is ruling us. But when we are able to eliminate the ego, then we are submitting. Then everything is the master. Failure or success is the master. We have taken the ego out of it. We have taken the I-ness out of it. Then you can give credit or discredit to the master. But as long as the mind is controlling us, then we cannot give credit to the master for anything. So the main thing is to eliminate the ego, and then there's a complete submission. Then whatever you do, you can say it's all the will of the master.

CRITICISM AND ANGER

307 *So many people ask you questions, and you are able to answer them with total love and understanding. I find myself judging a large percentage of my brothers and sisters. Some speak too soft, some speak too loud – whatever my mind says about what their question is. I have nothing but criticism. I wonder if you can speak to me personally or to us as a group about how we can deal with our criticism of others.*

Brother, we should not mind anybody's criticism at all. I can tell you, critics are the best guide in life. We should always keep our ears and eyes open to our critics. We must weigh their criticism without any ill will towards them. If it has any weight, we should try to learn from that criticism and try to improve ourselves. If it is just for the sake of criticizing, you can just ignore it. But our critics are the best guides in our lives, for our improvement. Without our critics, we would never be conscious of our shortcomings, our weaknesses. They are very essential for us to improve ourselves.

308 *How does one keep from judging and criticizing others and thus taking on a posture of self-righteousness? How does one control one's temper in the presence of such a person? How does one deal with such a person?*

Everybody has to train his own mind. We have to develop our mind to that extent that we are not affected by any criticism, we are not affected by any public opinion. In fact, we have to train ourselves rather than train the other person in that situation. We must train ourselves to fit into that situation. If the other person loses his temper, we cannot help it. It is for him to control his own mind. But we can control our own mind. If there is one fool under a roof, why do there have to be two? We must control ourselves.

309   *I have read in the Sant Mat books that if a person is being slandered by other people, this is a kind of blessing in disguise. So my question is, why and how is this a blessing?*

Anything which turns our attention towards the Father, reminds us of the Father, reminds us of our home and pulls us towards our home is a blessing. Anything which keeps us attached to this creation, I won't call it a blessing. You may think that the Lord giving me ten million dollars is his blessing. I won't call it a blessing. That may keep you attached to this creation forever. You may think that God has blessed me with four or five beautiful, healthy children, and I love them all, but it may not be his blessings. You may be so absorbed in their love that you may even forget the Father. I won't call it a blessing. Any death in the family which can turn you toward the Father may be his blessing, though it is very painful to experience these things. Anything which turns us toward him is his blessing. Anything which keeps us away from him is not his blessing. In that light, you can yourself weigh what is a blessing and what is not a blessing, from a Sant Mat point of view.

310   *Maharaj Ji, why is it so easy for us to criticize and judge and hurt other people, and so difficult for us to admit our own shortcomings and faults?*

Christ said in the Bible very clearly that we don't see the beam in our own eyes, but we are very anxious to see even just a little straw or something in another person's eyes.[27] We don't sit in judgment on ourselves, but we are always anxious to sit in judgment on others. We don't look within; we always try to look out, to see how others behave. We never try to see what we are, how we behave, where we stand. We're only concerned with where other people stand. We want them to be perfect but we don't want ourselves to be perfect. Actually we love them more than we love ourselves. We hate ourselves. We're not concerned with ourselves, we're only concerned with others. We always want them to be perfect, to be pure, to be the best, because we love them, we are obsessed with them or we're attached to them – even through hatred we're attached to them – and we are not attached to ourselves. So we don't try to look within to see that we must love ourselves, that we must sit in judgment on ourselves and make ourselves whole, make ourselves pure.

311 Master, more and more I've become aware of anger in me that I don't understand. It's always unexpected and unreasonable, and it leaks out in the form of irritation and judgments of others. Where does that come from and how do you deal with it?

Well, brother, with the help of simran and meditation, we are definitely becoming better and better, and we do not find our associates coming to that level, and we start losing our temper with them. We start judging them, because we have evolved ourselves, we have risen from those weaknesses and we cannot tolerate people becoming a victim of those weaknesses. Our standard has become very different from what it used to be, so we become a little short-tempered sometimes, and we have to be very cautious about it.

You will often find in the life of great people who are very disciplined, very noble, that they are short-tempered and impatient. They cannot see how people can be undisciplined – they forget when they were just like them.

So we should be more liberal with others and not try to judge them too hard. If we have improved, we should try to help them to improve, but we should try not to judge them too hard and become unnecessarily impatient with their behaviour. It does happen; I've often seen it with many satsangis, even very good satsangis. And even with the great people – if you read their histories, you'll find that weakness in them.

Is there ever constructive anger between people?

I don't know what you mean by constructive anger. It depends upon how the other person takes your anger, whether he takes it destructively or constructively.

Are there times when the only way to handle a situation is to be angered, to be strong in defiance?

Well, I can only say that we have to be cautious and not be unnecessarily strict in judging people, not be quick to condemn people.

312 *Maharaj Ji, what should our attitude be if people whom we work with persistently make fun of us because we're on the path? Should we just smile at them and walk away?*

Why should you be touchy about their remarks? Why should we be touchy? Let them say whatever they feel like. They've every right to comment and you have every right to reserve your judgment. Don't be affected by what they say. As Great Master often said, you can't pick up the thorns of the world but you can definitely wear shoes. You can't make them quiet, but definitely you can be indifferent to what they say. It doesn't affect you. Why do we want to be appreciated just because we are on the path? Was Christ appreciated? Wasn't he put on the cross? Is that appreciation? Why do we expect appreciation? We should just do our duty and let people say whatever they feel like, and not get discouraged by public opinion.

313 *Maharaj Ji, how can we avoid the pitfall of criticizing others and judging others when we are simply trying to use discrimination in keeping good company?*

You may not criticize them. You can judge within yourself whether the person is worth your company or not, but you may not criticize him. You can avoid him. Where's the necessity of criticizing him? The question is, how to avoid criticizing. If you think he's not worthy of your company, avoid him.

The idea is to keep good company from a meditation point of view. If you find certain company not conducive to meditation, naturally you have no option but to avoid it. If you don't find a person's company helpful for meditation or he otherwise has tried to exploit or misuse you, naturally what can you do except avoid him? You may not criticize him, but you can definitely avoid him.

314 *In the book* Thus Saith the Master, *one answer suggests that we should have a loving attitude toward ourselves.*

What is your self? The soul. So we should have a loving attitude towards the soul. We should try to help the soul. When we have a loving attitude towards others, automatically we have a loving attitude towards ourselves. When we love others, we live in love. When we are good to others, we are good to ourselves. Then you are happy with yourself, then you live with yourself.

If you're angry with somebody, if you have a spirit of revenge against somebody, or if you have any malice towards somebody, you can't live with yourself at all. You're unhappy with yourself. You don't actually hurt the other person, you hurt yourself more. If you are loving to another person, good and kind to another person, actually you are being good and kind to your own self. You're living with yourself and you're happy with yourself. Automatically we become loving to ourselves. Then we have a loving attitude toward others.

The peace and happiness we get by being good and noble to others is the greatest reward one can get. We should try not to expect a reward from the other person by being good and noble to them. We are giving a reward to ourselves. The happiness which we build by being good and noble to others is itself a great reward. What other reward do we expect?

315 Should we always try and hold the truth in our minds when we make any criticism?

I don't say that we should compromise with the truth, but there is a way of putting a truth to another person. Our approach should be one of love, of helpfulness. But if we think we are superior, then we are only using the truth to humiliate the other person. That approach is not right. At times, silence is golden. Most of our problems in this creation come from our tongue. If we can control it, I think we have solved 80 percent or 90 percent of our problems – if we know how to control our tongue, how to use it. Controlling our speech is very good, and then to use it rightly is even better. If we can't use it rightly, at least we should try to control it. The truth shouldn't be used as an excuse to humiliate another person. It depends upon the approach, how you reach out to a person and what your motives are.

316 I know we should not criticize. If you have someone working with you and the work they do is not satisfactory, how do you go about changing their behaviour?

Sister, you can tackle the same problem in two ways. You can be polite and lovingly explain with constructive suggestions, or you can condemn the same action. It all depends on how you approach the subject. So even if we have to criticize or correct anybody, there must be love behind it, with the aim to reform the other person.

317 If you criticize someone, do you take on their karma?

We are all filled with weaknesses; we should try to clear up our own weaknesses, rise above our own weaknesses, and try to help others. Why criticize anybody at all? We should try to be helpful to them, not try to let them down or unnecessarily criticize them.

> *If someone criticizes you, what should you say back to him?*

You should rise above the opinion of the world. Christ said: When they can persecute me, they can persecute you also.[124] When the world can torture Christ, when they can crucify their saint, then why should we bother if people criticize us or malign us? We should try to rise above these things and try to keep our own goal in mind and not worry about public opinion.

318 When people criticize the path, should we try to defend it and ourselves?

I know we are very sensitive to public criticism. We have to rise above public opinion. It shouldn't bother us. When I know there is a horse before me, even if the whole world says it is a donkey, it doesn't bother me. I am convinced from within myself that it is a horse. There's no sense in my arguing and trying to convince anybody that it is a horse, not a donkey. Let them say what they like – why bother with them?

319 Master, what should we do if we hurt the feelings of another, and secondly, will meditation eventually enable us to avoid hurting people's feelings completely? Through meditation, will we be harmless to other people someday?

We should not unnecessarily sit in judgment on others or try to hurt people. We judge others when we think we are superior and other people are inferior to us. We think we are much better human beings and they are an inferior type of human being. We think we have no weaknesses of our own at all and other people are full of weaknesses, so we always feel superior to them. Then we try to show off or taunt them or tease them or hurt them about their weaknesses. This is not a right attitude. We can be helpful to them, we can feel sorry for them, and we can be a source of strength to them rather than hurt them or condemn them.

Naturally the purpose of meditation is to eliminate the ego. When you are able to eliminate the ego, then you don't think you're superior at all; then you think you're inferior to everybody. Because you see that light of the Father in everyone and you know your insignificance before the Father, everybody becomes superior to you. Then you start realizing what your real self is, your insignificance. When that realization comes, we don't see humans at all, we see his light in every human. We become humble before the Father. Then the question of hurting someone doesn't arise at all; the question of condemning anybody doesn't arise at all; the question of feeling superior to anybody doesn't arise at all.

Christ said: Judge not, that ye be judged.[26] When we try to judge anybody, we also expose ourselves to judgment. So it's better to judge ourselves rather than judge others. We should be helpful to them; we should be a source of strength for them.

320 *Master, could you explain the extent of the damage we do by feeling revenge?*

When the mind is so closed, when mind is so full of malice, how can it concentrate? How can it attend to meditation? It has to be relaxed. It has to be absolutely receptive. When it is full of revenge, how can it be receptive to the Lord's grace within?

321 *Maharaj Ji, let's say you're working closely with somebody, and you can see that the person is going to become an alcoholic because he's drinking a lot, and so you confront him. You tell him: "Look brother, this drinking is going to be a bad thing." But what if your confrontation hurts the person?*

In hurting, one has to look at the motive. Is your motive to hurt him or to help him? The motive makes all the difference. And your approach to the person, the situation, and the problem makes all the difference. Whether you are telling him just to show your own superiority, or whether you are really wanting to help him – you really love him and you want to help him – it depends upon your approach and also your motive. If you just want to make him conscious of his weakness and of your superiority to him, then you are not helping him at all. Then of course you're hurting him. But if you are humble, if you really love him and you really want to help him, and you lovingly approach him and want him to get out of it, then naturally you are not hurting him at all.

322 *Maharaj Ji, Christ and many other saints have written that to injure somebody's feelings is one of the greatest sins of all. What about the situations where there was no intent to injure somebody's feelings, but someone didn't like what we had to say, or didn't agree with what we had to say and their feelings were hurt?*

Our motive should not be to hurt anybody. That is the main thing. If some people are extraordinarily sensitive, we can't help that. But your motive should not be to hurt or injure anyone, and if you feel that your words or expression or deeds have hurt anyone, you can apologize. One should never hesitate to apologize or feel shy about it.

323 *On the question of anger, when living in this world, this society, there is a good deal of frustration. I do not know the difference between frustration and anger. I find that I can handle it much better if I can give some kind of outward expression to the things which are making me angry. Then I can get rid of it.*

You mean, just to lighten yourself? Well, prepare the others that I am just lightening myself. [Laughter] There is no harm if sometimes we do become a victim to strong expressions, but we should not keep any grudge in the heart. We should be honest enough to clear any misunderstanding that has arisen, and then just feel light about it.

324 *Master, if we feel anger, is it better not to express it at all? What do we do with it when we feel it?*

Well, we are trying to conquer all these enemies. How can we say we should express whatever we feel like? We have to fight with the mind not to become angry at all. But if we do, it's better to keep our lips sealed rather than express it. It's better not to feel it, but if you feel it at least don't express it, and if you do express it, express it very gently and lovingly.

325 Let's say a person is prone to anger, so he suppresses it, but still inside he feels it, only he doesn't show it.

That's good.

This is good?

Why show it? Anger only hurts another person when your face shows how you are feeling. If it is held within, it doesn't harm anybody at all. You may be able to throw it out slowly and slowly. But at least one should learn not to get angry, to at least control your emotions, your feelings, your anger. That is a great achievement.

You've talked in the past, though, that by suppressing the mind, it might come back twice as hard if you hold it down.

No, slowly and slowly you can get rid of the anger.

326 I've read that if we knew the effect of anger, we would never become angry. Could you explain that?

Try to look at your face in the mirror when you are angry. Then perhaps you wouldn't want to become angry. The pity is that we don't see our face, our expression when we are angry. So many changes take place, so many expressions come and go. Nobody wants to show themselves in a poor light. If we knew how we looked, we wouldn't want to get angry. We lose our balance. After all, anger doesn't solve any problem. It has not reformed anyone. We just hurt our own self and hurt another person, nothing else, with no gain for anybody.

327 Master, I'd like to know the best way to handle anger. Sometimes I suppress it and say simran. And other times I let it out and voice it, and then I say simran.

Which way makes you feel better?

Letting it out and voicing it.

When you voice it, is the other person receptive to your voice or does he voice it back? If he voices it back to you, then you again want to voice it back at him. Where does it lead? If there is one fool under a roof, it is better not to have two. We should try to digest our anger within because anger doesn't solve any problem. You can be firm in explaining your viewpoint and do it diplomatically rather than angrily. When we get angry, we harm ourselves more than the other person because the other person is not affected by our anger. Rather, he would think ill of us, what type of man we are. Neither is he improved by it. So we damage our own self.

But these are general instincts of the body, so it does express itself sometimes here and there. As far as possible, one should try to avoid losing one's temper. Getting angry can become a habit. If we start expressing it because we think that by voicing it we can get rid of it, rather it builds more and more. It's always better to rise above it.

328 I want to ask you about cursing. In the West we use four-letter words when we get angry sometimes. And I was brought up in an area where people express themselves when they're angry.

You see, if anybody gives you such compliments, don't accept them. [Laughter] You only get what you receive. If another person is giving you something and you don't receive it, it doesn't affect you. If he's cursing you and you don't receive the curses, it doesn't affect you at all; it doesn't upset you at all. But if you receive them – if you receive a gift, naturally it becomes yours. If you're affected by those curses, if you receive them, then you unnecessarily make yourself unhappy and miserable. Let the other person give them to you, but don't you receive them.

What should I do?

Make your ears deaf! It's not always good to hear everything. And everything's not always worth hearing.

What about my habit of cursing?

That is more important. When you don't like anybody else to curse you, then how can you justify your cursing anybody? Get rid of it, don't do it. If there's one fool under one roof, why have two? One is enough.

329 *Master, while one is angry, it's impossible to get out of this anger at the same moment. One has to wait ...*

Sister, that is right. At that moment you can't help it because you are just being carried away by the wave of emotion. But in the future you can always think that you should not throw yourself into the wave to be carried away by it. And if you go on thinking like that, and putting in an effort not to be angry, then you will get out of it.

330 *Maharaj Ji, like anyone else, as disciples we experience a whole array of emotions. My question is, how should we*

best deal with the emotion of anger? Should we express it
when we feel it, or should we try to keep it inside?

Why not throw it out without expressing it?

It's not always so easy.

Well, try to do it. You see, if you keep your mind in simran
and try to attach yourself to the spirit within, you will rise
above these little things which unnecessarily perturb you and
make you angry. One should try to control one's anger and try
to divert one's mind at that time to some other direction. It is
always better to do simran or try to be in touch with the spirit
within. Then you will rise above the anger.

331 Are these karmic things which bring about anger?

We try to justify in this way all that we are seeing and all that
is happening in this world. We can say it is all due to karma,
but to take that attitude is definitely a weakness and we must
take steps to overcome it. In order to overcome all such evil
tendencies we must realize that they are weaknesses. And the
only way to realize that and to overcome these weaknesses is to
attach our mind to shabd.

FORGIVENESS

332 Master, will you speak about forgiveness?

We are all knocking at the Lord's door to forgive us for all the
sins we have committed, all the karmas we have committed,
right from the beginning of the creation. Since we have been
part of it, we have collected a lot of karmas. Unless we are

forgiven for all that we have done, the soul can never go back to the Father.

Meditation is nothing but seeking his forgiveness, nothing else. "Whatever we have done or we are too weak to do every day, please forgive us." Meditation is nothing else. It is not vain words to say to him, but practically we pray to him for forgiveness by attending to meditation. It is the same as repentance. When we are sitting in meditation, we are actually repenting for what we have done in the past. We are repenting and seeking his forgiveness. We are sorry for what we have done in the past and now we are asking the Father to forgive us.

So repentance and forgiveness go together. Unless we repent, unless we realize what we have done, we will never ask for forgiveness. First, repentance comes within us – we realize we have done something wrong – then we go to another person to seek his forgiveness. So we do realize what we have done, that we have been doing something wrong in the past and now we seek the Father's forgiveness for what we have done, for what stands between us and the Father.

So as far as forgiveness in the world is concerned, if we don't forgive what other people do to us, we build karmic connections with them, and then we may have to come back to forgive them. They may have to come back to seek our forgiveness and we may have to come back to forgive them. We want to escape from all that. So we don't want justice at all, even if others have trespassed against our rights. We just want to forgive them so that we may not create any karmic link with them that might pull us back to this creation.

That is why we should also try to forgive whatever anybody has done against us – it is immaterial whether the person even asks us for forgiveness. We should not have any idea of revenge within us – that he has done this to me and if the opportunity comes, I will do it to him. We should not have that attitude, even if he's arrogant enough not to ask for forgiveness. Even then I think we should forgive the person, because we've had enough and we don't want more of these karmic relationships.

So we should just forgive the person and call it quits. The Lord knows best how he's going to account for all that, but at least we should have no karmic relationship with that person. Whether you go to a court as the accused or the complainant, you still have to go to court. We don't want to go to the court of justice at all, even as a complainant. We want to escape from this court of justice, so we just forgive. If you want justice, then you expose yourself – you have to go to the court for justice, so then you will be judged too. But we want to rise above all that.

So whatever we have done in the past, we can seek forgiveness by meditation. Whatever anybody has done to us now, we should always be anxious to forgive. We should just try to forgive them. We shouldn't have anything weighing on our mind at all. Then we don't create any karmic relationship. That is why Christ said: You go and ask for his forgiveness while you are on the way,[16] meaning while you are living and he's living.

So if he leaves – if he dies – then you have no one to ask for forgiveness. That is added to your karmas and you have to ask the Lord for forgiveness. But while you are both living you can seek his forgiveness and you can forgive him also. So forgiveness is always best.

333 *Maharaj Ji, it says in the books that the Lord himself finds it hard to forgive us when we break the heart of another person, or we hurt their feelings. Could you explain what it means to break someone's heart and why the Lord finds it so difficult to overlook that?*

You see, unless we learn to forgive others, we cannot expect the Lord to forgive us. We have to forgive others when they have done something against us. The Lord will forgive us if we learn to forgive others for what they have done against us, and we can only get forgiveness from the Lord by meditation.

What is forgiveness? There is a block of karmas between the soul and the Father. That is why we are separated from the Father. That layer of karma doesn't let the soul go back to the Father. Forgiveness means to forgive us for all those karmas, all those sins which you have collected in the past birth. Whatever seed we have sown, before it comes up, we can uproot it. But once it becomes a plant, we can't uproot it. Then we have to taste its fruit.

If you hurt another person, if he is still alive he can forgive you and you can forgive him and that karmic relationship is finished. You've uprooted the seed. But if the other person leaves the world, you have no opportunity to ask for his forgiveness – then that karma goes to your debit. You have to account for that karma. You will have to come to this world to account for it – you can account for it by meditation, or you can ask the Father to forgive you for that karma. But the Lord will only forgive us if we also forgive others.

Christ has given a very beautiful parable in the Bible: One servant of a king owed some money to him and he implored the king: I'm not in a position to pay you the loan, so please forgive me.[60] In those days, the custom was that if anybody is a debtor, he could be put in prison. This custom, this law, was quite prevalent in India, even till some thirty, forty years ago. So he implored the king, and the king felt that this man was really not in a position to pay. So he forgave him all that he owed him. But that very man also was owed some money by a fellow servant. So he went to him and said: Give me my money. And that man pleaded with him the same way: Please forgive me, because I'm not in a position to pay you and I am helpless. There was a drought, there's been no rain. I couldn't produce any crops, so forgive me. Someday later on, I may be able to pay you. But he didn't forgive him; he had him put in prison. When the king came to know about this, he called that person. He said: Look, I forgave you, but you have not forgiven your fellow man. So I won't forgive you anymore. Then he put him into the prison. This is just a parable given by Christ to explain to us that we can only provoke the forgiveness of the Father if we first learn to forgive our fellow beings for whatever they do against us, whether they trespass our rights or we feel hurt by their actions. If we learn to forgive them, then we can also pray to the Father to forgive us for what we have done to others. If we don't learn to forgive, how can we expect the Father to forgive us?

Real forgiveness can only come from the Father by meditation. Clearing our karmic account is forgiveness. Eliminating the karmas which stand between us and the Father is all his forgiveness. When he wants to forgive us, he puts us on the path. He brings us into the company of the mystics. He gives us that environment where we can meditate. This is how he forgives us. It's not just vain repetition of prayers which provoke his forgiveness.

Forgiveness and repentance are the same thing; there's no difference at all. We repent for actions we have done by not repeating those actions again. Whatever we have done, we are sorry for it; we want the Lord's forgiveness, and we promise not to repeat those actions again. That is repentance. That is why Christ said: Repent, the kingdom of God is within you.[3] The Lord is nowhere outside; he's right within your body. But you have to repent before you can see him within yourself – repent for what you have done in past lives, which stands between you and the Father. Unless that is forgiven – unless you're able to repent for those actions, those karmas – your soul can never be forgiven; that is, your soul will never be able to go back to the Father.

The Father forgives us by putting us on the path. He attaches us to the spirit within, and with the help of that spirit, by worshipping the spirit, all our karmic accounts are cleared. So we are forgiven for all that we have done. By just mere praying to the Father, we don't get forgiveness. We have to work hard for it in meditation.

As for repentance, we can repent only if we know what we have done. But we don't know what we have done in past lives. When we don't know, how can we repent? Repent for what? What has a child done to repent for in this life? He's so innocent; he's a babe. He has to repent for what he has done in past lives, in previous births. Since we don't know what we have done in past lives, how can we refrain from repeating those actions again? That is why we can repent only through meditation, by worshiping the spirit. Christ says that the spirit will make you free; the truth will make you free.[98] He means free from all these sins, all the karmas we have collected in our past births. We become free when we have been forgiven or we have been able to repent. It is the same thing.

334 Would you speak to us about the role of nonresistance in the life of a disciple?

You mean nonviolence, that we should not retaliate? When Christ said, whatever you sow, so shall you reap,[133] he meant that if another person sows a bad seed, he will have to reap or harvest a bad crop. Why should you sow any bad seed at all? Why should you commit any karma for which you may have to come back? And if you also retaliate against someone, you become like the other person. Then you both may have to come back to this creation, whether you come as a debtor or a creditor.

If we go to court, whether as a complainant or an accused, we don't know whether the judgment will be on the side of the complainant or the accused. Christ is saying that you should not seek judgment at all; you should not be a party to what the other person does. If there's one fool under a roof, then there is no necessity for two under the same roof. The other person will pay for his own actions. Why should you have any spirit of revenge or retaliation, for then you may also have to come back, whether as a debtor or a creditor. He will pay for his karmas, but you should not involve yourself in that karma so that you won't have to come back, even as a creditor.

335 *Master, do you believe that all things have seeds – that the law is an eye for an eye and a tooth for a tooth? Is not this the karmic law – God's law – that we give a karma for everything that we do? Is it an eye for an eye and a tooth for a tooth?*

Sister, what Jesus meant to tell us is that we should not be revengeful in our heart. If somebody should take our eye, we should not think that we should also take out his eye. Rather, we should give him love, affection. If he slaps you on one side, then put the other side before him. Love thy neighbour,[67] love one another – that is what the teaching is. It is the teaching of peace and love, and certainly not of hatred and revenge.

When that love comes in you, then you do not have any ill-feeling against anybody. Unless your heart is pure, you will not be receptive to the Lord's grace. That is what Christ says. When you are praying to the Lord, if you have not forgiven someone, you must first forgive him. Only then will you get forgiveness from the Lord.[15] That means that your heart must be pure when you pray. Your heart must be receptive when you pray, and it will be receptive only when it is pure, when it is unconscious of the world. If you are carrying a grudge against anyone or have hatred in your heart, it is not pure, as its tendencies are always downward. Then you cannot receive what the Lord wants to give you. So, if we have no ill-feeling against anybody, we have become pure and receptive; and we receive his grace, his love. There is no hatred left in us when his love comes in. A heart full of love has no room for hatred.

336 *Master, as far as the new karmic seeds we're sowing, is there a way that we can have instant karma, when for seeds that we've sown in the present, we can pay them off in the next few days or the next month, or do they go into our store of karmas?*

Definitely meditation helps us in many ways to clear all that, but if we still have ego in us – for example, I refuse to apologize to that person and I only want to clear that by meditation – it would be difficult for you to clear that karma. Ego is there, and it will not help you to seek forgiveness, even from the Lord. If the other person doesn't forgive you and you have exhausted all opportunities to seek his forgiveness, then you can depend upon the Lord to forgive you. But if ego is in your way – you don't want to bend before him, you don't want to apologize to him, you would like to clear all that only by meditation – then you won't be able to clear it by meditation. So if we really feel that we arc guilty and we definitely have to apologize, we should never hesitate. We have to be honest with ourselves.

337 *Master, when we find it very hard to forgive somebody for something that they've done to us, what makes us hold on to that grievance?*

We have to analyze ourselves, we have to think rationally that it is to our own advantage to forgive that person. As long as we don't forgive someone, we are actually punishing ourselves. The grudge we keep within ourselves, the malice we keep within – we are also punishing ourselves. We are punishing the other people too, but we are punishing ourselves also. We feel so light and happy after forgiving. The happiness you get by forgiving, you don't get otherwise at all. You get more happiness by forgiving than by seeking forgiveness. When day and night we are asking the Father to forgive us, there's no reason why we should not forgive anyone who asks for our forgiveness. How can we receive the Father's forgiveness when we are so closed that we cannot forgive another person? We must set our example before the Father, that we have been able to forgive, so you should also forgive us. If we are so closed that we can't forgive, how can we expect the Father to forgive us?

338 *Maharaj Ji, could you discuss the qualities of forgiving and forgetting?*

We generally do forgive, but sometimes it becomes difficult to forget. It still weighs a little on our conscience. We should even forget that we have forgiven. If you forget that you have forgiven, then you will forget the original incident. If it is always weighing on your mind that "I have forgiven, I have forgiven," it means you've not forgotten at all. It shouldn't weigh on your mind. Forget the incident, absolutely. We do forgive people, but we don't forget that we have forgiven them. So a scar is always there. The wound is gone, but the scar is always there. We shouldn't be conscious of even the scar.

339 *Maharaj Ji, how do we know in our heart that we have truly forgiven someone for some past ill-treatment we feel has been dealt to us?*

If we really don't want any revenge and we have forgiven, then it doesn't bother us at all. If that instinct to take revenge from the person is gone, then it means we have forgiven him. And we forget the incident also. If the incident is always obsessing us and we are always thinking, "I have forgiven him, I have forgiven him," then you have not forgiven him at all. If you forget the whole incident, if you don't even recollect it, then you've really forgiven.

340 *Master, I've read a lot in the Sant Mat books that to hurt the feelings of another person is a great sin, and sometimes on the path we become really sensitive, and maybe we hurt the feelings of other people or they hurt our feelings. How do we deal with that graciously and just realize that people are going through their own transformation process?*

We should never hesitate to apologize if we really think we are at fault. We should never go out of our way to hurt anybody at all. We can be firm in our faith, firm in our belief, but still we can be loving and kind in our expression. Naturally we can't oblige everyone for everything. We have to refuse sometimes, but we can lovingly refuse. We shouldn't go out of our way to hurt anybody unnecessarily.

341 *If we hurt someone's feelings by accident, are we held responsible for it?*

Well, sister, sometimes we hurt somebody's feelings; not purposely, but unknowingly, without intent, innocently. But if we have hurt another person even innocently, we should try at once to make amends. There's no harm. When the motive to hurt is not there, you cannot be blamed. It always has to do with a motive. That's when we have to suffer for hurting people's feelings. If something happens unconsciously, then you shouldn't worry. Yet there's no harm in making amends even then.

342 If we slandered another and the other person does not forgive us, though we ask for forgiveness, what should we do?

Sister, the most important thing is that you have to forgive yourself for that behaviour. If you have honestly tried to make amends and are truly sorry, then it should not bother you whether the other person has forgiven you or not. And the other person will only be convinced that you are really sorry by your behaviour. The mere word 'sorry' does not solve any problem. He has to know from your behaviour that you are really sorry. You can always express your repentance, not by mere words but by deeds. That is how you can forgive yourself, and when you forgive yourself, you become happy.

How can we forgive ourselves when we hurt others?

We can forgive ourselves only if we cease hurting others. If we keep repeating the same behaviour, it is self-deception to say that we have forgiven ourselves. In order to forgive ourselves, we must cease repeating that mistake. When we really repent and do not repeat that mistake again, then we can say that we have forgiven ourselves. Forgiving ourselves means not to repeat that mistake again and to forget absolutely what we have done to another person. That sense of guilt should leave us when we have reformed ourselves.

We should never hesitate or feel ashamed to apologize if we have hurt anybody, if we have injured anybody's feelings; whether the other person forgives us or not, at least our apology helps us. When we have apologized, we feel light, we feel much better with ourselves. It is for the other person to forgive us or not, but at least we have forgiven ourselves by apologizing and sincerely showing our regret.

343 If there is a misunderstanding between two people, should not the guilty person apologize in order not to lay the blame on the other, and perhaps not make him feel badly?

When we want to clear up a misunderstanding, the question of pinning the blame on one person or another does not arise. When we want to finish that topic, when we want to forgive, we should never try to decide whether you were wrong or whether I was wrong. We should always try to say that you forgive me and I forgive you, and we had better forget whatever unpleasantness has happened between us. The question of thinking and trying to analyze whether you were wrong or whether I was wrong will lead to another type of trouble again. So if we want to forgive ourselves and forget, it is better to express our regrets sincerely and then forget what has happened between us.

344 I'm sure I can't remember all the people I've offended. Will meditation help to burn it off?

You have to forgive them from your heart. We forgive from the heart. You don't want to have any revenge. If anybody owes you anything, just forgive him. But if you have done wrong to others and they are living, you can ask for their forgiveness. If they are no longer living, then ask the Lord to forgive you. But don't have, in your heart, any grievance, any feeling of revenge, any spite against anybody. Your heart should be clean.

345 In order to get rid of our karmas, do we ask forgiveness of those we have hurt or do we ask God to forgive us?

I'll tell you – you ask for forgiveness as many times as you possibly can.

I ask the people I have harmed?

Naturally. Whom you can forgive, you must forgive. If they ask you for your forgiveness, you should forgive them at once. And you should ask for the forgiveness of those whom you have harmed. If they don't forgive you for what you have done to them, then the Lord will forgive you.

A PEACEFUL AND RELAXED LIFE

346 You often speak of living a calm, relaxed life. How can we do this?

Well, everybody wants to be happy in this world. Nobody wants to be miserable. So why not be happy? Why not lead a relaxed and happy life? Why worry about the past and the future? Why not live in the present? Relaxation comes only when you're happy within. When you are able to obtain that peace within, then wherever you go, you radiate peace. If you are relaxed within, wherever you go, you will relax the people around you. If you are miserable within, you will just share your misery with others. If you go to a miserable person, he will make you miserable in two minutes. If you go to a happy person, he will make you happy in two minutes. So we must obtain that peace and happiness within – we can never get that from outside, from worldly and sensual pleasures. That has to be obtained from within. Then your whole attitude towards life becomes relaxed. Then you will attend to everything in a relaxed manner, with a relaxed attitude.

If you're always living in tension, in worry, in misery or in a sense of guilt, then it becomes difficult for you to give even a smile to anyone, and the other person also has to make his face just like yours because if somebody's weeping, you can't go and laugh before him. You have to make your face as miserable as his.

Most of our worries are our own creations. Life itself is very simple, but we have complicated it so much that we now find it hard to live. We have created all these problems and complications, and now we find it very hard to go along with them, because we can't solve them and they become a source of misery. What do we really need in this world? If we look broadly at our needs, how few we have! How much can one eat? How much can one wear? How many places to sleep do we need? These are our necessities of life. But how much do we really need? And how much effort have we expended to fulfil these needs? We have so many rooms in our house, so many dishes on the table, so many restaurants and hotels to feed us, such variety of clothes and dresses to wear – wardrobes full. You can expand your needs as much as you like, or you can bring them to the minimum.

We have created all our problems, by demanding more and more, more and more, by not being satisfied with what we have. So how can we relax? We're racing to keep up with our neighbours, so how can we relax?

We invented all these gadgets to save time for ourselves, to sit at leisure, to be happy. If a lady used to cook her food in three, four hours in the olden times, now she can probably cook a meal in twenty minutes – so many short cuts and facilities are available to her in the kitchen. But can she use any of the time she has saved for herself? She still has to rush and rush and rush and rush, and ultimately she throws herself dead tired on the bed at night.

We used to walk from one place to another place. Then we had bicycles, then carts, then cars, and now we have jet planes, but we haven't saved any time. It used to take us about a month or so to reach London by ship, and now we fly in airplanes in nine, ten, eleven hours. But those twenty-nine days I've saved are not at my disposal for sitting at leisure. I've not gained anything.

These things are good if you gain time for yourself, if you can live a relaxed, happy life. Then these things are at your service. But now you are their slave – they possess you, you don't possess them at all. All these modern conveniences are possessing us, so we are miserable. We find no time for ourselves. We can't sit with nature, we can't enjoy each other's company, we can't talk or gossip. We're always running and rushing, so how can we relax and be happy? We look at everything from the commercial point of view, from the business point of view, so how can we relax?

We have made so much progress in society and we are also making progress in the mental hospitals. There are more and more patients every day, more and more suicides, more and more broken homes, more and more undisciplined children. How can we be happy in this atmosphere?

We have no time for ourselves. Unless we have time for ourselves, we can never be happy. We always live for others, we never live for ourselves. We always love other people's company, we never love our own company. We have become so self-centred that we can't tolerate anybody's criticism, anybody else's viewpoint. So how can we be happy? How can we be relaxed? We have complicated our life so much that now we find it difficult to live with those complications.

Unless we are able to obtain peace within, we can never be relaxed, we can never be happy. And meditation is the best relaxation one can have. Nothing relaxes you more than meditation. The more your mind is scattered into this world, the more miserable you are; the more your mind is concentrated within yourself, the more happy you are. The more you need, the more miserable you are; the less you need, the more happy you are. So we have created this misery, and now we find it difficult to relax.

347 Maharaj Ji, I think that people are not sincere in wanting peace.

We come to this world to reap the fruit of our good karmas and our bad karmas. We have a little peace when we are reaping the fruit of good karmas, but what about when we get the result of bad karmas? We are at war – with each other, family to family, nation to nation, country to country. And that is why this world is known by the saints as a world of happiness and unhappiness. It's a combination of both good and bad which brings us back to this world. So while taking the fruit of bad karmas, we have got to be unhappy; and when we are unhappy, how can there be peace? There can never be peace in this world, and saints never come here to create peace in this world.

First, we used to probably fight with our hands. Then we started fighting with bamboo sticks, then with swords, then with guns, and now with these tanks, the atom bomb and all that. But still we are fighting. We have improved our method of fighting, but where is the peace? History doesn't encourage us. When we research the bad things of history, there never has been peace in this world. Now with all this civilization and everything to our credit, scientific achievements to our credit, we are not better human beings than we used to be. We still have the same jealousies and we are still cutting each other's throats. I personally think that people were happier in olden days than now. Then they used to sleep under a tree, and now we sleep in concrete and steel buildings. We are more unhappy in our soft beds. Before, people could sleep seven, eight hours a night. Now we have to sleep by pills or by injections. With all our physical comfort, we don't get better sleep or have better health.

I have seen with my own eyes the change in the attitude of the people, the masses in the villages. Just about thirty years ago, all village folks of their own age group would collect under some tree or in some common area and would talk and chat and joke and enjoy and laugh with each other. Now everybody is confined to their own house. Nobody comes out to a common place. They can't stand each other and don't want to see each other!

We have got civilization from the West now and we confine ourselves to independent rooms. At first the villagers would come together around a fire and solve all the problems of the village – about some daughter or boy not behaving, or some marriage problems and all that. Elders were respected and whatever they would say was accepted. And if anybody was misbehaving, he would try to avoid the elders of the village. But now the elders are being abused! He says: "Mind your own business. You have no right to interfere with me. It's my own life; let me waste it. I'll spend it as I think best."

We are becoming more and more self-centred now, and the more self-centred you become, the more unhappy you become. We can hardly express ourselves anywhere to anybody – we have to rush back to our pillow and weep. What else can we do when we are unhappy now? There are hardly any good people to console us or to laugh with us or to make us light or to hear our burden. No, our pillow is the only place now left to weep. And we don't want anybody to even know that we're unhappy. That is another suppression. We can't tolerate our neighbour knowing that we are weeping. So we try to suppress our tears within also.

348 Master, you were telling us about the safety valves of the Indian women who fall down and faint. What can we Westerners do to let off steam?

Nature has given a safety valve to everybody. When emotions build up too much, tears come out of our eyes. Don't we weep?

That is a safety valve. We cry, we howl. These are natural safety valves the Lord has provided everyone. We can't keep those emotions built up within us, so we release them in these natural ways. And this is quite natural. These days our problem is that we are living in so-called civilized society, where we can't even weep – we don't even know how to weep. We have forgotten how to laugh, we have forgotten how to weep. We are always worried about our cosmetics or other things when we weep. When we laugh, we also are worried about manners and appearances, that I shouldn't smile too much or laugh too much. Nature has provided these things for humans. Weeping and laughing are our safety valves.

Otherwise, if you go on keeping everything within and within and within, it's not good. That is why we now have so many mental cases. Because in modern society we don't open ourselves to anybody; we just try to keep everything within ourselves and we become so isolated. The more civilized our society, the more self-centred we become. And the more self-centred we become, the more we have to keep all those things within ourselves, and we go on building and building and building, and then we can't take it and we burst. But before that, if you are in agony or misery, just weep and cry and you will become light. If you're happy, you just laugh – the heart's content. You're not bothered with what other people think. These are the natural safety valves the Lord has kept within everybody.

349 Is it possible to be a good satsangi and be a good artist at the same time?

All work delights the mind. Any job you do gives you job satisfaction – and that delights the mind. I do my duty as a husband, as a father, as a mother, as a child, as a friend – it delights me. We can't deprive our mind of this pleasure, but at the same time we have to attend to meditation. Similarly, the art we create delights us – it's all right. It's a most innocent pleasure. It doesn't harm anybody.

There's no work which can be done without putting the mind into it. If your mind is a little derailed, you can't work. There's no work in this creation which you can do without the mind. You have to put your mind in the work – only then can you get anything out of it. If you are teaching a class, if you're a professor, you have to put your mind in teaching. If you're a mason, you have to put your mind in that work. Without putting your mind in work, you don't achieve anything. So similarly, the artist has to apply his mind to project that art. It doesn't come in the way at all, in any way. But at the time of meditation, he should withdraw his mind from the art and put it to the side.

350 *Master, I play a guitar, and sometimes as a sort of a break, or a recreation, from either meditation or worldly duties, I will entertain myself this way. Now I know that it is advisable to keep simran going all the time, but at present I can't seem to do both things at once – do concentrated simran at the eye centre while trying to concentrate on guitar playing as well. I somehow feel that my guitar is good company for me, but now I'm not so sure, as I would like to do simran as much as possible. Is this one of the types of pleasures which should be sacrificed for attaining the goal which we seek?*

You see, this is a very innocent hobby. You can't do simran all the twenty-four hours of a day – the mind and body definitely need some relaxation. There is so much tension from the world, and you have to get rid of that. By your own self, you can amuse yourself, entertain yourself. What's the harm in it?

Well, I had gotten a little bit afraid that it was drawing the attention downward, and that this was the opposite of Sant Mat.

No, no. Sant Mat makes us normal human beings. Sant Mat doesn't believe in suppressing or running away from worldly activities. It's natural to have a little recreation, and this is a very innocent thing. There's no harm in it.

351 *Would going to movies or theatres or reading novels scatter our meditation?*

Well, sister, we shouldn't be obsessed by these things, but there's no harm in enjoying them sometimes.

352 *Master, why do you like photographing flowers so much?*

Flowers are your best friends, always smiling. You can stand before them weeping and they will still be smiling. They were made for that – so many colours and shapes, different expressions and shades. Nature wants us to enjoy these innocent pleasures.

353 *Maharaj Ji, where do talents stem from, if they don't stem from God?*

Well, sister, talents can come through many sources. A person's interest in poetry or music may be inherited, or may be due to a person's past karma. Maybe he has taken birth to express that interest in a much better way. There can be many reasons for that.

I've seen many musicians who are born into families of musicians. They get that atmosphere in which they can develop their own music, or they can get that training. But God-realization is something very different. Even a simple person who's not a man of letters, who knows nothing about poetry, music and art, can be much nearer to the Father than those people. Their gift doesn't show that they're nearer to God.

These musicians definitely inspire us, and that helps you concentrate, and that concentration gives you happiness. The attention or concentration you get from that beautiful music gives you happiness. In other words, concentration gives us happiness. Whatever you can concentrate on becomes a source of pleasure for you.

354 Master, what is the role of humour in Sant Mat?

Sant Mat should make us better humans rather than pull us down to the level of animals. You see, except for humans, nobody laughs. I don't think you have seen any bird laughing or any dog laughing or any animal laughing. They may smile, but the privilege of laughter is given only to humans. So if we want to remain human, humour has to be there, just to help us relax. But we have so much association with past species that we find it very hard to laugh. In spite of being humans, we're hardly human. You see, humour is something which another person also enjoys along with you. Humour is not taunting, humour is not hurting. Joking doesn't mean that you taunt another person or hurt another person or malign another person. That is not a joke at all; that is not humour. And also, you always give what you have. If you are happy within, you will radiate happiness wherever you go. If you're miserable within, you will share misery with others. If you go to a miserable person, he will make you miserable in a second. If you go to a happy person, he will make you happy in a second.

355 Master, there is one thing we never learn – just sitting quietly. People call that laziness and our society seems to have no room for that.

Because we are so used to working, we can't sit still for even five minutes in one place. And we hate ourselves – we always love others, but we hate ourselves. We don't like being alone at all. We all hate our own company; we always want the company of other people. If we love our own company we can sit quietly with ourselves in a room, but we can't because we always love other people's company and hate our own company. We are not happy with ourselves, we are just happy with others. We say, "Loneliness is killing me." But other people are not making you happy either – they also are killing you. You become more frustrated and miserable from them also.

356 Maharaj Ji, the Great Master has written that to hurry is satanic.

I was reading in some newspaper, many, many years ago about somebody from England who has written about his experience. He said, "I found everybody on the road hurrying and rushing, and I thought: Let me see where everyone is hurrying to. Where are they going?" So he said, "I followed one gentleman. He had a paper in his hands, and he was rushing to the bus stand, so I rushed after him. He caught the bus, so I also got on the bus. Then he went to a park, and he rushed to find a bench, and he sat there in the sunshine for two hours and was enjoying his newspaper!" He said, "I just cursed myself. What was the sense of my running after him? I could have come to the park seven, ten minutes later."

This is what we do. We rush and rush and then we start gossiping and wasting time. We don't space our activities properly.

All these modern gadgets should be to our advantage, but now we have become a slave of civilization. What a modern wife cooks now in fifteen minutes, our elder ladies perhaps used to cook in one or two hours. But these modern wives have not saved that time. They are busier, they rush more. So what is the sense of all this? People used to walk, and it might take them a day to reach a place. Then they had bicycles, so they saved time; then there were cars; now we have airplanes. People used to go by sea; now we go by air, by the fastest plane. Have we saved that time? So what is the sense of all these inventions if we have no time left for ourselves? This modern civilization should give us more relaxation, more rest, more time for ourselves. But we have no time for ourselves.

~ 15 ~

Facing Life and Death

ATTACHMENT AND DUTY

*357 Can we still love our family and friends and yet love the
master?*

Well, sister, if you read Saint Matthew, Christ makes it very
clear about our worldly relationships with our children, with
our mothers, with our friends. He says: I have not come to make
peace in the world, I have come with a sword.[39] Don't think that
I have come to make this world a better place for you to live
in. I have come with the sword of the holy ghost to detach you
from everything to which you are attached in this world and
to take you back to the Father. He says: I have come so that a
father may be detached from his son, a wife from her husband
and a mother from her child.[40]

Unless we are detached from each other, we cannot go back
to the Father because these attachments are always pulling us
to their own level. However, you can only detach yourself when
you are attached to something higher. Then you will automatically be detached from your worldly relations. Christ says: If you
love your children or your worldly relations more than me, you
are not worthy of me.[42] 'Worthy of me' means worthy to become
one with the Father; and if you want to become one with the

279

Father, you have to love me. You are not to love your worldly relations because your attachment to them is pulling you back to this level. I have become one with the Father. Through me, you can also become one with him.

Then he talks about worldly relationships. Somebody said to him: Your mother and brother are standing behind you, perhaps desiring to speak to you. Christ answered: Who is my mother? Who is my brother? Who is my sister? Those who live in the will of my Father, they are my brother, they are my sister, they are my mother.[47] I have no worldly relations. All this is only an adjustment of karmic accounts. We have been allotted certain karmic duties with each other, and we have to carry out those duties.

Actually, we are not meant for one another at all, we are meant only for the Father. Just as on a stage every actor is allotted a certain part to play – one person plays the part of a hero, another the heroine, another the villain – after playing their allotted parts, they leave the stage and they end their relationship with each other. They are no longer husband and wife or villain and hero. Similarly, mystics tell us that this world is nothing but a stage and we have all been allotted a certain part that we have to play on this stage.

We should not be so involved and obsessed with each other, nor so attached to each other, that we forget this is a part given to us to play on a stage, which we have to leave one day. For we become so attached to each other that we forget we are playing a part, and this attachment pulls us back to this world again and again.

That is why Christ says: Your householders are your enemies.[41] He uses very strong language. He says they are not your well-wishers, they are your enemies, because they are always pulling you back to their own level. They obsess you so much, they keep you so absorbed in themselves, that they give you no time for the Father. You sacrifice many things for their sake, and yet they are never able to become yours. God knows how many children we have had in our past births, how many times we have played the part of a husband, a wife, or a mother. When we have forgotten all those past relations, we are certainly not going to remember the ones in this world to whom we are so attached now.

So Christ implies that the purpose of a mystic or a saint is to detach us from each other and attach us to the Father. That is why he comes with a sword – to cut the ropes that are tying us to each other. The main reason for getting this human form is to realize the Lord within ourselves, to go back to the Father. If we keep that purpose in view, then naturally we attach ourselves to the spirit within and that spirit will automatically detach us from each other and make us one with the Father again.

358 How should we learn to live in relation to one another and to create a detached attitude?

You see, we have certain obligations and certain responsibilities in society. We have certain responsibilities to other people, to our country, to our community, to our family. We have to discharge all that as a matter of duty. We have not to run away from those responsibilities.

But our main attention should be towards the Father, towards the Lord. Only attachment will create detachment in us. When we are attached to something higher within, then automatically we are detached from this creation. Then we will mix with people as a matter of duty, just to discharge our responsibilities and obligations. You see, both a manager and the proprietor come to the office, but there is a difference in their attitude. The manager is not worried much about profits or losses, but the proprietor, the owner, is very concerned about everything. The manager works eight or nine hours honestly and sincerely, and that's all. He doesn't get heart attacks, but the proprietor does.

Similarly, we should think that nothing belongs to us in this creation. Everything belongs to the Father, and we have been allotted certain responsibilities and duties which we have to discharge. So as a matter of duty, we must discharge those responsibilities and duties truthfully and honestly.

We are all actors on a stage, but an actor always knows when he is acting, knows that there's no reality in what he is doing. There are love scenes on the stage, there are so many fights and quarrels, but the actor has neither love nor hatred in his heart. He's acting. That part has been allotted to him, and he's discharging his part very beautifully. You even find tears in his eyes, you find smiles in his eyes, but still he's acting – he knows that nothing belongs to him, that nobody is really dead and that he will not be deprived of anything at all. When he leaves the stage, he has no connection with anybody. That is the attitude we have to develop.

We have certain karmic responsibilities – as a son, a father, a husband, a citizen, a friend – which we have to discharge as a duty; but we have not to align ourselves so much with the acting that we forget it is just acting. Our problem comes when we become part and parcel of the roles we are playing. We meet so many travellers, so many fellow passengers on a train, and if some passengers are pleasant, we have a very pleasant journey. But when our railway station comes, we just say "bye-bye" and get down. You never get so attached that you forget to leave the train and stay with your fellow passenger; neither does he come down with you to the platform. But still, you have had a very pleasant journey. It is the same in a hotel – so many guests come and you have such a jolly time. And on sea voyages, so many people come from different countries. You meet, you dance, you are happy, but then the moment you leave the ship, you forget about them. We have to develop that attitude, and that automatically is developed with the help of meditation.

*359 Then why is it that we can still feel love or loyalty or duty
to those attachments – our parents and loved ones?*

As long as you are travelling on a train, you should be very kind, polite, helpful and entertaining to each other. I don't say that you should have sullen faces, that you should not meet each other. But all the same, you should not forget that you have to get down at your destination. You can't live in that atmosphere forever. You people go to different hotels; you have such loving company – dinners, lunches, swimming pools. You meet so many people and have such a good time, but when your flight comes, you just fly away. You know that you cannot stay here permanently. Our only permanent relationship is with the Father. We belong to him and he belongs to us. We are grateful to our parents – they have given birth to us, they have brought us up. We have to do our duty; we have to discharge our responsibilities, obligations. Sant Mat doesn't tell us to run away from all that. But we should not forget that these are karmic relationships. They will not last forever. We have to leave them, and they have to leave us.

*360 Master, do you think a batch of people that collect like
we do here, from all over the world – do you think there
would be any karmic relationships among us from previous lives?*

That's right. You see, when you are on a train travelling together, if you get a good companion, your journey is very pleasant. But you don't get to know the companions so well or get attached to them so much that you forget to get down at the station when you reach your destination. It's pleasant to have a companion on the train, but not so pleasant that you forget to get down when your destination comes. We should always strive to keep our destination in our mind. We are all fellow travellers together. Everybody has a different station to be dropped at, a different destination, a different time to separate. We shouldn't get so attached to each other that we start weeping and crying when we leave each other or that we forget to leave each other. We have good companions, but when we have to leave, we have to leave.

The world is just like a bridge; never build on it, just pass over it. It is the same with our karmic relations in the world – we should not get so attached to each other that we forget our real destination.

361 *Maharaj Ji, we learn that we have to detach ourselves from everything in this world. Sometimes we go through situations where we feel that new attachments are being formed, and our intellect tells us that we don't want them because they might not necessarily be good for us. How do we assess whether this is in our karma, or whether we should just avoid the issue?*

Well, brother, we should never think that these attachments are in our karma, no matter how good or noble they may be. Attachments are attachments. And neither should we ever try to analyze whether it is my destiny or whether I'm creating a new attachment. We should never try to analyze these things. We should just attend to meditation. All attachments automatically fade out, whether they are old, whether they are new – whatever they are. The only way to get rid of them is to attend to meditation. Get attached to something higher, then they start fading out. Otherwise, if you start justifying, "This is in my destiny, I cannot avoid this attachment, I should relish it; I should avoid other attachments, which are not in my destiny," you are just deceiving yourself.

362 *Master, what can we do about the feelings of those who feel that detachment happening and feel that we no longer love them?*

Well, sister, we try to mix our responsibilities with the attachments. We should not mix our responsibilities as a wife, as a mother, as a sister, or in any capacity the Lord has kept you with our attachments. Attachment is something very different from the responsibilities which we have taken on our shoulders. We must perform our responsibilities with a detached mind. Nobody will bother you. People are more interested whether we fulfil our responsibilities toward them or not. They are not concerned with our attachments to them. This is just a justification, to say that "I love you, so I expect this from you." Actually these are our needs which we try to fulfil from each other. And we call it love. Actually these are the obligations or responsibilities which we have to discharge in this world. And if you attend to meditation, you will be able to discharge them much better, and also you will be able to detach yourself from them.

363 *In becoming attached to God, does that mean one is no longer attached, for instance, to one's husband or wife, or brother or mother, or someone like that? I mean, does that exclude them?*

Sister, there is a difference between attachment and duty. A wife has a certain duty towards her husband. A husband has a certain responsibility, a duty towards his wife. Yet there may not be any attachment. If there had been real attachment, there would not have been a single divorce in the States. This attachment that couples have is just a self-deception. They feel that they are attached, and when a situation arises, they feel that they hate each other. Where does that attachment go then? Those attachments are simply karmic relations of give and take. Certain responsibilities have to be fulfilled, and we have to play a certain role accordingly, whether as a husband, a wife, a child or some other relationship. We try to feel we are attached and yet within our heart we know we are not. If that attachment had been so strong, we would not have forgotten our own mother and sister and father and we would not have fallen in love with another person. We were feeling so attached to parents, but on finding another attachment or with the lapse of time, we forget them. Where has that attachment gone?

Attachment really means forgetting the whole world, except the object of attachment. But we are shifting every day from place to place, from person to person, so we really are not attached. We are to live in this world as a matter of duty, taking full responsibility as a wife or a husband, as a father or a son, as a citizen, and so on, and yet not be attached to them nor be affected by them. For example, when a married daughter goes to her parents, she visits her brothers and sisters, she works in the house, is affectionate and very loving to her parents, and yet she is attached to her husband living thousands of miles away from her. Her mind is not where she is. It is somewhere else. We are to live in this world like that. We have to be in the world, doing all our duties, yet our heart should be where it belongs. If a bee sits on the edge of a bowl of honey, it will enjoy the taste of the honey and fly away with dry wings. If it jumps into the bowl of honey, neither can it taste the honey nor will it be able to extricate itself; it will die.

If we keep our attention, our mind, our heart in the Lord, we will enjoy this whole world. If we forget him, this whole world will become miserable for us, for then we are in love with the things that he has given us and have forgotten the Giver. We are not grateful to the Giver but are drowning ourselves in what he is giving us. We can only enjoy what he gives us if we are grateful to the one who gives. Instead, we are attaching ourselves to what he gives and are trying to detach ourselves from him. So we have to attach ourselves to him and to nothing else. By doing so, we enjoy this world too, just as the bee can enjoy the honey and fly away at will, unscathed, as long as it does not leave the security of the edge of the bowl and get stuck in the honey.

364 To what extent is a person – for example, a husband or a father – responsible to others? To what extent is he responsible for a person's mental illness? For his wife or child? Is he karmically responsible for the illness of the people with whom he has lived?

Brother, you are just to do your duty as a husband, as a son, as a friend, as a relative, and do whatever you can possibly do for the other person, according to your role in that relationship, and don't be affected mentally. Everyone has to pay off his own karmic debt. Neither are you responsible for the other person, nor is he responsible for you. We are each responsible for ourselves.

To the extent that we are related to each other, we are responsible to each other. That is a matter of duty. We have to do our duty by living in this world in whatever position the Lord has placed us, whether as a husband or a wife or a sister or a brother or any other relative or friend, and not be much affected by them, because ultimately, with the help of meditation and the sound practice, we have to detach ourselves from them. We are not to attach ourselves to them. And when you are detached from them, you will not be affected, whether or not they are mentally or physically ill. They have to pay for their own karmas. That does not mean that you are not to do your duty as a human being. You are to help them to the best of your ability. You have to help them, but not be affected by them.

365 *Maharaj Ji, can you tell us how we can love our family and fellow man without feeling or being attached to them? How can we love them and at the same time be detached from them?*

Sister, when we love everybody, we are not attached to anybody. Loving everybody means loving that power which is in everybody, and not just in certain individuals or in one particular person or creature. We should try not to justify our weaknesses by saying that we are loving his creation when we are loving one particular person. I shall tell you a little portion of a mystic's example, written in his lifetime. He was going down the street, followed by some of his disciples. He always used to remain in devotion and love of the Lord, in his own mood. As they were walking, a dancing girl came happily dancing towards them in the street, in her lax manner, and he just kissed her and said, "O, how beautiful is the Lord." Because the master kissed her, his disciples also kissed her and said, "O, how beautiful is the Lord." The master saw that. As he went a little farther, he saw a blacksmith hammering a molten hot plate. The master went up to that hot plate and kissed it and said, "O, how beautiful is the Lord," but the disciples held back. Then he said to them, "Where is your love for the Lord?" Sometimes we just try to justify our weaknesses in this way and we say that we are not loving the person, we are just loving the Lord in that person. For everybody, the real attachment should be to nam or shabd, for that alone attaches us to the Lord.

366 Master, as long as we haven't reached the state of attachment to the Lord, is it possible to love family and friends in a detached way?

There is no question of possible – we are attached to them since we are not attached to the Lord. But we have to fulfil all our obligations. You have to just do your duty. Your attitude should be to help them in every way, to discharge your obligations in every sphere of life. This applies not just to your wife and children but to everyone. You have to be a good citizen, good friend, good brother, good father, good husband – kind, loving to everybody, helpful to society. That doesn't mean you are attached to them. To have a sympathetic heart is very different from attachment. If you are driving and see a dog that has been hit by a car, you just stop the car. You take so much pity on the dog that you even shed tears, seeing him in such a pitiable condition. That doesn't mean you are attached to the dog. You don't know the dog at all. It is only having a loving heart, a compassionate heart, which is bleeding for the dog. We have a wrong concept of attachment. Another person might just drive away at the sight of the dog – he doesn't even bother to stop. That doesn't mean that he is detached from the dog. It's a question of attitude. You must have a kind and loving heart, a sympathetic and helpful heart.

But if we are attached to our family, should we make a conscious effort to try to be detached from them, or will that only come naturally as we attach ourselves to the Lord?

You have not to be conscious of detaching yourself at all. You have only to be conscious of attaching yourself to the divine melody within. That will automatically detach you. If you fight with your mind – I am not going to love my wife, I am not going to love my child – you will love those attachments much more. The more you fight with your mind, the more your mind will run to them. But if you fight to attach yourself to the shabd and nam within, then automatically your mind will become detached. Only attachment can create detachment; detachment never creates attachment in anybody.

367 *We put in so much effort, and it seems like nothing comes for a while, that we're in that vacuum you speak of. We're putting in all this effort to give up our ego and give up the world, but my mind rebels. How do I deal with my mind? What can I say to my mind?*

Brother, what do we give up of the world? What are we supposed to give up of the world? What is your concept of what you have to give up? You don't leave your families. You don't leave your children. You don't leave your job. You don't leave your house. You don't leave your friends. What do you give up? Do you give up the sensual pleasures? One can enjoy those in a family life. What is there to give up?

You see, we don't give up our self. We want to rise above our self. We have to detach our mind; we don't give anything up. We have to live with people, and yet we have to detach ourselves from them. And that can happen only when we are attached to something better than the sensual pleasures, the worldly faces, the worldly objects. When we are attached to something better, we automatically become detached from everybody. Physically we don't have to give anything up at all.

When a girl falls in love with a young man, she automatically forgets her parents and brothers and sisters. There's no effort on her part to forget them. So when we get that taste of nectar within, that living water within, we automatically withdraw from the senses. They don't interest us anymore at all.

Worldly fame, worldly objects don't interest us anymore. But we do live with them because we have to discharge our karmic obligations. Whatever part the Lord has assigned us to play, we have to play, but with a detached mind. If a honey bee sits on the edge of a utensil containing honey, it will taste the honey and fly away with dry wings. If it lands right in the middle of the honey, its wings will become heavy and it will not be able to fly away – it will die.

So living in the world, discharging our obligations, we have not to forget the purpose for which this human birth was given to us. When that purpose is before us, automatically, naturally, we become disinterested in worldly things. But we don't run away from them.

368 Master, is the love between a man and wife an illusion of the mind?

There's no real love in this world at all; it's just a self-deception. Nobody belongs to us; we don't belong to anybody. We deceive ourselves; people deceive themselves. They're living in an illusion that we belong to each other, that we are meant for each other. We belong only to the Father; the rest is just karmic relationships with each other. It's like actors who come on the stage and play their part. After that, they get off the stage, and then they have no relationship with each other at all. So this is just a play we are going through – acting our parts with children, wife, husband, friends. But we think they're real, so we get involved with them, and then our whole trouble starts with that. When we have forgotten our past relations, our past karmic connections, we're not going to remember these present ones.

Somebody said to Christ: Your mother is standing behind you, perhaps desiring to talk to you. He said, who's my mother? Who's my brother? I have no mother, no brother. Those who live in the will of my Father, they are my real relations.[47] So these are only karmic relationships. Our relationship with the Father, when we live in his will, is the real relationship – that is a permanent, everlasting relationship. As Christ said, ultimately there'll be one shepherd and one fold.[107] So those who come in that fold are permanently related to each other around the shepherd.

369 Would you continue the discussion on love?

There's only one love, and that is spiritual love. Worldly love is a self-deception. There can be no love with each other. It is just self-deception. It's good to remain in that self-deception for some time because then you can spend your life more easily – it becomes easier to go through your life. But a real love is only just spiritual love.

370 How does one determine the difference between attachment and worldly responsibility?

To do your duty is something different from being attached. We have to do our duty as a citizen, as a husband, as a son, as a brother, as a friend. But we should not be so obsessed by these duties and people that we forget the real purpose of life, the real destination, the real path. We should not be so attached to them. When they are with us, we should be happy to be with them. When they are away from us, we should not feel so miserable as to miss them and long to be with them. That is attachment.

We have to do our duty – we can't run away from that – but when we do our duty, we have to do it with a detached mind. But it is very difficult to detach ourselves from something unless we are attached to something better. If you tell a girl, before her marriage, that she should cut herself off from her parents and friends before you can marry her, however hard she may try, she can never succeed. But when she falls in love with you, she automatically turns away from everybody else. That is the nature of the mind.

When the mind is attached to the holy spirit within, to that holy light within, it is automatically detached from the senses. As long as the mind is running outward towards the senses, the tendency of the mind is outward. It remains attached to the world. When the tendency of the mind is turned inward, after coming to the eye centre and becoming one with that holy spirit, it starts getting detached from the senses.

If you keep yourself attached to the holy spirit within, then whatever type of work you do in this world, you always do it with a detached mind. Otherwise you are doing everything in the world with an attached mind. Your attachment to the spirit within automatically detaches you from everything else.

371 *The books emphasize that our only true friend in this life is the master. If we fully accept this fact, how can we also have friendships with other people in this world, even if they are spiritually inclined?*

We have a karmic relationship with everybody in this world. But this relationship exists only so long as we live in this body. After we leave this body, nothing from this world will go with us. We will have to leave everything. I often give the example of a play. Each actor comes on the stage and plays his own part. He plays the part of a husband, of a wife, of a child. But after playing his part, when he leaves the stage, he has no relationship with the others at all. Similarly, we have no real relationship with each other at all. It is only a karmic adjustment; for a karmic adjustment of our accounts we are brought together in one form or another.

You have read in the Bible that somebody said to Christ, when his mother was standing behind him: Your mother is there and wants to speak to you. And he said: Who's my mother? Who's my brother? I have no mother, I have no brother, I have no relations. Those who live in the will of my Father, they're my real relations.[47]

So ultimately our real relationship is when we are tied together with that bond of spirit, that bond of word, that bond of nam and shabd. That is our real relationship, because eventually there is going to be one fold and one shepherd.

This physical relationship is only a karmic adjustment of accounts. Mothers come, fathers come, children come – we are all playing our part on a stage. But when we leave this world, we have no relationship with anybody at all. So the real relationship is only with the master, because he's going to merge back into the Father. And we are in love with the master, and through him we are going to merge back into the Father.

Finally, as Christ has said: You are in me, and I am in the Father, so you are in the Father.[122] That is the real relationship – when we all become one in that bliss, in that Lord. These worldly relations are merely adjustments of the karmic accounts.

372 *Maharaj Ji, it has been stated that if you are married you will not make it this time?*

I do not think I have read anywhere, in any book, that married people do not make any progress.

That is what I thought, too. We had a discussion about that, and the discussion was that if you have karma to pay, you cannot go within until your pralabdh karma is liquidated.

Sister, how do you know what your karma is that has to be paid? I do not think marriage makes any difference at all. It is attachment which pulls us back, and I think that marriage is more of a duty, a responsibility, than an attachment. Those attachments that we feel in the beginning in marriage, sooner or later we discover that they are not attachments at all. They are for a certain selfish purpose, and as soon as we realize that, I do not think anybody can keep us back. We can perform our duties much better as a husband, a wife, a son, a brother, or as any relative, provided that we know what our duty is; though living with them, we are not attached to them

We have something better to be attached to. That is the main thing. When we are attached to a bulldozer and at the same time we are holding a dog by his chain, the dog cannot pull us back. If we keep the dog's chain in our hand, even if we forget that we are attached to the bulldozer, the dog cannot pull us back, but the bulldozer will pull us, and the dog may even be pulled along with us. So when we are attached to that sound, that audible life stream, the shabd, though being in this world and performing our duties here, we are not being pulled back into it. We think that worldly people are holding chains in their hands and pulling us, but compared with the pull of the shabd, those people are so light that they are just being pulled towards us by those very chains. So if we are living in Sant Mat, these duties do not bother us, do not make any difference. It is the mind, not so much the body, that matters. Therefore, we have to do our duty and keep the mind in shabd.

You will find that most saints were married. They had families and they were householders. There are certain advantages in marriage, for then there is not too much suppression of certain desires and not too much thinking about those things. They come and go; otherwise, there may be suppression, there may be an unconscious pull downwards, which one is not even aware of sometimes. So from nature's point of view, it is always better to be married, to be a householder, an honest householder, and then also to do our duty.

Actually, we never leave anything in this world. We may think we have withdrawn from the world, but really we have not withdrawn from the world. Even if you run to the forest, even if you take shelter in the temples, in the churches, what do you leave? We need clothes to cover ourselves, we need food for our stomachs, we need shelter, and we get these things. Even there we require all these things; so we do not leave anything. These are natural instincts of human beings, to which we are not to become a slave, and yet the natural instincts will take their own course. We should do our duty, and at the same time do our main duty. We should not forget that duty for which we got this human body. If we keep that destination in view, keep that part of this human life in view and walk in that light, then these things do not even bother us.

373 Master, how much is a satsangi's family or relations affected by his being a satsangi?

What brings us back into this life is our attachments. If we are attached to anything or anybody in this world, that attaches us to this world. In that way we are leaving our roots in this world, and these roots bring us back into this world. If a satsangi is attached to shabd, to the master, naturally that of course is pulling him much more than his worldly attachments. He has detached himself from the world, from his relations, and has attached himself to the master, the audible life stream or the supreme Father, and he is being pulled to the Lord by his attachment.

A satsangi's relations and people around him are attached to him. Their attachment to the satsangi will bring them to him, and the satsangi's attachment to the Lord will bring him to the Lord. So those who are attached to you are being helped in that way, for eventually they will have to come to the path to reach the same place where you have gone. If, on the other hand, you are attached to them and not attached to the master or shabd or the Lord, you will be pulled back by your attachment to them. When we are attached to a bulldozer, and a dog is attached to us, he cannot pull us back. He will be drawn along with us, and thus gets the advantage of our being attached to the bulldozer.

Actually, it is the degree of attachment that matters. Their attachment to you will help them because you are attached to something more powerful with an upward tendency; but your attachment to them would help neither them nor you.

What is the bulldozer?

The master, shabd, word or nam is the bulldozer.

374 *In one of the books it says that the master helps the relatives of initiates eight generations back. Why would the eighth generation back be affected by our initiation? Because of attachments?*

You see, it's not a question of eight generations. As Christ has said: If you build your treasure in the world, you will come to the world. If you build your treasure in heaven, you will go to heaven, because you go where your heart is, where your attachments are.[22] So attachments pull us to their own level.

Now, if you are attached to the sound or the holy spirit within yourself, this holy spirit will pull you to its own level. And the people who are attached to you will be pulled along with you, towards that holy spirit. But if you are not attached to the holy spirit, if you are attached to them instead, they will pull you down to their level. If you are attached to something higher, you will be able to pull all who are attached to you to that level. For example, if you are attached to a bulldozer, it will pull you. But if you are not attached to the bulldozer and you are holding a dog on a chain, the dog will be able to pull you back.

So if you want to help your relations, the first thing is to help yourself. Detach yourself from everybody and attach yourself to the holy ghost. Then, when you are attached to the holy ghost and your relations are attached to you, they will find their way according to their attachments to you. And you are no longer with them; you are with the holy ghost. Ultimately they also will find their way because of their attachment to you. That is the whole theory.

It depends on what people are attached to and how strong their attachment is with each other. When you see a railway engine, there are many carriages attached to it. But each carriage that is attached to it will pull all the other carriages. So if you are attached to an engine, and the others are attached to you, they will also be pulled along with you by the engine. But if you are not attached to the engine and only attached to the carriage, you will all stay where you are. Nobody is there to pull you. You will stay with the stationary carriages. So this is the meaning of what you have read in that book.

375 Are our relatives helped by the fact that we are initiated?

In a way they are helped. If the initiate is attached to the spirit within, he will be able to help himself to rise above the realm of mind and maya. And if his relative is attached to him, through that attachment, the relative will find his way to the initiate and be helped in that way. But if the initiate is attached to the person and is not attached to the spirit, then that person can pull the initiate to his level.

Christ said, we go where our heart is.[22] We go where our attachments are. If we want to help our relations or friends, we must help ourselves first. When we are able to help ourselves by attaching to the spirit within, then automatically our relations will also be helped.

What if the two people are both satsangis?

Well, sister, that's a very good thing if both of them are attached to the master. Naturally they will both be able to detach, ultimately. But Christ said, no man can serve two masters.[24] Either you are attached to the Father or you are attached to the mind. As long as we are below the eye centre, we are attached to each other. When we are above the eye centre, we are attached to the spirit within. Then we are not attached to each other at all. Then we are only doing our duty, as a wife, as a husband.

So these attachments automatically become loosened. When you become attached to the holy spirit within, when that time comes, then you will just do your duty without becoming attached or obsessed by each other. Then you become a better wife and a better husband.

376 *I understand that for initiates and satsangis there is also, after death, a certain amount of grace that will be given to their loved and dear ones. Is this true? In other words, mothers for instance, even though they did not at the time of their incarnation here receive initiation?*

Brother, it is again the question of attachment. When we are attached to the word, the shabd, the master – when we have his love and devotion within us – we are attached to the Lord. Our attachment will take us to the master, who is merged into the Lord, so we will merge into the Lord along with the master, in his love, in his devotion. If our friends and relatives are attached to us and we are attached to something much stronger than what they are attached to, their attachment will eventually take them to the Lord.

If we are on the path and are attached to the master through spiritual practice, it will help them to be attached to us, because they have to come where we are, as they are attached to us and we are attached to the Lord. So they in turn will also be attached to the Lord, because their attachment to us creates such a karmic relation that they will ultimately find themselves on the path and come back to us, where we are. If, on the other hand, you are not attached to the Lord through shabd or nam, but you are attached to them, then your attachment cannot help them.

We can help our relatives and our friends only when we are attached to the sound inside. When we are attached to the master and to the word inside, then we will help them also. But if their attachment to us makes us forget our destination, our path, our devotion to the shabd or nam, then we will be driven back to them. If you are attached to a bulldozer and you are holding the chain of a dog, the bulldozer will pull you and the dog along with you. However, if you are not attached to the bulldozer, but you are holding a very strong dog, he will pull you back. Similarly, we always help our friends and relatives by meditation, by attaching ourselves to the sound and by detaching ourselves from them. Their attachment will bring them to us, and our attachment will take us to the Lord. So we are also gradually putting them on the path, and eventually we all will reach the same destination.

377 *Master, are we to help our relatives if they need help? For instance, a mother who has young babies, would that be considered as an attachment when we render service to them?*

No, sister. Nonattachment does not mean that we are not to render service to our relations at all. We have certain responsibilities towards our parents, our other relations and friends. We must carry out these responsibilities; otherwise we are not the right type ourselves. I must say, we should always do our best to help – especially older people who need our help, who need our respect, who need our strength to pull through that age and that time. To help them is something quite different from merely feeling perturbed the whole day and worrying about them and yet not doing anything for them. That is no use. We should help them practically and yet not be worried about them. We must do our duty by giving them respect and help. We owe them certain obligations that we must pay; otherwise we would not be able to live with ourselves. Our conscience would bother us if we did not do our duty, and we would have no peace of mind.

A mother and a father do so much for their children, to help them, to give them a good start in life, to guide them. They sacrifice so many things for their children, and children also have responsibilities to their parents and benefactors in their old age. We must do our duty. They did theirs, and when we become parents and do so much for our own children, then we realize how much our parents did for us. We are greatly indebted to them. We feel frustrated when our children are not attentive to us and we say that we have done so much for them, but they do not care for us. At the same time we forget what we are doing to our own parents. They may happen to be frustrated and have the same feelings towards us that we are having, now that we are parents. So if we are dutiful and devoted to our parents, we can expect the same from our own children.

378   I have a niece with babies. As an aunt, should I help if she needs help?

These are just individual matters – you can make up your own mind about what she needs and what you can do; I am just discussing these things in general. We should be helpful to each other. Only a human can be helpful to a human. Animals cannot come to our help, so we must give a helping hand to each other whenever we can.

379 If one were put in a position where one had to choose between duty to one's father and duty and help to one's daughter, which has precedence?

You want to know whether you have more allegiance to your father or to your daughter? Well, you have to help both. You have a certain responsibility towards your father and a certain responsibility towards your daughter. You have to deal with both of them, and only you can decide how far you can ignore your daughter and how far you cannot ignore your father, and how far you cannot ignore yourself in dealing with the situation. I think the answer must come from you.

380 May I ask whether this factor of attachments tends to favour cremation rather than burial? Going back to the grave as people do, a great deal of attachment is avoided by cremation, with no definite place to go to mourn over the remains.

I think, brother, we generally do not try to face reality. We must face reality. The one who has gone has gone forever. He will not come back to us. When we visit the grave and all that, we do not go for the sake of the dead. We go because of our own weaknesses. We go because of our attachments to those people. We do not go for their sake.

381 Would it be possible that, in the same family, we could be weeping and rejoicing for the same soul – when a grandfather has died and a new child is born?

Yes, sometimes attachments bring us back to the same family. Is it not strange that you leave this world as a grandfather and come back as your own grandson?

Afterwards, do they still see everything that is going on, the same as before they left?

No. They have severed their connections as far as that particular birth was concerned, and whatever contact we may think we have with them after their death is due to the projection of our own mind. They have gone to where their karmas have taken them and are engrossed in their own karmas. All our grief and worry does not help them in the least; rather, if they are attached to us, we are thereby attracting them back to this world. It is our strong attachments that act as roots which we leave behind and which in turn attract us back here again. So it is much better for us to have our roots in shabd, which will merge us back into the Lord, and ultimately all those who are attached to us will merge along with us. That is the best way to help those whom we love and those who are attached to us.

382 Master, is it possible, in a family where the husband is not a satsangi and won't accept any of the teachings but yet is tolerant of the family's faith, that in his next life-time he will become a satsangi?

The relationship of the soul to the Father is an individual one. It is not like a marriage relationship. Christ said: Who is my mother, who is my brother?[47] These relatives are people with whom we have karmic relationships while we are in this world.

But our spiritual relationship is the direct relationship of the soul with the Father.

As far as helping your husband who is not on the path is concerned, the best thing to do is to help yourself first – then you may be in a position to help him. If you are attached to him, then your attachment to him might pull you to his level. But if he is attached to you and you are attached to the spirit within, then your attachment will take you back to your destination, and his attachment to you ultimately will enable him to find his way towards you. So in that way you might help him, but not in any other way.

383 *You were saying that we have to develop disciplined emotion for the master – that's the manifestation of our love for the physical form of the master. Now, if the disciple has discipline but has no emotion, and the master leaves the physical body, does that mean that the disciple has to take another birth in order to develop that emotional feeling toward the physical form of the master?*

It depends upon his karmas. You see, if the disciple is attached to something in this creation, he will come back, even if he has some meditation to his credit, even some progress to his credit. If on the other hand he's not attached to anything in this creation, though he may not have any spirituality to his credit within, nobody can bring him back.

It is the attachment which pulls us back to this creation, but generally it is the shabd which detaches you from this creation. When you're attached to the shabd, you automatically get detached from everybody in this creation. It has nothing to do with an emotional link. When you're attached to the shabd and nam within, that is an emotional link. The link is only of shabd and nam to the Father. You cannot have a better link than with shabd and nam. That is the only link to the Father, and your meditation will create that love and devotion – it will help you to develop your love and devotion.

*384 In other lives, have we been with the people we are closest
       to in this life? And will we be with them again?*

We have a permanent relationship with each other only where we are going to live permanently, forever. Only those have a permanent relationship who will not come back to this flesh at all. But those who are taking birth here have no permanent relationship. Sometimes they are our sons and daughters, sometime we are their sons and daughters – we don't even know who our parents were in our last birth. When we have forgotten them, naturally we will forget our parents in this life also, these relationships also. But that does not mean that we have to forget these relationships now or run away from them and not do our duty. We must pay whatever is due to them according to our karma. We must do our duty lovingly and devotedly, but not be attached to them so much that we forget the real purpose of life.

*385 Saint John said: Greater love hath no man than this, that
       a man lay down his life for his friends. Does a saint have
       to die to save his friends? It says in the books that saints
       give up their lives in Sach Khand to come down to Pind.
       Could you explain that?*

Yes, the mystics and saints spend their whole life for their friends. They live their whole life for the sake of their friends, not for their own fame or ego or for ruling people or collecting funds. They give their life, they die for them, they live for them, they exist for them. Just read the history of all the mystics. That is the real friendship. Otherwise, other relations are just karmic.

Somebody pointed out to Christ: Perhaps your mother is desiring to speak to you – she was standing behind him. Mystics always find excuses to share their spiritual truth with us, so he said: Who is my mother, who is my brother and sisters? Those who live in the will of my Father, they are my real relations.[47] So these are just karmic relationships. How many mothers have we had, how many brother and sisters? How many times have we come here? How many friends have we had? If we have forgotten them, we will forget the present ones, too. But those who live in the will of the Father, they are the ones with whom we have real relationships; they will stay together forever. Christ says that ultimately there will be one shepherd and one fold.[107] That is the real relationship.

Soami Ji calls them thugs – all our worldly relations are thugs, he said. Great Master used to call them beloved thugs. They so much entrap you in their love that they make you forget your destination, the purpose of your coming into this creation. And you willingly, happily, waste your life for them and only realize what you have done in the end, when it is too late. That is why Great Master called them beloved thugs.

You see, there are three types of people who take away our possessions. One is a thief, another is a dacoit, another is a thug. Their object is the same; their modus operandi is different. The thief likes the owner of the house not to be home or to be deeply sleeping so that he can take away his belongings. He doesn't want the owner to know that he has taken away his belongings. The dacoit doesn't care whether you see him or not. He has a sword or a gun at your chest, and you cry and howl and weep, and he takes away what he wants. The thugs entrap us in their love, become our own, and we willingly, happily give them everything, and then in the end we realize what we have done. So that is why Great Master used to call them beloved thugs – because they look so sweet to us, so loving to us.

386 Is it true that we are born alone and that we live and die alone?

You see, currents in a river bring together so many scattered pieces of wood, but another current comes and just scatters them again. A wave of karma comes, we all collect together; another wave of karma comes, we all scatter to our own destinations. That is why we say the world is like a stage and we are all actors. An actor never gets so attached to another actor that after getting down from the stage he starts crying. He knows he has been given a part to play – maybe of a husband or a wife or a child – but after he gets down from the stage he has no relationship with them. So the world is just like that. It is self-deception to think that the part which is given to us is real.

That is our whole problem and misery in this world. If we could only remember that we are all just playing parts on a stage. People come and go in different roles in this life. There's no real relationship. If today we have forgotten all our friends, all our loves, our romances in each of our past lives, how are we going to remember our current relationships? We are not going to keep remembering them forever. They come and go. We will forget them also.

387 Christ says, they are not my mother, they are not my brother, yet later on in the Bible, he says: Each disciple is my sister, is my brother. What did he mean?

I'll tell you what he means. He tells us: Honour thy father, honour thy mother.[51] This means you have certain obligations to your parents which you must discharge in this world. But do not be so attached to them that you forget the real destination for which you have taken birth. He doesn't say not to respect your mother or your brother. These are karmic relationships. But don't get so attached to them that you forget the real purpose of your life. They are not your permanent relations at all. You will leave them. Your real relationship is with the Father, and with those people who live in the will of the Father. But about worldly relationships, he doesn't say that we should leave them and shirk our responsibilities.

If you read Saint Matthew, he says, honour thy father and mother. You have a certain obligation to your parents, and you must discharge that obligation, husband to wife, wife to husband, son to father. We have certain karmic obligations. We must discharge them smilingly and lovingly, but not get so attached to them that we forget the purpose for which we have been given this human form. They are not the end all and be all of your life. The real purpose is something different. So this was just a way to explain to his disciples: Don't get so attached to your worldly relations that you forget the purpose for which you have come. He did respect his mother, his brothers, but he indicated that these are only karmic relationships. We are all playing our part on the stage, whatever part the Lord has given us. But the real relationship is between the soul and the Father. And there is no other relationship.

388 *You could be playing your part very well, but others could misinterpret what you are doing, and therefore you could cause friction and trouble.*

You see, the question is how concerned are you with others. Actors and actresses are never concerned with the audience at all. They're conscious only of their parts. They are not concerned with what the audience is going to think. They know the audience will forget, after the play, because they have no relationship with them at all.

MARRIAGE AND FAMILY LIFE

389 Master, we are told that we should try to maintain an atmosphere of peace and happiness in the home, as this is conducive to our meditation. But sometimes the decisions taken by one member of the family affect the others adversely. Should one submit, knowing it is not right, or should one oppose the decision?

We have so many hurdles we have to cross to live a family life. So we have to create understanding in the family. There are so many problems which we have to mutually resolve. I know it is not easy to live together, whether for wife and husband, brother and sister, father and son, mother and daughter. It is very difficult for two, three people to live together for very long. We are so self-centred, especially in these days. But we have to put an effort to create that atmosphere in the family, especially if the whole family is fortunate enough to be satsangis. Then we should make use of that atmosphere and attend to meditation. We should forgive and forget. We must base our living and understanding on love for the other and create that atmosphere in which we can build our treasure. We have to help each other.

390 Master, what part must love play in a marriage and how necessary is it to be in love to stay married?

Understanding in a marriage is much more essential than this so-called love. Infatuation may bring us together, but that infatuation doesn't last forever. It fades out after some time. That is human nature. But then the responsibility, the obligation we have taken on our shoulders to live together, to be parents, good parents, good citizens of society – that should bind us together. This so-called love doesn't last forever. Understanding is more essential. If love creates that understanding, it's most welcome. I'm not against love. But understanding is much more essential for a couple to stay together. If love were so binding, then there would be no divorce at all, because everybody thinks he is in love when he marries. Perhaps my views are about forty years old. That's possible. We change along with the time and along with our age.

391 *If you have a husband or a wife who is not a satsangi, who throws the books away, who does not allow you to attend satsang – you have said that we must keep harmony, but where do we draw the line between harmony and choosing ...?*

To stay or leave? Why create disharmony at home? Don't attend the meetings; you can sit in your house and attend to your meditation. And slowly and slowly, persuade him lovingly. If you need him, he also needs you in many ways – the relationship of husband and wife is such that both need each other. If you have to adjust to certain things, he also has to adjust to certain things – otherwise, naturally, besides this thing, other things would create conflict. So understanding has to come from both sides. If you are unnecessarily rigid in your attitudes, then he also becomes rigid toward your attitudes, so naturally conflict arises. If there is understanding on both sides, there will be no conflict at all. It's a give and take on both sides. If the general attitude of the couple is to adjust, then if the adjustment is there, there's no problem. Otherwise, very small things become big issues. One has to handle all situations very tactfully and lovingly.

392 *I'm a divorced satsangi, and it seemed when my wife and I divorced it was so easy to say, "Well, it's our karma." Now I'm engaged to be married, and I get the feeling*

that I need to attach some importance to this marriage, maybe along the lines of my attachment to the Creator, in order to weather the difficult times and make this marriage a lifetime union. I know that a good marriage helps you in meditation. So, what I'm asking is: Isn't there an attachment that you must make to the marriage – not so much to the husband or wife but to the marriage – that is similar to our attachment to Sant Mat in order to maintain it for a lifetime? And if you do not have that, couldn't your marriage end in divorce?

I don't know what makes people divorce each other. I don't believe that marriages stand on attachments. Infatuation never lasts for very long – it fades out quickly. Then we start looking right and left for another one, and the same happens there. So we shift from partner to partner. It leads us nowhere.

In marriage, besides our likings, we have to also share the responsibility, the obligations we take on each other's shoulders for the rest of our lives. That infatuation may not last but those obligations, those responsibilities which we have taken on before God, remain with you forever. We have to live through our life to discharge those responsibilities and those obligations.

We also have a responsibility for our children, whom we have brought into this world. We can't throw them in the road and run to another woman or another man. We are running after attachments, but these attachments don't last forever. That is why there are so many divorces. Hardly after a year or two, that infatuation fades out and we run to the right and run to the left, and then again the marriage ends in divorce. We forget there is some obligation attached to marriage – to live together, to support each other and be responsible to the children. That is a great responsibility which we have taken on our shoulders. Running away from our responsibilities is not fair to the children. You have to take mutual responsibility for each other. And think ten times before you share that responsibility.

No marriage runs smoothly. There are storms in every marriage. But we have to pull through those storms, pull through those ups and downs, and then again walk on that path of marriage. If you can't tolerate each other, and it takes no time to break up the marriage, then there'll be no end to this. Our Sant Mat books are full of questions and answers about divorces. There's nothing which I have not written, nothing which I have not condemned. Now I've stopped writing anything at all because my advice hardly makes any difference to anybody. People do what they want to do. They only want my thumb imprint to justify what they have done. So I've told Professor not to write anything about anybody's domestic problems. Nor will I. Let them deal with it themselves, because they are going to do what they want to do. They've already decided what they have to do. Why drag us into it?

393 Maharaj Ji, is it true that if husband and wife are both satsangis and practice meditation every day, after they're dead their souls will continue on the inner path together?

Would they want to continue together? I'd be more than happy if they continue together in this very life. Ninety percent of my correspondence concerns couples who don't want to continue together – 90 percent!

There's no soul mate in spirituality. Everybody has an individual relationship with the Father. Some people have a concept of a soul mate, but it's absolutely wrong. God knows how many wives, how many husbands we've had in our previous lives. If we're not continuing with them, how can you expect that we'll continue with the present ones after their death? This is just a karmic relationship, and it finishes here.

394 If there is disagreement between married satsangis about having children, who should give in?

Couples must travel together in family life, help each other, support each other on the path. The path doesn't create disharmony at all; rather it should make you happy. You must learn to adjust to each other. Happiness always lies in adjusting to another person. Never make another person adjust to you. Happiness lies in submission, always, and not offending another person.

395 If you are a satsangi, and your husband gets angry and directs his anger at you, how should you act?

I think you should act lovingly. You shouldn't react as he's acting; but you should respond lovingly to whatever he says and smilingly try to answer his question, try to satisfy him. And if even then he's not satisfied, you shouldn't become angry like him. It's sufficient to have one angry person under one roof rather than two under the same roof. So you should always try to handle such situations tactfully, lovingly and smilingly.

396 For the past year and a half I have attended satsang almost regularly, and my wife has offered very little resistance. She is coming here this afternoon for the first time. Is the lack of resistance from her an indication that deep down there is an acceptance that has not come out yet?

I do not know about that, but it is very clear that this is an indication of her affection and love for you. I do not know whether this is an indication that she is being prepared to understand or to see, but it definitely indicates that she has affection and respect for your principles. She wants to please you. You should take it only in that light, and then leave the rest of it to her own fate, her own karma.

We should never try to force the teachings on anybody else. We can help anybody who is interested. But if a person is not interested, we can help him much more by trying to live the life ourselves and not force our views on him. At least in this country, there is so much independence of viewpoints, so much individuality. Everybody has his own background and he has to stand on his own convictions, on his own principles. And everyone has his own time, so we should never feel frustrated if our partner is not interested in Sant Mat, as long as the partner is not an obstacle in our way.

If we are really fond of each other, we will also respect each other's individual convictions, each other's individual views on life, especially regarding spirituality. So we should be happy and grateful if the other partner is not an obstacle in our path in any way. Of course, we are always happy if both husband and wife can come on the path. They can be of great help and strength to each other. But the alternative is, if one does not become a block in your way, you should appreciate that too.

397 Where does the concept of male and female, man and wife, come from, which is taught by those masters and yogis of the lower planes? At one time I was associated with a master that taught this. That is, he claimed to be a master, and he taught that you had to unite as man and wife in order to progress up the spiritual path, and I just wondered if you knew anything about the basis of this teaching. He did not consider you whole unless you married a woman and united as man and wife, male and female.

You mean that an unmarried woman and an unmarried man can never tread on the path?

That was his teaching.

I had better not discuss it. There is no such bar, I may tell you, brother. That may be a justification for marriage, I do not know; but there is no such bar. Some people have the erroneous concept that we always have a soul mate, and unless we meet that soul mate, we will not go back to the Lord. That is absolutely wrong. There is no question of a soul mate.

Everyone is an individual, an individual drop of that ocean. And we have to work individually through our karmas to merge back into that ocean. Our karmas bring us in contact with certain people who become husbands, wives, children, friends, relatives, business associates, or with whom we have to have some dealings – pleasant and unpleasant – during our lifetime. We meet all types of people and have all types of associations, due to the debt of our karmas. But it is not true that unless we are married we can make no spiritual progress. Definitely, being a householder has certain advantages on the path, which you can see – but it is nothing like that, and that too, only when the householders are both going straight. If the married couple has a divergence of views and is always fighting, that of course is no good and of no help to either of them.

398 *Last night somebody asked me if Sant Mat advocates divorce.*

I am sorry if anyone has that impression about Sant Mat. Sant Mat rather unites families, tries to create harmony in families. I always advocate that meditation makes one a better husband, a better wife, a better son, a better father. If it does not, then it is we who have failed in our meditation. It should bring us together. We should understand our responsibilities, our duties in life – not to escape them, but to face them, to face reality. I hate to see people getting divorced, especially if they are sat-sangis. It actually pains me.

Getting divorced, as far as marriage is concerned, is not right. Divorce, in a bigger sense, we all get by meditation or divorcing ourselves from worldly attachments. We are divorcing ourselves from worldly roots and taking our mind and soul up to the Lord. We are getting divorced from the world and getting attached to the Lord. That you can say. But in family life I am very much against divorce. That is my personal view. But I never force anybody.

399 *Master, in many of your books and teachings you suggest that all satsangis be married, if possible. Could you comment as to the reasons?*

There is no harm in remaining single, if you really remain single. If you are just trying to avoid marriage and still need company or you live with someone, then what is the sense of deceiving yourself and deceiving society? Why not marry? Or else be strong enough to really remain single. It is better to be tied down to one lady than to run after a hundred ladies. When the mind is always running and wants to flirt with so many, why not get married and settle down? What is there about marriage to avoid? Or else we should be strong enough to remain single. I am not against remaining single. Baba Ji [Baba Jaimal Singh] was single, and many mystics have remained single. But if that's your choice, then you should really be single.

400 *Would you advise satsangis to continue family religious practices?*

We are part of society, we are part of a certain chain, and we don't want to look abnormal. If our family traditions demand our presence, say in a church or some family gathering, then what is the harm? Don't we go to the movies and to the theatre? We shouldn't be narrow-minded. If our duties and our family obligations demand it, there is no harm in doing it. As long as we are firm in our meditation, firm in the principles of Sant Mat on which we have to base our meditation, there's no harm in going anywhere. We must be very open-minded. We may even get something good from going to a church or temple. If it pleases other family members, what is the harm in accompanying them? We shouldn't be fanatical about these things. We must be open-minded and face the reality of life.

401 *Maharaj Ji, what should we do if a great conflict arises in the family between the teachings of Sant Mat and traditional religious practices?*

Sant Mat doesn't put any restrictions on us about what to do and what not to do, as long as we build our meditation on the four principles. But when we really follow the principles of Sant Mat and adapt our way of life according to Sant Mat and attend to meditation, then our mind doesn't go to these things at all. Restrictions may not be put on you, but you will not feel at home in doing those things. You will not want to do all those things – you will not want to go there at all. But this must come from within, rather than anybody asking or forcing you to refrain. We discuss rituals and ceremonies every day in satsang: that they are meaningless, that there's no depth in these things, that these things will not lead us anywhere. But at the same time, we don't put rigid restrictions on anybody that they mustn't do this or that. Then the mind rebels, revolts against those restrictions. But when that awakening comes, by understanding the real teachings of Sant Mat, you automatically leave these things.

Sant Mat must stand on its own legs and not on the weakness of other religions. So when our legs become strong, then we automatically understand the futility of doing all these things. And then our mind doesn't run to those things unless there are some traditions in the family. Then we may participate, just so we don't annoy anyone. But then we know that these traditions have no spiritual significance behind them, so we don't give them much importance.

402 *I belong to a family who believes in going to the cemetery once a year to bless the graves. If you refuse to go, aren't you being hard?*

Well, sister, if you can please people by this, go with them. What difference does it make? If you can please them by going, where is the harm? You can go. You may not get anything by going there, but at least you please some people by going.

403 *How can we help those in our own home who refuse to listen?*

I think you can help them best by not forcing them to listen. Be an example to them, according to what you have gained from the teachings. By our living example, we automatically influence them. If it is in their karma, they will run after you to understand what they want to know. When you try to force people, I think you are driving them away instead of attracting them. There is nothing to be forced on anyone. It must come from within. And that will come only when you are a living example for them. So you help them most by not trying to force them to understand.

My family are all so much against my talking about Sant Mat or even bringing up the subject, and I just do not dare to talk to anyone about it.

There is really no need to talk to anyone.

> *Yet I wonder what to do about it. I have had an adopted son for almost thirty years now, and I know so many things are all wrong. What can one do about it? Can I tell him? I do not dare to talk to him much because it disturbs him, and the answers that I get from him leave me disturbed. What can I do about a case like that? I shouldn't ignore it entirely, should I?*

You can just try to help and explain with love, and do not feel much concerned or worried about it. There is no other alternative. You cannot ignore it entirely, but with affection and love you can try to help him understand. Then, if he does not want it, you should not worry about it. You have done your duty. We should not unnecessarily raise unpleasant issues. In a family we have to overlook many things in order to live together harmoniously.

404 *Master, sometimes an older member of the family becomes senile or very difficult to handle. The person I'm thinking of is a satsangi and we hate to put him in an institution, and yet he has become so difficult, wandering out at night and this sort of thing. It's difficult to know what to do, because it does somewhat interfere with meditation. How far do we really have to go to take care of these people?*

Unfortunately, the attitude towards elderly people in your country is very different. In India, we have elderly people but they are looked after very well by the younger people – family members always take care of them. Everybody has to pass through that stage, and young people should always remember that.

In India, in our houses we have what we call *deodi*, which is the main entrance to a big house. The elderly generally shift outside to that main entrance of the house and stay there. There's a story that one very cold winter, an old man asked his grandson for a blanket. So the grandson told his father: "Grandfather wants a blanket." The father said, "There is one old blanket which we use for the horses, so you can go and give that to him." The son cut it into two pieces and gave half to the grandfather and brought the other half back. The father asked, "Why have you brought this half back?" His son said, "I have kept this half for you." So the man realized his duty, that he would be in the same state someday and started looking after the grandfather, his father.

You see, it is our responsibility to look after our elders, and we should take care of them in every way. But actually youth is such that we think we are never going to become old, that we will never have to face that situation at all.

CHILDREN

405 To what point, as parents, can we influence our children, knowing that they still have to go through their own destiny in this life?

As parents, we should try to do our duty to influence them rightly. But then, whatever has to happen, will happen – we have no control over that. But we shouldn't neglect them. We shouldn't have the attitude of just letting them go through their destiny, thinking that we shouldn't bother about them. We have certain responsibilities, certain duties as a parent towards our children that we must discharge. But if, in spite of our best efforts, something happens, that must be their destiny. Let them go through it.

406 A lot of us here have children and grandchildren. They come to us and want to know what we are doing when we meditate and so forth. How far can a young child go before being initiated in this work? I mean, how would you answer them?

You can just explain the principles to them and tell them to try to have devotion to the Lord in their mind. Children naturally pick up from their parents, but I think we should, in this modern age at least, make them feel that they are making their independent choice to follow Sant Mat. We should guide them, explain to them, be good examples to them and let them grow up to make their own decisions as to what they want when they reach maturity.

407 What can we say about Sant Mat to children?

Actually, we should try to give the children a good spiritual background and then, when they reach maturity, let them decide for themselves what they want to do. We should try to give them facilities and opportunities, and prepare their background from a spiritual point of view. It is very easy to give them a spiritual atmosphere in the home. If parents are spiritually minded, naturally the children are influenced by their spiritual outlook on life. If parents are in love with God and are meditating, automatically they are also influencing their children. But still, we should allow them to grow up and make their own decision.

408 Master, do the children of satsangi parents receive your protection, and are they marked for initiation in their present lives?

Everybody has their individual karmas. So even if they are the children of satsangis, it doesn't mean they must be initiated. Those who are marked by the Father automatically come to the path, whether or not they are the children of satsangis. But if parents become a living example to their children, naturally the children are influenced and may become interested in the teachings and spirituality.

409 Master, does the child choose the parent or does the parent choose the child?

I think they both choose each other. The child has certain karmic accounts with the parents, so he comes to them as a child. The parents have certain karmic obligations to the child, so they get that child. They become either the parents or the child, depending on the karmic relationship they have with each other.

410 Master, my question relates to a satsangi parent's responsibility to his or her children, children of an age sufficient to understand and accept the teachings, but tempted by play. To what extent should the parent encourage participation in group meetings and other activities?

Parents always guide their children. If the parents are loving and affectionate, if they maintain an atmosphere of love and harmony in the house, this will automatically affect the children. Certain children are born into a satsangi family. But this does not mean that their natural desires are to be so suppressed that they do not know about the world, so that when something happens, they experience a reaction. They must understand what is good and what is bad. They should be influenced through understanding, not by removing them from society. That could lead to suppression, which may cause a reaction once they go out into the world. They should have everything explained to them lovingly. Parents do influence their children to a great extent.

411 What is the best way to bring our children up in Sant Mat?

Bring them up lovingly and do your duty as a parent, and try to prepare them for love and devotion for the Father. Don't try to condition their minds with any philosophy, but give them the general teaching of love for the Father. You have to prepare them for the Father and then let them make their own decision. Children are influenced by their parents and automatically start following them. So be a living example. That will be sufficient.

412 Due to this confusion which exists in organized religions, would it not be better to try to raise children without exposing them to these organized ways of thought and to try to teach them the principles of Sant Mat directly?

You can do that, brother. I never said that you shouldn't do that – do whatever you think best. What I mean to say is that we should not try too hard to condition the children's minds. We should let them develop in such a way that they can make their own decisions, and try to create a spiritual outlook in the children in whatever way we can. We're not to raise them as Christians or Hindus or Sikhs or Muslims. We have to give them a certain spiritual understanding so that they can understand the necessity of the Father, and then they can make their own decisions. I don't want children to be conditioned by even the teachings of Sant Mat, but we must give spiritual understanding to every child.

413 Sometimes in America we run into situations where your child might be going to a Protestant school or a Catholic school or something of this nature where they're being taught different concepts of religion or spirituality. Should we try not to combat that type of thing, but also to tell our children about the path?

We all come from different religious backgrounds. We are not all born into satsangi families. We have come from different ways of thinking, different concepts of religion. Yet we all grew to that level where we were open to understanding other ways of thinking. So we should give children general knowledge about religion, about spirituality to make them receptive, to open their minds to alternatives to traditional beliefs. Then, when they grow, let them decide for themselves.

414 What happens to the baby of a pregnant woman who is meditating, whose soul leaves the body?

Nothing will happen to the baby. Withdrawal is only of that person who's withdrawing to the eye centre. The soul of the baby is not affected. But the soul of the baby is already conscious of its past. It forgets everything when it takes birth.

But definitely meditation has a good influence on the baby, because children in the womb are always influenced by our way of thinking, our way of living. If you are attending to meditation, it will definitely have a good effect on the child. If you keep bad company, that will definitely influence the child in a bad way. The child is always affected by the way of life of the mother. So it's always good to meditate at that time – babies will definitely be influenced in the right direction.

415 Maharaj Ji, I would like to ask a question about children. The fact that they seem to have such a pure understanding

of love and of the Lord when they are small, is that because
they bring this knowledge with them from a previous life,
or because their minds are open and undisturbed?

Children generally pick up these good qualities from good
parents. Children's minds can be easily influenced. Maharaj Ji
[Maharaj Sawan Singh] used to say a child's mind is just like a
sheet of blank paper. You can write anything on it. Our papers
are absolutely blackened; so much is written there. Our mind
has been conditioned, but their mind is absolutely a white sheet
of paper. Whatever you tell them, they will follow it. And they're
generally influenced by their parents – by their words, by their
example – very easily.

Is it possible that they bring with them knowledge from a
previous life when they're very small?

At least their mind is not scattered yet. They have not become
a victim of the senses. They have not yet learned to conceal,
cheat and deceive. Their mind is not very active in that direction, so they are very innocent. As far as bringing all that with
them from their past, due to their karmas, they do take birth in
certain families. It is due to their past association with a certain
family that they come as children in a particular family. They
are easily influenced by their parents.

416 *Is it all right to tell our children that the master's with*
     them?

You can create some sort of confidence and faith in them so that
they don't get frightened at night. I remember my daughter used
to study in a convent, and the first time she came home she had
a picture of Christ which she always kept under her pillow. I
said, "What is this?" She said, "He will protect me at night." I
never said anything to her, so she kept it and she always slept

with confidence. So you can give faith and confidence to a child in whatever way that works, and then when the children grow and understand, they can make their own decisions.

417 *Maharaj Ji, for those of us who have small children, how much responsibility do we have in seeing that they adhere to the strict vegetarian diet?*

If the atmosphere is of vegetarianism in the house, they'll automatically be influenced. But since they are going to school, they also have their own associations and friends who influence them. So it depends on how much influence you have and how much influence people of their own age have. If your influence is greater than the other influences, children will automatically remain vegetarian.

You can explain to them, but you can't force them. It depends on your approach. In my case, we have all gone to colleges and boarding schools. Our parents never told us to remain vegetarian, but we had been brought up in that atmosphere and we remained vegetarian, even as children. Children who have been bought up in that family atmosphere tend to remain vegetarian. It depends on how much we can influence them at home, how much they are affected by our atmosphere in the home. If both husband and wife are satsangis, then it's very easy. When children go to their school, they mix with other children from different types of families, so it depends on what they start off being influenced by. But after all, you were not all born vegetarians. So when the time comes, we all make our own decisions.

If left to us, we should try to make them vegetarian. If husband and wife are both satsangis, there's no reason why their children should not be vegetarian. There's no problem in the house, and vegetarian food is healthier than any other food.

But when they leave the house and are influenced by the outside atmosphere, then how much you can hold them depends upon the parents.

418 *Master, if a very young child asks a question about the path, how should we answer them, if we know that they won't quite understand the answer?*

General spiritual truths should be told to the children by way of stories, by way of fairy tales. But in the end, when the child grows, he'll forget everything but the spiritual truths which he has heard, which are the outcome of those stories – they will stay with the child forever. That is why the old women tell their children and grandchildren fairy tales – they are actually impressing upon the children certain spiritual truths. The stories themselves are meaningless, but the children carry the moral of the stories with them their whole life. What impressions you create on children depend upon the mother and father, more the mother than father. She can mould the child towards meditation, towards the Father, lovingly, spiritually, talking about the Father, talking about his grace, his love, telling the child to thank the Father at every step for what he has given us. She can create love and devotion in the child, but she can't explain the path to him because he is too young. The best way to do this is to make yourself an example. Children always try to copy their parents. If the mother sits in meditation, the child also will try to copy that behaviour. That creates a habit in the child, and that habit grows.

419 *I have a question concerning disciplining my children. I've been raising five children by myself for the last ten years, and I know you've given me tremendous strength*

to be able to raise them by myself. Sometimes I find it difficult to know exactly what type of discipline to use when they don't listen, when they do something that I don't feel is correct. This is especially true for the last several years with my oldest son, who, when he was very, very young, used to ask and cry for initiation. We wrote to you and you told me to tell him that he should listen to his parents. And now that he's older, he's forgotten about his attachment to the path, and we get into power struggles.

Well, sister, I can understand your concern as a mother about the welfare of your children, but we should know they have their own lives to live. The children come through us, they don't belong to us; they have their own destiny to go through. Moreover, there's a generation gap. Our way of looking at things is different from theirs. It is not always that we are right, though because of our age we may be more experienced, or at least we are supposed to be more experienced than they are. But we are not necessarily wiser than they are. Sometimes they may be right; we may have been wrong. So we, as a parent, should try to do our best to guide them, to do our best for their welfare, but then if they don't listen, leave them to stand on their own legs, make their own future, realize their own mistakes and learn by their own experiences. But as parents, we should naturally feel concerned – we want to do our duty, but there is a limit to what we can do for them. We can't do everything for them; they have their own destiny to go through. Sometimes we are helpless spectators, knowing full well that they're jumping in the dark. But we should be a good spectator then, because we can't help them, we can't do anything for them – they refuse to listen to us. We shouldn't lose our own balance. We must stand on our own. We must be content within our own self and try to help them as much as we can, and not worry much about them.

420 *This is from the father of a satsangi. He is having prob-*
lems with his satsangi son because the son has aban-
doned his family.

Sister, we all have problems in life. Our children look from a
different angle. They think their parents are wrong; we think
our children are wrong. There is a generation gap. They have a
different outlook on life. They come through us, but they have
their own lives to live. And we have our own lives to live. We
have to play our part, and our children have to play their own
part in life.

421 *What is the best way to discipline children?*

The best way is to be a good example. One has to make a lot
of sacrifices for one's children and one always has to set a good
example for them. Their mind is just a clean slate, and their
parents are always their heroes. They look up to their parents and
notice how they are behaving in this world. That always leaves
a deep impression on them and lasts a long time. Whatever we
want to teach them, we can do best by being a good example
to them. Supposing one smokes and does not want the child to
smoke. How is it possible to impress upon the child that it is
wrong? If the child has seen the parent smoking, how can that
advice be effective? If we give advice but are not living up to all
the good advice that we give, the child knows; so that advice
does not have any effect at all.

> *Master, since we are talking about these things, does a*
> *parent have a right to punish his children?*

When one corrects a child with the intention of helping him, it
is not really punishment. The disciplinary measure is a punishment when you want to take some revenge. In order to discipline

children you have to explain things, you have to be firm and sometimes also a little harsh – but always in the interest of the child and not to satisfy your own instinct of ego or anger. While explaining or disciplining, one should not lose one's own balance of mind, but should always keep calm and cool. Sometimes we have to be firm and strong in our views and even in our actions.

ANIMALS

422 *Regarding animals and our relations to them, is it det-rimental to our own progress to have affection for an individual animal? One satsangi has pointed out that if you enjoy pets you are retrograding to the level of the animal. Does that not also work in the opposite way?*

Sister, it depends upon the attachment. If you are attached to an animal, naturally, it will pull you down. If the animal is attached to you and you are not attached to the animal, but you are attached to something much better than the animal, then you may pull that animal up. If we are meditating and we are attached to that sound so strongly that it is pulling us, and if the animal is attached to us, we will also pull him along with us. If we are not attached to the sound but to something else, whether man or animal, and he is pulling, we will be pulled down. If a dog is very strong and you have his chain in your hand, he will pull you, but if you are stronger, you will pull him.

All this depends upon the chains of attachment. If we are too attached to those things and we ourselves have nothing to hold on to that is stronger than that attachment, then natu-rally we will be pulled down. If we are tied to something much stronger than these pets and all that, we will pull them to us, ultimately. It is all a matter of attachment.

423 In our association with animals, can we help their progress? The animals we have, the animals we love, when they die, do they come back because we help them to come towards the path?

If a dog is attached to you, you will pull him up provided you are attached to something higher, which will not let you go down; but if you are attached to the dog and not attached to something higher, you will go to the dog. Actually, it is our attachments that bring us back. If the initiate is attached to the master, he is bound to go up and merge into the master, and if the dog is attached to that initiate, naturally the dog, after reincarnating as a human, also comes on the path and gradually travels upwards because of his attachment to his master.

424 Then love is never lost, regardless of whom we love?

Yes – if you love your dog, you will become your dog. Because your love will make you lose your own identity and become another being. That is the characteristic of love. Whomsoever we love, we become. So if you want to become that being, then love him. Since we want to become one with the Father, we love the Father. We go where our treasure is. Christ says that if you build your treasure in heaven, you'll go to heaven, and if your build your treasure in the world, you'll come back to the world.[22] And what is that treasure? That treasure is attachment, love. If we are attached to the Father, we go back to the Father. If we are attached to the creation, we come back to the creation. Because we become whomsoever we love. If we are attached to the birds or animals or even humans, their love and attachment will pull us to their level – we will become them and remain separated from the Father. Love will play its part. Love will make us merge into the other being. But it depends upon in whom we want to merge.

425 I found a cat who was so badly injured that I knew she would die soon of her injuries. She was crying and miserable, so I took pity on her and put her out of her misery. Will I incur karma for that?

You have taken mercy because you couldn't face her suffering. It's your weakness, not the cat's weakness. You can't bear to see her suffering, you can't face reality, what the cat is going through. You are weak, you are not strong enough to face it. The cat is suffering from her karma. She doesn't want to die – she is brave to face what she has done. You are a coward. You can't face what she has done, so you want to finish her off. It is you who are weak, not the cat. Definitely you incur karma. Until now people could be in a coma for years and years and linger on, and there was no law that could put them to death. We are suffering due to our weakness. So should we kill someone because he is suffering, and we can't face it?

426 My son has a ranch and they have a lot of trouble with moles, gophers and so forth getting into the irrigation ditches and they cannot farm the ground. What is the proper procedure when we are not supposed to kill things?

Sister, we should try to avoid killing as much as we can, but sometimes we just cannot help it. There is a certain type and amount of killing which you cannot avoid for your existence in this world, but one should not try to justify that killing. You should not go out of your way to kill these things, but when you have to do it for your existence, you cannot help it.

427 Master, what is our position regarding spraying of gardens to prevent insects and so forth from eating or otherwise destroying vegetables and flowers?

Brother, some of these things are necessary in order to live in this world. We have to draw a line somewhere. If we analyze minutely, we will find that even now, as we are breathing, we are killing many insects. This whole room is filled with insects; as you walk on the ground, you kill many insects; when you drink water, you kill many insects – what you call bacteria, you may give them any name – the very air you breathe is filled with souls. So it is impossible to live in this world without killing anything. One cannot even breathe or take a single step without doing so. Therefore, saints always advise us to carry the very least load that is necessary to live in this world, so we are allowed to take vegetables, even though they also have souls. Now scientists have proved that vegetation contains life.

We cannot help killing insects and rodents by spraying or otherwise protecting a crop; but naturally there is a difference in the degree of karma incurred, just as there is a difference in degree of crime in our worldly laws. We should not try to find a justification for killing, nor should we kill unnecessarily. Where we have to, we may, for we have to in order to live and exist in this world. This whole world is full of crime and creatures killing one another. As you have just heard in the discourse, this whole world is nothing but darkness, and one cannot live without killing. The eating of vegetation and protection of crops is more or less innocent killing, as we have to live in this world, and in order to live we have to do all sorts of these things. The main thing is that we must do the least possible killing for our existence – only as much as is absolutely necessary to maintain a healthy body.

PHYSICAL AND MENTAL HEALTH

428 *If God is all-knowing, and he knows when we are sick and when we are to be healthy – when health is to be*

restored – why are there physicians? Where does the role of the physician enter into healing, and of what value then is the pursuit of human knowledge to sharpen the skills of being a better physician?

Do we have faith that God is everywhere? Do we have faith that he will really cure us if we don't take medicine? If you have that much faith that he's always with you and he will cure you, then you don't need medicine; but we don't have that much faith. We commit all sorts of sins in this world knowing that God is everywhere, so what is the point of our knowledge? If a five-year-old child is standing before me, I dare not even take anybody's pencil. I tremble to steal. We don't fear the Lord even as much as we do the child, despite our saying that he's everywhere.

When it suits us to believe that he's everywhere, we say he's everywhere. When it doesn't suit us, we don't believe he's everywhere. We have no faith in these things at all. If you really think he's always with you, that you are being watched, that everything you're doing is right in his presence and you are accountable to him, that he's the one who is going to treat you and nobody else, then definitely you don't need a doctor. But we have no faith in him at all. So we need everything in this world.

The Lord has given knowledge to doctors to cure us and given us understanding to go to the doctor for treatment. How can we cut one portion and accept only the other portion? He's the one who has given us the understanding that for illness, we need a doctor. And he has given knowledge to the doctor so that he can cure patients. The Lord is playing all the parts. So naturally we need a doctor, and yet that doesn't mean that the doctor's medicine will definitely cure us. If a doctor's medicines are so effective, then why are there so many deaths? Everybody doesn't get cured. Only they will be cured who are destined to be cured by those doctors. Only they will go to the doctors who are destined to go to those particular doctors.

We have karmic relationships with the doctor, the chemist, the Red Cross van and so on. Karmas must play their own part. Whatever you sow, so shall you reap. It is a give and take in this world. I may be indebted to so many for my illness in this world, and I have to pay them with that excuse of my illness. How can I run away from my karmas? I have to pay the doctor, I have to pay the chemist. There have to be factories to make my medicines. They have to be transported to a particular shop. Certain people have to play their part in all that before I can be cured. How can all that be eliminated from my karmas?

429 *Master, one of the Sikh gurus is quoted as saying essentially that if you harm the creation, you offend the Creator. Does this mean we should not harm the body by neglecting its care, since we are told that it is a temple of the living God?*

Naturally. You can yourself imagine how much we look after our churches, our synagogues, our temples, our holy places simply because we feel the Lord lives there and he can be reached there. So when we become conscious that this body actually is the living abode for the Lord, that it is the real temple, the real church in which the Lord resides and where we will be able to reach him, you can imagine how much we have to care for this body temple. We have not to misuse it, we have not to make it dirty by eating dirty things. We have not to have any malice or hatred in it for anybody. Naturally we have to look after this body because it is the temple of the living God. We have to keep it neat and clean, without any disease.

What are the diseases of the body? Not the physical diseases but the other diseases, like jealousy, greed, hatred and revenge. These have polluted us. So we are to make it clean by getting rid of all these diseases. Then we are really looking after the temple of God. You can imagine how much we take care of our man-made temples. We should give at least that much respect to this body. We should take that much care of this body, which is the real temple of God. Once you lose this opportunity, you don't get it so easily again. A temple that is destroyed can be rebuilt. But if this temple of the body is destroyed, you won't get it very easily again, so the more care we have to take.

Of course, we have to keep our body physically healthy. But I am referring to the diseases of the mind which we have created ourselves: backbiting, greed, hatred, jealousy, revenge, malice. These are the real diseases of the body.

Of course, physically you can keep the body clean by exercises, by yoga and by so many other means. But you have to mentally clean it, spiritually clean it if you want to make it fit for the Lord. You can imagine how much we clean a cup when we want to fill it with any liquid. So imagine how much this body needs cleansing when we want that nectar within us, when we want the Lord to reside within us. What do we not do? We have beautiful carpets, beautiful cushions, chairs, and then we think that now this place is fit for me to sit in. When we want the Lord to reside within us, are we worthy? Is our temple clean enough for the Lord to reside there? Is it not full of all the dirt and dross of the world? So how can he sit there? We have to make it worthy for the Lord to sit there. We are so particular about where we sit, so naturally we should also be particular about where we want the Lord to sit – whether this place is really worthy for the Lord to reside there, how much cleanliness it needs.

430 *Do we have an obligation to take care of the physical body?*

Yes. The Lord has given it to us, and we should make proper use of it so that we can attend to our meditation. We have not to adore it, but we do have to preserve it so that we may utilize this time in his love and devotion.

431 *If I meditate all night long, how does the body get rest?*

Try it. Try it one day. Then you will know how the body reacts. The body has a strong connection with the mind. If your mind is healthy and happy, you won't mind any fatigue – it doesn't bother you at all. If your mind is not happy, any little thing can tire you out. The mind goes a long way to relax the body. It makes us happy in the body. It has a strong connection with the body. Now doctors have also started to treat the mind along with the body, so that the body may become fresh again. You can't ignore the mind and just treat the body.

432 *Master, there are doctors in America who treat patients by having them visualize the sick part of their body, and through imagery or visualization – for example, imagining that that part will get better – healing occurs. Does that run counter to our spiritual path?*

Well, sometimes healing can occur even without our doing anything. Healing is a natural process. Healing occurs even without our doing anything at all. Nature does heal – medicines only help nature to heal a little quicker, nothing else. Otherwise, healing is done by nature.

The best healing of the mind is meditation. The mind is healed by meditation. Then you gain self-confidence in your mind, that this will become all right. You use your mind and willpower to believe that this will become all right – that helps you to heal also. You don't have to go to anybody for that.

433 Master, recently a faith healer from England went to Mexico, and some of our satsangis were very interested in her, so much so that several of them asked for an entire session with her so they could learn and apply the same principles. Now we expressed some doubt about it and turned to what you have said about these things.

I hear that many people go to faith healers for treatments, and yet when they come back, they are suffering from the same disease again. I've hardly seen anybody being healed. There may be some cases, I can't say. If you are able to build faith in your mind, you automatically heal yourself. If you are able to build faith in the Lord, that whatever he does is right, that it is in your own interest and for your own ultimate good, you'll heal your soul. You follow my point? Meditation is nothing but trying to build faith in the Father, that whatever he does is for our ultimate good. We submit to him, we resign ourselves to his will. And by doing this, we are healing our soul.

434 Maharaj Ji, if a satsangi gets an incurable disease, is he required to submit to intensive medical care or can he refuse?

Brother, we should do our best to get ourselves medically treated. How do we know that it is not in our destiny to be treated by medicine? How do we know? It may be in our destiny to be treated by medicine, by medical doctors. So we should do our best, then leave the result to the Father. It may be in our destiny that the medicine helps us to recover.

There are so many diseases nowadays that are really incurable, but they are deploying very heavy treatments even so.

Yes, they are, but the medicine may help you to at least get relief from suffering to some extent. There's no harm in using medicine.

> *If it's in our destiny to use the medicine, then why do we have to worry about it? Won't we just automatically use the medicine?*

Yes, if it's in your destiny to use the medicine, your mind will be conditioned in such a way that you will want to take it. If it is not in your destiny to use the medicine, you will be conditioned in such a way that you'll refuse to accept the medicine. Nothing is in your hands. The decision to accept the medicine or reject the medicine is also destiny.

435 *I am aware of the requirements of a satsangi, and the reasons for these are clear. I wish to know whether medication is permitted and, if not, the reasons.*

Sister, there is no harm in taking medicine. We do not want these medicines for sensuous pleasures, and it is wrong to take them for such purposes. We only want to preserve or regain our health so that we can devote ourselves to the Lord. So there is absolutely no harm in depending upon medicine in the time of need.

436 *Master, I have heard that pain is curative. Are we to endure pain as much as we can, or are we allowed to take medicine for pain?*

If we are ill and we have pain and we think that we should not take medicine because it will interfere with our karma, that is absolutely a wrong conception of karma. We should always try to take an objective view of life. All the scientific achievements and all that we have available to us should be put to use for our physical comfort, not forgetting the end, as I said yesterday. There is no harm in consulting a doctor to try to get relief from the pain. If it is in our karma to get relief, then only will we get relief from the pain. If it is in our karma to go to a doctor to get relief, naturally we will go to a doctor, follow his instructions and use that medicine or remedy. So we should not think that we will interfere in our karma if we try to get rid of this pain. That is not a practical, objective outlook. We have to live in this world.

Is it also equally possible or proper to administer help when we find others in similar circumstances?

We should try to help anybody and everybody in that situation, whether by medicine or by advice or by consoling them. We should try to help everybody.

437 *Master, sometimes doctors prescribe injections of animal cells to their patients. Are satsangis allowed to have such injections?*

There are so many substitutes now. There is hardly any injection which has no artificial substitute. We should try to avoid animal products as much as we can. If we can find any substitute, we should never use these animal products.

438 *Maharaj Ji, the question is about transplantation of organs in human beings.*

If it is in the karma of the donor, he will give the organ. If it is in the karma of the patient, he will receive it. If it is in the karma of both of them, the transplant will be successful. If it is not in their karma, it will fail.

439 Master, is it permissible to donate any part of our body to science, like our heart or our eyes?

After death, if our body or any part of it can be of any use to anybody, donation is a good thing. There is no harm in it. It is a thing of merit because you are not in the body, and if anyone can make use of it, why not?

There's no karma involved then?

What karma? When you leave the body, there is no karma left with it. Your soul is not there and your mind is not there. What is the karma then?

I wanted to know if perhaps the heart or the eyes might involve karma.

Absolutely not. When the soul has left and the mind has left, the body cannot be accountable for any karma.

440 Is yoga beneficial?

There are different types of yoga. Generally, the yoga the world understands today has to do only with physical postures. But yoga does not mean physical postures alone. This path is also yoga. We call it *surat shabd yoga*. Yoga means something which unites. This path unites the soul to its Creator. But generally, in the West, yoga is understood as physical exercises.

441 What about pranayam?

Breathing exercises are pranayam.

What about the visual exercises associated with pranayam?

This is another mental development, but still it will not take you very far. It will help you to concentrate to some extent, but it is not very easy in these modern days for the householder or for people who are so busy with their own work to do all these things without proper guidance. For pranayam and hatha yoga, you constantly need a teacher to guide you at every step; otherwise there are so many complications. And with all that, what you gain is just good health. You can control your breath, and you can control your mind to some extent, but it does nothing for you beyond that.

What I am trying to do with this is to settle my body and my mind down to such an extent that it is reasonably restful.

Naturally, a relaxed body and a relaxed mind are good for meditation. A tense body and a worried mind cannot attend to meditation, so the yogis used to just relax the body with exercise and relax the mind by breathing exercises, with pranayam, before they started their meditation. But this was just the means and not the end or objective. Nowadays people have taken these things as an end and think that this is meditation. That idea is wrong; otherwise, there is no harm in doing these things.

There is no harm in doing pranayam or other yoga exercises?

It is all right if one has the time for it and can get a good guide or teacher. If you say that by reading books you can do it, that is not possible, because there is always the likelihood of complications. I know of many cases where, even under proper guidance, there were many complications, because modern times are not suited for these things. In olden days those who practiced these things used to be absolutely celibate and they lived in the forests. They could do it, and probably that was their need also; but now the atmosphere in the world is entirely different. If one can do it, it is very good; but one should not do it for meditation – that is what I mean to say.

Then, too, it depends upon your physical fitness. Some people have a weak heart and it is harmful for them to do the pranayam and some of the other yogic exercises. I have seen many cases where these yogis or their teachers have never bothered about or tested the student's heart beforehand; and when the student tried the exercise, it resulted in heart failure. Because they do not know the physical aspect of the body, they have the same set of exercises which they try to teach everybody, whether one is a blood-pressure case or a diabetic or a heart case or a nervous person. They have the same set of exercises for everyone, and sometimes it becomes quite a complicated affair.

442 *Is there suffering in the astral plane? Or is this the plane for offsetting our bad karma?*

There is no physical suffering there. Mental suffering is there, in the sense that we are away from the Lord. Physical suffering is only in the physical body.

443 *Master, I have questions concerning insanity. Is it something that can destroy the five senses? Where does it fit in the pattern of our karmas?*

Insanity or any other disease is always due to our karmas. Whatever we suffer in this world is due to our karmas. We are reaping the consequences of whatever we have sown in the past. But we should try to get ourselves treated, try to get medical help, and try to do our best. But definitely, we only suffer because of karmas.

444 *Sometimes psychologists and psychiatrists can help clar-*
ify our problems. Is that an advantage or disadvantage?

The problem is that in our modern society, we've all become very
self-centred. We don't have any faith or confidence in anybody.
We don't want to discuss our problems with a friend because
we don't trust anybody. So we store up our problems within
ourselves and then run to psychologists and this and that. What
do they do? They just listen to you. They just help you to open
up and let out what you are keeping within. We pay to buy their
friendship, to share our inner self with them, nothing else. We
go to them because we don't have any friends nowadays. Even if
we have a fine wife and family, they have their own limitations.
Everybody is so busy or so full of their own problems. So we
build up all these problems within ourselves. All the pressure
and tension is built up within ourselves. That is why there are
so many mental cases, so many psychological cases – because
we have become too self-centred in modern society. So now
we have to pay people to be our friends, to help us, to listen to
our problems. And then when we give vent to them, when the
pressure is let out, we think we have become very light. What
problems do the psychologists actually solve? By meditation you
can rise above all these problems.

445 *Maharaj Ji, for those of us who work with people with*
psychological problems, is there any basic rule of thumb,
any clear principle to hold in mind?

One has to be a good friend. One has to open another person.
He's so closed. He's keeping his own problem within himself. He
doesn't want to divulge. He doesn't want to share with anybody.
He doesn't trust anybody. He wants to keep it within himself.
So he's just becoming miserable because he can't off-load it. You

have to try to win his confidence. Try to become his best friend, so that he may open to you and lighten himself.

That was the purpose of confession in the churches. What did they do? They never redeemed anyone from their sins, they just made them light. They heard their problems. They wanted to tell somebody what they could not tell to anybody else – heinous crimes they could not share with anybody. They were frightened, but they trusted the father [the priest]; they confessed and then felt light.

That is the purpose of a psychologist. He has to be their friend. He has to win their confidence. Every patient doesn't trust the psychologist. He tries to keep everything within himself unless he feels that he can trust the other person, by his love, by so many other ways and means. It is for the doctor to open that patient. Medically, treating the patient means just giving him a pill, giving him medicine. Psychologically, treating him means you have to become his best friend so that he will share all his problems with you. His problem will be solved the moment he shares.

446 *I was wondering if a satsangi can come under the influence of negative occult forces?*

Mostly it's superstition, this black magic and occultism. These things don't affect anybody at all. They make our willpower weak, and then we're exploited by people who practice these things. It's all superstition.

Even possession, when people are possessed by other people?

No, there are evil spirits – I don't deny the existence of evil spirits. But they're not within anybody's control; they can't be set against us. Some people are so attached to each other that if they suddenly die, they become spirits, and the people to whom they were attached are haunted by them. I don't deny that, but all these spirits or ghosts are not in anybody's control so that they could be set against us. That is all superstition.

447 *Master, is it true that the harmony in the whole Sant Mat group can be influenced badly by black magic?*

Sister, black magic can't do anything to a satsangi. Black magic can't influence those who are devotees of the Father. It is people's own minds which are creating disharmony, not black magic.

448 *Are there such things as spirits and ghosts, and if so, can they harm us in any way?*

Well, sister, there are. There are spirits and there are ghosts. They haunt us only because of our attachment to them. I'll give you a rough sort of example: Supposing two people are greatly attached to each other and suddenly death by accident or otherwise takes one away. They are so attached to each other that one spirit starts haunting the other. There are spirits and ghosts, but they don't harm a satsangi. If you are attending to your meditation and you're not conscious of those attachments and those faces, they cannot cause you any harm.

> *Master, sometimes we hear of spirits that invade a house and sometimes throw things around and frighten the people who live there until they can't bear it, and the people move out.*

Actually, the spirits are not harming them. In their subconscious mind they feel that the spirits are there, and it is that fear that is harming them. It is not the spirits which are harming them. So with the help of meditation they can rise above these fears, as these things come out of the subconscious mind. As a result of meditation, the mind becomes clear and one is at peace in that bliss and happiness within. Then one does not feel frightened of anyone or anything and cannot be harmed. Even otherwise, the spirits won't harm you. But the fear which you have developed in your mind is harming you, and with meditation you get rid of this fear.

449 Is there such a thing as demon possession? If so, in what way can or should a satsangi help this kind of individual?

Evil spirits? Well, brother, evil spirits are there. But I don't think they bother humans unless humans are attached to them or they are attached to the humans. Sometimes it happens. For example, when a couple with a great love for each other experiences a sudden tragedy in which one of them dies, sometimes the surviving partner will feel as if he is being haunted by the spirit of the person who has died. But if the survivor is strong, these spirits can't do any harm at all, and certainly not to satsangis. Satsangis should not worry about these spirits and all that. They can't harm satsangis at all.

> *They can scare them. There's a satsangi who married a nonsatsangi whose former wife died, and she saw the deceased wife in the house. After a month she said to her husband, "You know, I see your dead wife here!" And he said, "I didn't want to mention it, but so do I!" [Laughter] They moved and the dead wife didn't follow them. She didn't do anything to them, but it became bothersome.*

Most of these things are psychological. I know about one or two cases where a wife has died and a man marries another wife and the second wife feels haunted by the spirit of the first wife. The second wife is in the same house where the first wife used to stay, with the same furniture and photos and all that. It's probably psychological. She starts feeling that she is being haunted, in dreams and otherwise. But actually it's nothing like that, although there are cases where they're actually being haunted. But satsangis shouldn't worry about these things, because they don't bother satsangis at all.

SUICIDE

450 You say that to commit suicide is wrong, but you also say that everything is destined. So wouldn't suicide be karmic?

Sometimes it may be destiny. It's very difficult to say what type of karma suicide is, whether it is destiny or whether it is sowing a future seed. Sometimes it may be destiny – you can't help it; you have to go through it. Sometimes it does happen. But since we cannot know whether it is destiny or a new seed, we have to treat it as a new seed. It's not even right to think of committing suicide. Besides the aspect of karma, you have been given an opportunity – such a beautiful opportunity – to finish with this prison of life, to escape from this prison of birth and death. We have to make use of this opportunity and fight to go back to the Lord, rather than try to escape from our karmas through suicide.

Why do we commit suicide? When we think we cannot face a situation, when we think we cannot cope with a situation, and we have certain wishes, desires we want fulfilled and we cannot fulfil them. So we want to finish with our life, to escape. But there's nothing in this world worth shedding tears about. So we should face each situation as it comes. Why try to escape it?

451 Is suicide part of destiny?

It can be, and it also may not be. But still we can't justify suicide, whatever way it may be. This opportunity to get a human form is not so easily available, so we should try to make best use of it. Who knows, we may or may not get this opportunity again. Or we may take birth in such a place where we could never even dream of thinking about the Father. So why lose this opportunity? Who knows when you will take birth in a better atmosphere? You may take birth in a worse atmosphere than this. You may have worse problems to face in your next life. Why not face these problems now? It's not right, this attitude of suicide; actually, it's not right.

452 Do you think the motivation of people who commit suicide is that they get tired of the world and want to meet the Lord?

No, no! They do not commit suicide to meet the Lord. They are cowards not to face the world. They commit suicide because there are certain desires which they cannot fulfil, and they cannot stand that. So they will have to come back to fulfil those desires.

Is suicide the greatest sin?

I think so. We do not get the human form so easily, and just to waste it is the greatest sin, no doubt.

453 I was appalled at your reaction when someone talked about somebody committing suicide. You didn't seem to pardon it very easily – if at all.

You mean, you don't like my criticizing suicide?

I understand it, but I just thought you were very hard, as if you have never had anybody you loved commit suicide, which is a silly thing to say to you, I suppose, but that's the way it felt to me.

No. You see, if a surgeon operates, he does not want any pus to remain in the wound. He scrapes the wound with a knife, but he doesn't worry about the crying of the patient – he worries about the patient's healing. I cannot treat the subject of suicide lightly. You can't expect me to encourage people to commit suicide. Naturally, I have to be hard. Why should these people not make the best use of this opportunity which the Lord has given us? Why should they think about committing suicide at all?

454 *Do you not think the suicidal tendency is sometimes sublimated into wanting to leave the body, such as in meditation?*

No, it is not wanting to leave the body. It is rather not getting what you want while being in the body.

I mean, is meditation a sublimated way?

No. One should never have this approach to meditation. That is a cowardly approach and a betrayal of the privilege of having the human body.

FACING ILLNESS AND DEATH

455 *Will a satsangi's death be painful?*

If you have progress within, then it will be easier to face. If you have already done the rehearsal to die, then death is no problem to you.

*So whether a person dies in that in-between state between
life and death or goes on to the higher planes would just
depend on the person's growth?*

It would depend on the person's individual destiny, individual
growth, individual attitude towards meditation, towards life,
towards this creation, his attachment to the creation.

If a muslin cloth is thrown on a thorny bush, if you try to
pull it, it will be torn. But if you take it from one thorn, then
from another thorn and then from another thorn, you can easily
remove the cloth. So one who has done the practice of removing the cloth from each individual thorn takes it off very easily.
Another person, for whom the cloth has to be pulled all at once
from the thorny bush, naturally will feel it.

If our attachment is very spread out into this creation,
when we are withdrawing ourselves to the eye centre and trying to pull our roots from those attachments, it will be painful
because the mind refuses to leave them. So it varies with individuals. You can't generalize these things.

*456 As a result of meditation, does our soul detach itself at
the time of death?*

Sister, that is why we are told that slowly, gradually, we have to
withdraw to the eye centre. If you put a fine cloth on a thorny
bush, and you pull it all at once, you will tear the cloth. Similarly, if suddenly you withdraw to the eye centre, it becomes very
painful. For this reason saints always advise us: Slowly, slowly
try to withdraw. Pick the cloth off one thorn at a time and you
will be able to save the whole cloth. So this process is very slow.
Then it's not painful at all. But if suddenly you have to withdraw,
naturally it is painful. Therefore, we are always advised to try
to withdraw slowly.

*457 At the time of death, does the master always come for the
disciple, on this side, to take him across?*

Sister, it depends upon the individual. You can't say as a matter
of guarantee that the master always comes, but the soul is always
taken care of, whether the master appears at that time or not.
If you have already progressed sufficiently within, and you are
not much attached to anybody in this creation, the natural pre-
sumption is that the master will come. But if you are pulled too
much towards the creation or towards worldly faces, master may
or may not appear, because your mind at the time of death runs
to your attachments. Your attachments just come before you
like on a cinema screen. If you are not attached to anything in
this creation – if you have been able to overcome these worldly
attachments – then master must appear. But if you are attached
to so many things in the world, then master may or may not
appear before you, because generally attachments come before
us at the time of death.

*458 Master, is it true that some satsangis know when their
time is up, and so they can prepare for death?*

Some satsangis are fortunate to know when their time is going
to be up. Others may or may not. Christ asked: Whom will I
raise at the last day? He says, not everybody. They must fulfil
two conditions: First, they must have seen me; second, they
must believe in me.[92] They must be initiated through me – take
a new birth – and then they must follow my teaching, live my
teaching. Believing in a mystic is to live the teaching, to follow
his instructions. He says that only they will be raised by me
at the last day. Others may be raised, but that is entirely at his
discretion. That is why he said that unless you take a new birth,
you will not go back to heaven.[77] Why does he refer to a new

birth? Because a child always grows after birth, grows and grows to become a man. Similarly, we take a spiritual birth at the time of initiation, and after initiation we start spiritually growing to ultimately become the Father. Unless we take a new birth, we cannot grow to become the Father. When we are growing to become the Father, then we will also know our end.

459 *If the disciple sincerely does not want to come back, attends to his meditation and asks the master to remove any subtle attachments that might bring him back, is the master gracious enough to let that soul go in and stay in and not come down again to the creation?*

If we are not attached to anything in this world, nothing can bring us back, even if our meditation is insignificant. If, on the other hand, we are attached to this creation – its objects and faces – even if we have lot of meditation to our credit, we will come back.

When we attend to meditation, automatically all those bonds are cut. Those attachments become meaningless to us; they become superfluous. It is only the grooves on the mind, our deep attachments which pull us back to this creation. Otherwise, we meet so many people – they come and go. Today we love them; tomorrow we forget them. That is no attachment. But there are certain grooves we make on the mind – very, very deep attachments that we can't get rid of. We get obsessed with them and they pull us back. But meditation helps us even to rise above all that.

460 *If one were to die without thoughts of the shabd or master, through not meditating sufficiently and so forth, would master still take over the direction of that soul when it left?*

The principle is that even if we have not made much spiritual progress within, but we have lived the Sant Mat way of life and are not attached to anything in this world, we will not come back to this world at all. On the other hand, even if you have some spiritual growth within to your credit but still have strong desires or strong attachments to this world, you may have to come back to this world. Ultimately it is the attachments which determine whether you come back. And our whole meditation is for the purpose of detaching us from this world.

The master wouldn't interfere with the direction of that soul if the attachments were still there?

That is for the master to decide. Sometimes our attachments are taken care of at the time of our death. Sometimes they are taken care of even in dreams. He knows best how he wants to do it – whether it is in the interest of the disciple to take another birth, or whether it is in the interest of the disciple to stay in those regions and then make progress. The master has to decide, because his responsibility is to take the soul back to the Father. How he accounts for what is due to Caesar is for him to decide. There is no hard and fast rule about it. But Caesar must get his due.[66] Whatever we owe to this creation, we have to pay that, but the master stands as our ransom to Kal and then takes us back to the Father. The master helps us through meditation, through love, through devotion, through service – he wants to help us in so many ways because he is responsible to take us back to the Father. So you can't say that if any desires or attachments are there, you will have to come back, because that is for the master to decide.

461 *I have heard from satsangis that if you are quite ill and you still carry on with your meditation, it counts as double time. Is that so? [Laughter]*

Meditation is nothing but a daily preparation for death. Why should we worry when the end comes, for which we have been preparing our whole life? We should rather face it gladly, because our whole life has been spent just for that moment. All of our meditation is nothing but a preparation for how the soul leaves the body. When the opportunity comes for the soul to leave the body, why should we howl and cry? We should be glad that now the opportunity has come to utilize that, to achieve that for which we have spent our whole life. So the fear of death should not arise in us. But as far as attachment is concerned, you may think academically you are not attached to anything, but the time of our death reveals whether we are really attached to anything or not.

462 *Master, when a satsangi dies, and he hasn't yet contacted the radiant form within, will the shabd come to his aid after his death to help him remember the Lord?*

Well, sister, shabd never forsakes the disciple. Once we are in touch with the shabd within, no matter how little progress we may have made in our meditation, shabd never leaves us. Even if we have to come back to this creation as a human, shabd is always there with us, even then, and will lead you to some master because all masters are the same. And again shabd will pull the soul back to the level of the Father. So shabd is our real master, not the body of any master.

463 *At the time of dying, for the satsangi who doesn't qualify to see the radiant form, what is meant by the words "the initiate will be taken care of"?*

You see, we find our place according to our own individual karmas, our individual attachments. We'll find our place after death. If we are to come back to this creation, we'll be sent back here. If the master or the Lord thinks it would be better for the soul to be in the inner regions and then make further progress from there, it will be placed in those mansions.

And does the soul, as it progresses at an inner level, then meet the radiant form?

What is your concept of the radiant form? I'll tell you: This shabd itself is the radiant form of the master, because the master inside projects himself from this shabd. Actually, what you see or what you hear is the shabd itself, but since you have seen the master outside, unless he appears before you as he does outside, you will not be satisfied and convinced that you are seeing your master. So he projects himself from that shabd and nam. That radiant form is nothing but shabd itself. So shabd is the one who takes care of the soul at the time of death, and even before.

464 I was wondering whether, during a natural death, one should try to do simran?

We should keep our mind in simran at a natural death, provided you are conscious of yourself, provided your mind still remembers simran. Sometimes you become unconscious – you don't know what you're doing. During a natural death, people go into a coma, people become unconscious, so what is in your hands?

If you are in the habit of doing simran and you have made some progress within, then even if you're in a coma, inside you may be in touch with the sound and the light. The body is in a coma, not your consciousness. It depends upon the individual. The mind will go to meditation at that time only if you are in the habit of doing meditation. You can't say, well, at that time, I will do meditation, I will keep my mind in simran, but there's no necessity now. Then your mind won't go to that at all.

Thoughts of the world, suppressed desires of the world will all spring up before you. Your mind won't go to simran at all if you are not in the habit of doing simran, if you're not in the habit of attending to meditation. If you're in the habit of attending to meditation, then even if you are in a coma, you will be in touch with that sound.

465 *Satsangis know that the master appears in his radiant form at the time of their death. Could you tell us about how much time is given to satsangis after their master appears? Is it two minutes, or five minutes?*

It depends upon the individual progress of a satsangi and his individual attachments, his individual outlook on meditation, his individual karma and the grace from the master. There are so many factors. It may be days, it may be years, it may be months, it may be two minutes, it may be just at the last moment. You cannot fix any time for it. It differs with every individual. If we are not following the path, not meditating at all, not living the way of Sant Mat, he may not appear. He is not bound to do so. He may if he likes, but we should try to deserve it by remaining within his commands.

At least there is usually enough time for a satsangi to say good-bye to the children and kiss his wife on the cheek?

You mean, you are still conscious of your attachments even at the time of death? You can imagine how much meditation has helped you! Devotees refuse to recognize that they have any wife or children at the time of death. They do not want to see them. They do not want to be drawn outside. They forget that they have any relation at all with anybody. That detachment we have to develop by meditation. That is the purpose of our meditation.

466 *Maharaj Ji, I think somewhere along the line I've heard that the master appears to a satsangi, gives him some forewarning of his physical death. Is that true?*

Who would like to know when we're going to die? Everybody's not prepared to know that. If we were told, then we would think: "Let me write my will, let me love my child, let me do this and let me do that." The mind would spread into the whole world at once. All those attachments will revive in no time. Those who are anxiously looking forward to that time, who are prepared for that time, who are anxious to face that experience, they are told. They know it, but then their mind doesn't go to the world at all. They are prepared for it. They have gone through the rehearsal for death so many times before, and they are anxiously looking forward to it. But those who are attached to the creation, to worldly faces, if they are told that they have to go, all those attachments will revive and they will have to come back again.

467 *Maharaj Ji, what help can a satsangi give to another satsangi who is dying?*

That is a very good question. We should all be a source of strength and help to each other. We can remind him about the teachings, about the path, we can fill him with love and devotion for master, for shabd, for the Father. We can read Sant Mat literature to him and we can draw his attention to the shabd and nam within. And we can create an atmosphere around him so that he can attend to his meditation, and keep away from him whatever is distracting him towards the world. Everybody is not fortunate enough to have just devotees around him. Many people are nonsatsangis, and he has dealings with so many people, both satsangis and nonsatsangis.

It's always better if we can build a devotional atmosphere – an atmosphere of satsang – around that soul, so that the soul goes peacefully and is not attached to anything in the world. Anybody who is distracting him and pulling him out, we should try to keep that influence away from him, generally.

468 *Maharaj Ji, at the time of our physical death, when does a soul leave the body? Is it a moment of hard stress, or do we just fall into unconsciousness?*

You see, when you die, the soul leaves the body – only then do you die. As long as the soul is there, death is not there. You are still living as long as the soul is in the body, whether you are conscious or unconscious. When the soul leaves the body – that is the physical death.

Sometimes our relations try to call us for farewell. Can they distract us from our master?

Sometimes they do, because your mind is concentrated on a certain thing within and they try to withdraw your attention outside. So they do distract. That is why it is always advisable at the time of a satsangi's death that no nonsatsangi be there, and that nobody should try to call him or draw his attention outside.

Therefore we should say to our relations that we are leaving them all? We can say it gently, without anger or hurting their feelings?

Naturally. You see, they are so attached to their relatives that they think they can help by calling him, by putting some medicine in his mouth. It depends upon the individual. If one is really attached within, then he should never be disturbed.

469 Maharaj Ji, if a satsangi is near a person who is not initiated, at the time that person dies, how should one behave?

We should accept facts, that the soul has left and our relationship has finished. We must accept facts. If you're attached to the person and you really want to help him, then you should attend to your meditation. Then you'll help yourself; by meditation you'll be helping the other soul also. But if you forget about meditation and start crying for that departed soul, then it's not to your advantage or to the advantage of the departed soul.

We must accept facts; the relationship is a karmic adjustment of the accounts. Somebody is a wife, somebody is a daughter – they come and go on the stage, as you hear every day in satsang. We must accept a death scene when it comes, that this drama has finished now. There's no use crying over spilt milk. We must accept facts and face life as it comes. It is always better, if somebody is dying in your presence, that you keep doing your simran with your attention on the sound, and do not disturb that soul, and also tell other people not to disturb that person. Even if he's not a satsangi, don't let other people ask him too many questions: "Where have you kept the keys? Where are your financial papers? Where is your will?" Let him keep his attention wherever it is. Don't disturb him at all. Leave him alone and quietly attend to your own meditation.

470 Why does the master sometimes take away those whom we love the most?

Well, brother, whether we love them or not, everybody has to go through his own destiny. When their end comes, they have to quit the stage. Everyone is always special to someone. Everyone is someone's loved one, but when their time comes, they have to go.

*471 If a child is born mutilated, paralyzed or terribly deformed
     and survives, as some children just exist but have no control
     over their own movements, or some cannot even move and
     are bedridden all the time, would mercy killing be allowed,
     if it is legal in that country? If you were a satsangi doctor,
     would you kill that child, if mercy killing were legal?*

I do not believe in mercy killing at all, and I don't think it is
legal anywhere in the world, yet. Though I know little of the law,
mercy killing is not allowed. Mercy killing is definitely wrong
from a spiritual point of view. In mercy killing, we are trying to
take something into our own hands that we think is mercy. If
we had to follow such a line of thought, I think half the world
would be killed tomorrow. Everybody is suffering; everybody is
in agony; everybody is in pain; people are starving; people are
diseased; people are unhealthy in this world. That does not mean
that we should start killing right and left. If we did, we would
have to kill ourselves too, for we are in agony with ourselves. So
the question of mercy killing does not arise.

The Lord knows best when to take life – he gives it and he
takes it. Nature always keeps its own level. The Lord knows best
how and when to kill. People are killed in wars, in storms, in
earthquakes and so many other ways that he alone can control.
Why should we try to be his rivals? We should be helpful to
the handicapped to the best of our ability and not try to take
away their life.

*Master, if one finds an animal or a bird that is badly hurt
and is in agony, is it wrong to take it out of its misery?*

Brother, if we start analyzing like this, probably we will have to
put an end to three-fourths of the world. [Laughter] Who is not
in agony? We should analyze within ourselves as to whether we
are at war within ourselves or not. Are we happy in this world?

361

Are we even physically or mentally happy to be in this world? If we will just analyze our own self, we will find that every one of us is most miserable with himself. Everybody is dancing to the tune of his own karma, and despite all that, no one wants to die. So whether human beings or animals or birds, we should try to help them, not put an end to their life. When you go to hospitals, you find that people are crying in physical pain. Do you think they should all be killed, straight away?

No, I mean an animal that was obviously dying?

But whether man or animal, we do not know whether he is obviously dying or he is getting a new birth. It is for that individual to clear his own karmas. We have to help him, whether it is with medical aid or whatever is humanly possible. We should give all the help we can, but we should never try to take it in our own hands to do away with his life. We have no right to do so. There is no mercy in killing. We should help to the best of our ability, wherever we can, but still, with our best intentions, in certain situations we really cannot help. They are paying for their karmas – whatever they have sown, they shall reap. But we have to help them with our best intelligence, capabilities and resources. It is only to the extent that the Lord wants us to succeed that we will be able to help them. So we should do our best to help them and leave the results to him.

If we start from the point of view of mercy killing, as I told you, I do not know how many people we might have to kill. Politicians throw bombs, wiping away humanity, and they also justify that killing. But whether the Lord justifies it or not remains to be seen. Whether we have done good or bad, he will tell us. We can judge only with our intellect. We may think we have saved many humans by killing a hundred thousand or two hundred thousand. But these are all justifications for our own weaknesses. We should help, not kill. Christ said, love one another.[115] He also said that if someone slaps you on one cheek, you should turn the other.[18] What does that mean? It means that we should have no malice against anybody – not even against our enemies. We have to show them love, devotion, mercy and give them love for hatred, not hatred for hatred. We will help them practically by giving them love, by giving them help, by giving them service. We do not help anybody by taking away his life.

472 *Maharaj Ji, would it be possible for disembodied spirits to affect embodied spirits?*

You mean those people who have left us, could they affect us? Well, we are affected because we are attached to them. That is why the Great Master always used to advise people that if we are attached to those who have departed and we do not overcome our attachment to them, sometimes we even hinder their progress by trying to pull them back. And if they are also attached to us and they have not found their way up, they sometimes also haunt us and pull us.

I remember an incident in the time of the Great Master when a very good satsangi had died, and his daughter was very much attached to him. Naturally, when he died, she was weeping and wailing. And the Great Master was trying to console her, saying that her father was to go, that he had lived his full life span and had provided well for her and the other children in this life, so she must face reality and forget him when he was no more. But the attachments are very strong with certain people. She could not overcome all that despite the advice. One day when she sat for bhajan, as she explained later to the Great Master, her father appeared to her. He told her, "Look now, my darling, what you have done to me. For three days you have been weeping and slapping your own face, and by doing so you have been slapping my face. How sore it is! Look what harm you are doing to me. You are pulling me and are not letting me go up. Why can you not forget all this?" She then wrote a letter to the Great Master, and the Great Master came and also consoled her inside, and took her father up.

Sometimes we have to experience these things to know reality. We must face reality, but we try to escape it. We know a person is dead – he cannot come back, he is no more – but we feel that he is living. We refuse to understand that he is gone. So, unless we live with reality, we can never be happy.

473 What is the meaning of "the last day"?

Our last day is when we leave this body. That is our resurrection. When we die, that is our last day, as far as the world is concerned. We will be judged at that time. But there is not going to be one last day for the whole creation; and there is no particular day when everybody will be judged. So our last day is only when we leave this world, when we leave this body. That is our last day as far as the body is concerned.

474 Maharaj Ji, is the day of resurrection, which is mentioned in the Bible, an individual affair and not universal?

That is right. Everybody faces that day of resurrection. So it hardly matters whether you cremate or bury or dispose of the body in other ways. There are so many ways of disposing of the body, according to the needs of a particular country. For example, Arabia is all desert. They have no wood, so they could not cremate. It was much more practical and economical to bury the dead by putting the body in the sand, and the body would decompose under the sand and there would be no bad smell. That was all right. In countries where they had a lot of wood or jungles, they followed the custom that most Indians do. They cremated the dead bodies. And now that electricity is available, it is also done by electric current.

It hardly makes any difference what you do with the body after death. We are concerned only as long as the soul is in it. Once the soul leaves the body, we are not concerned with that body. At one place people are weeping and mourning, "He has left us," and at another place people are blowing trumpets and joyfully proclaiming, "He has come – a child is born." It is the same soul, leaving one family weeping and sorrowful, and creating happiness in the other family. So it really looks like a strange drama. We weep for our attachments, our affections, our love, our own comfort, our own security, and not for the other person. We mourn because we feel the loss, and not because of our concern for the departed.

475 *The general point of view of the Christians is to go back to the grave of a person who has died because the person who has been interred is resting, so people go back and grieve and grieve and grieve. So does Radha Soami strongly favour cremation instead of burial because it would take away that incentive?*

Brother, I would not want to insist on anything. Whatever the family custom is or whatever way anybody feels like disposing of the dead body is all right. You can cremate it or you can bury it. For the soul, it makes absolutely no difference in what manner the dead body is disposed of. As far as Sant Mat is concerned, we do not differentiate between burial and cremation. I was reading in a book where some people expose dead bodies to vultures. There was a reason for it. It was a small island, and they had neither wood for cremation nor space enough to bury them. They were surrounded by water, and they thought that if they placed the body by the sea, the vultures would come and finish it off.

Every custom has a reason behind it. Without investigating the reasons, we become slaves of the rituals and ceremonies and dogmas, and forget about the purpose of doing those things. But circumstances can change, they can differ. For example, we always cremate with wood; but if wood is very expensive or scarce, or it is not practical to cremate in the open air, there is no harm in getting it done electrically. That is all right. Now even in modern India, some people think that it is not good to do it with electricity, that it should be done only with wood, and a certain kind of wood. These things are meaningless.

So I would not want to bring a ritual into Sant Mat by saying that cremation is the thing, or that burial or any other method should be advocated. Each and every satsangi is absolutely free to do whatever he or she wants to do. We have to overcome these notions that these outer things have any bearing whatsoever on our spiritual progress. When we have done our duty as long as we were given the chance to do it, then we must face reality. What will be the use to dwell on grief now? If the departed soul really loved us, he would not like to see us unhappy and miserable in his memory. He would like to see us joyful and happy and facing life lightly. He would not be happy where he is seeing us miserable and weeping here.

~ 16 ~

The Real Miracle

A POSITIVE APPROACH

*476   We have heard many times that the human body is given
to a person for the sole purpose of realizing God. We have
also heard that the life of a person who does not realize
God is wasted. How can his life be considered a waste?*

Our real purpose is to go back to the Father, to realize him. The
main purpose of getting this human birth is to go back to the
Father. This privilege is given only to humans, not to anybody
else. So if we don't use this opportunity to go back to him, then
we're wasting our time. Everything else we're doing, we've also
done in previous births, in previous species, in previous forms. So
if we are not doing anything to achieve our destination, to achieve
our goal of going back to the Father, we are wasting time.

Whatever step we take to go back to the Father, that is to
our credit. That's not a waste. But if our direction is the other
way and we don't think about our destination or try to do anything to reach that destination, we are just wasting our time.

*That does not necessarily mean just meeting a master –
it means doing anything toward meeting a master. Is
that correct?*

Yes. Anything you do to achieve your goal is not a waste – it's a step forward. When a child is born, ultimately he starts walking and running. So every step he takes right from birth is a step forward. He learns to sit; he learns to stand; he learns to lean. Ultimately he carries his own weight on his legs; then he starts walking; and then he falls so many times. Even a fall is a step forward for him, and then ultimately he achieves his goal of running. So the whole process is to his credit. Similarly, when we are trying to go back to the Father, all that we do to achieve that end is to our credit. That's not a waste. Every step we take is a step forward.

477 *Last night Professor Bhatnagar was saying that if some-one is so pitiful, the master will take pity and show compassion and take him inside. Even sinners can get up to Sach Khand because the master shows compassion because of the pitiful state they're in. I'd like to know if you would please tell us how pitiful we have to get before you'll take pity on us.*

It's not in our hands to get it. All we can do is be sincere and faithful to our meditation, and then leave everything to the Lord's mercy. We should make best use of the opportunity the Lord has given us – the environment, the atmosphere he has put us in. Then we should leave everything to his mercy. His grace, his mercy, his forgiveness are not in our hands. But he never lags behind. He's the one who has planted the seed of love and longing within us, and he naturally would like it to flourish. The gardener who has planted his seed wants to see it bloom into a plant. So we may be lacking in our devotion and longing, but the Lord is not lacking in pulling us.

478 Master, you've said that it's better not to ask for anything and also that the Lord knows best what to give us. Could you help me to understand the difference between that attitude and the attitude of begging?

You see, begging is not for worldly boons. Begging is for the Lord's grace, and meditation itself is begging. By meditation we are begging at his door for admission. We are asking just to become one with the Father. We are begging for forgiveness, to forgive what stands between us and the Father. We are not asking for any worldly boons. Instead of just making repeated prayers, "O Lord, give me grace, help me give time to meditation," why not just sit in meditation? Why not just give time to meditation? Instead of asking for his grace, attend to meditation – that itself is grace. Instead of asking him to open your inner vision, attend to meditation, which will automatically open your inner vision. Asking doesn't change the situation. There's a positive step, which is attending to meditation. Otherwise, we are all beggars at his door.

479 Master, I have a question about our attitude toward our weaknesses. When we observe our weaknesses, there's a tendency to dwell on them, but you've said that we should be grateful to the Lord when we see our weaknesses. But instead it seems like they become blocks in our way.

We should have a positive approach, which is to get rid of our weaknesses. And only by meditation can we help ourselves rise above our weaknesses. Just to feel guilty and not to do anything about it also doesn't solve any problem. We have to repent by not repeating our mistakes, and then we have to try to rise above our weaknesses with the help of meditation.

480 Maharaj Ji, this question has to do with the subject of forgiveness. A lot of times we walk around with a 100-pound weight on our shoulder feeling bad about something that we did in the past, and we feel that the master is upset with us. Could you please talk about self-forgiveness, how we can go ahead with our lives?

Well, brother, this self-pity and self-analysis doesn't help us. Brooding on the past doesn't lead us anywhere. We have to step forward now. We must have a positive attitude now, for the future. Forget about the past. Attend to your meditation. Live the Sant Mat way of life and be a good satsangi. Don't worry about what has happened – that won't solve any problem at all. We must take a positive step.

481 You often say, "do not analyze." Why not analyze so much?

It will lead you nowhere. We just start feeling self-pity, and where does that lead you? Instead of analyzing your own self too much, attend to meditation. That will take care of the coming events in a more practical way than brooding over the past, over the present, over the future. Why not prepare yourself to face the present and face the future – by meditation.

482 Sometimes I worry that if I miss my meditation, something horrible will happen to me.

You should attend to meditation not from any fear of the Father, but with love for the Father. You should base your meditation on love, not fear – lest I do this, this will happen; lest I do that, that will happen. Never have that approach. We should approach the Father with love. When that love is there, then we don't bother about punishments. When love for the Father is there, then we also don't carry much of a sense of guilt if we fall here and there. To think "If I don't sit in meditation, I'll be punished, I'll be sent to hell" is the wrong approach. The basis of religion is love, not fear – at least it should be. Saints have to explain that side to us also, but they don't tell us to meditate out of fear. You should meditate out of love for the Father.

483 *Maharaj Ji, on the path, does one experience a stepping backwards, as it were?*

On the path, we are always going ahead and ahead. But we have to pass through so many phases; so many human failings are there. But we ultimately overcome them. The Lord doesn't commit any mistakes. If he has marked someone, he has got to pull him to his own level. We commit mistakes, but not the One who has marked us, who is pulling us from within.

484 *Master, I'd like to hear what you have to say about this line from Paltu. It says: "In the game of love I cannot lose. If I win I get you, and if I lose you get me." Is that right?*

If I win, naturally I'll be in your lap. If, in my struggle, I lose, you will pull me to your level. So there are no failures if I am doing my best. One only loses a battle if one fights it. You can't lose a battle sitting at home. When you are fighting, either you win or you lose. But you are fighting. As Maharaj Ji [Maharaj Sawan Singh] used to say, in Sant Mat there are no failures, because you are trying to follow it. A child who is learning to run, well, he falls, he gets bruises, he gets up again, he tries again, tries again and starts running. If he is always frightened of falling, he will never even learn to walk. So even if we lose in this battle of love, we win.

It's a very strange battle in that master pulls us first, then we come towards him, and then he seems to go away.

He doesn't go away. We come and go, come and go. He is always pulling, but we are not always receptive to his pull. Christ gave the parable of the sowing of the seed. The seed falls on marshy ground. It grows, but along with the weeds.[50] One is attending to meditation and is receptive to the pull, but is also a victim of his weaknesses. The pull is always there, but we are not 100 percent receptive to it.

485 *If a person were to be cut off from life before he makes progress in nam, what happens?*

Sister, it depends upon many things, but mostly on our desires, our cravings, our longings, our karmas, our attachments and the grace of the master. Even if we have not made much progress during our life span, but we don't have many unfulfilled desires, we have not much attachment to people, places or things – if we have no strong attachments, nothing can bring us back here. We are then taken to certain stages inside, and from there we can work and make our way up. On the other hand, even if we have progressed to some extent inside and we still have very strong attachments with the world, we are brought back to clear those attachments, to get rid of those attachments and make further progress and go back to him.

So it depends on the individual situation. Generally, we never go backwards. There are no failures in Sant Mat. We always go ahead. If you do not make any progress in this life, you will get another life in which to make progress. You will be born under much better circumstances, as far as meditation is concerned, as far as devotion to the Lord is concerned – not from a material point of view. If you do not make progress, you will get another birth to make your way up, to improve yourself. You will be in still better circumstances for meditation. Ultimately you will have gone every step, every part of the way forward, not backwards. So, there is nothing to fear. We should try to do our best during our life span and then just leave the rest to him.

486 *Master, you've said that everything will be just fine when we rise above the mind, but I think it would be true to say that most souls don't rise above the mind until they've been on the path about fifty years, it seems.*

Not just fifty years – we are lucky to escape the clutches of Kal after even two or three lives. [Laughter] We have to calculate how long we've been separated from the Father, how long we've been part of the creation. According to that span, even three or four lives is nothing.

But it could be three or four lives before we even get to the eye centre or rise above the mind.

We should always think that this is our last birth, that I'm going to achieve everything in this life. We should never, never calculate that this is my first life. We should always think that this is my last life and I'm not going to come back – I'm going to get to my destination. That should be our endeavour, and then we should leave it to the Father and let him do what he wants.

487 *How much capacity do we have in planning our future, Master? Is it set for us when we're born?*

We have only one future: to go back to the Father. There's no other future.

A FRESH PERSPECTIVE

488 Maharaj Ji, I have a question that's been fascinating me for some time and also annoying me. When you say the soul and the mind are covered in layers, when does this lift off? Does this material world start to look different for that individual, as they start making progress within?

Even this very world changes before your eyes in your lifetime. And at a certain stage, things which you've been so attached to, which you thought were very beautiful, very fascinating, you close your eyes when they come before you. Same world, same faces, same things – they start looking different to you because your approach, your attitude has changed. The world is the same, but our attitude and approach to it changes. The world always remains the same, but we go on changing. Our attitude goes on changing. We are getting detached, so we are changing – we think the world is changing – and that is a level of consciousness. This world becomes meaningless to you. You enjoy that bliss and peace within, and that is the world for you. Nothing else exists for you there, except the contentment and happiness of that level of consciousness. And that is your world, which you enjoy.

There's no dearth of good people in this world, and you can find everything and anything in this world. But the question is: What catches your interest? Something may catch your interest which another person won't even like to look at. So many tourists come to India and go to the Thar Desert and many other historic places. And I have seen many satsangis who have just come straight to Dera and gone straight back, without perhaps even looking out of their hotel window in Delhi. The same world exists for everybody, but the difference is in their attitude, their approach.

It has to come from within, whatever it is. I don't condemn one or the other. But I'm telling you, it's different with different people.

489 *When one makes contact within, goes in and sees the master, does the awareness take place only in the spiritual realm, or does it also take place in the physical realm?*

Well, it does take place in the physical body also. Yes, you feel changes in yourself by meditation. You yourself feel quite detached. Your outlook on life automatically changes. Things do not please you anymore. You do not feel like being in that material atmosphere and you start shunning that society which you are so used to. So, practically, you yourself feel what changes are brought about.

490 *Maharaj Ji, some people refer to God as the divine mother. Isn't the world a beautiful place when you see that divine spirit everywhere?*

Well, brother, that mother or that power or that God, whatever name you give it, is within every one of us. Unless we realize that power or that mother within ourselves, we won't see that power or mother within anybody else at all. Once you realize it within yourself, then everywhere you look, you will find that love, that affection, that devotion, that mother and that father in every one of us. But to come to that stage – living in the world and not being affected by it, not being attached to it – we have to work our spiritual way within the body. Then whatever you see, you will find that bliss, that love within every one of us. You have to realize that within yourself in order to realize it in the world.

For example, when you are in love, when you are happy within yourself, you'll find happiness everywhere, even in a little pebble. You're just dancing – when you're dancing inside, you're dancing outside. Everybody you come across looks lovely to you. Everybody looks like a very fine person to you because you are very fine within yourself, you are very lovely, very devotional within yourself. When we develop that love, that power within ourselves, then wherever we look, wherever we go, we find the same Lord, the same power within every one of us. Then the illusion of this world doesn't bother us at all. Being in the world, we're not of the world. We're in our own love, we're in our own devotion for the Lord. Then this world doesn't affect us at all. But to develop that detachment, we have to know that this world is an illusion and not be tempted by it.

491   I just wondered if at this level one is at all aware of what one's meditation is doing.

Sister, meditation changes the very attitude of our life. That's different from what we achieve within and how far we still have to go, but meditation definitely changes our attitude towards life. You see, even if we don't experience anything within, but we attend to meditation, we at least can enjoy the fragrance of meditation, if not the experience of meditation. A blind man goes to a garden full of scented flowers. If he can't enjoy the beauty of the flowers, at least he can enjoy their fragrance. So meditation changes our outlook on life. It makes us humble. It makes us more loving, more kind, more God-fearing. We don't try to deceive anybody, cheat anybody, hurt anybody. In so many ways it moulds our life. If we do anything wrong, it weighs on our conscience and we try to get rid of our guilt. These are the effects of our meditation, and if one is lucky enough to enjoy the experience, there is nothing like it.

Won't even pluck a leaf mindlessly

492 *I suppose, Maharaj Ji, that any satsangi who does his meditation daily, diligently and devotedly for two and a half hours or more in the morning hours can reasonably expect to reach his spiritual destination?*

Definitely. You see, you not only make spiritual progress within, but with regularity in meditation and living the Sant Mat way of life, your whole attitude and approach to the world and worldly problems changes. The time comes when you feel you're not attached to anybody at all. And that is the main factor in our not coming back to this creation at all, no matter how little progress we have made within. Our whole attitude and approach to life changes by meditation, by living this way of life, and automatically we get detached from everything. And that detachment pulls us out of this creation.

493 *As we meditate and progress spiritually little by little, do we at the same time increase our freedom from the creation little by little? Is it a gradual process of becoming free or is it a sudden process?*

We make progress very slowly. In meditation we always make progress, but slowly. When a child starts growing, it takes him time to grow. We have all passed through so many phases before we have understood what life is, before we can face life, before we know that we can stand on our own legs. Think how many phases we have been through! It is the same with meditation. Just as a child, after birth, grows to become an adult, so similarly a soul, after initiation, spiritually starts growing to become the Father. That is why Christ says, unless you take a new birth, you will not be entitled to go back to heaven.[77] Every mystic says that you will have to take a new birth. After that, slowly and slowly, we spiritually grow. Through meditation our attitude to life is changed. Now our tendency and attitude is all towards the creation, towards the illusion, whatever form it may take. But with meditation, our attitude of mind starts changing and its tendency is no longer outward and downward. Its tendency becomes inward and upward, and that is the great progress we are making, when the tendency of the mind turns upward and inward. Because the more it goes upward and inward, the more we are getting detached from this illusion, and this very detachment ultimately leads us back to the Father.

494   Master, there's a beautiful hymn by Saint Paltu about the Lord's relation to the creation that I would like to hear you explain.

He says that the lovers of the Lord find the Lord everywhere, in everyone. The Lord is in everyone. He is in the guru, he is in the disciple. He is the Creator, he is in the creation. He's in the patient, he's in the doctor. He is the one who creates, he is the one whom he is trying to make worthy of judgment. He's the one who is judging, and he is the one who has to be judged. He is to be worshipped, and he is the one who makes us worthy of his worship. I often say, "He worships himself through us."

The lover sees none but the Lord in this creation. He doesn't see anything else at all. Bulleh Shah has said the same thing. He says there is only one thing to talk about – the Lord, which I see all around, everywhere. What else is there to talk about? Books have created confusion. They are just mental acrobatics by intellectuals to confuse people. What is there about the Lord to talk about, to write about? He is and he's everywhere. So this is a certain state, when lovers don't see anything else but the Lord. He's the Creator, he's the creation. He is the one who makes us worthy of his judgment, and he is the one who is to judge us. There's nothing besides him in this creation.

495 *Master, after the satsang I turned around and saw thou-*
sands and thousands of people, and suddenly I felt very,
very small, like a drop, and I felt this ocean around me
of all these souls, and I felt engulfed in love, and to me it
was very beautiful.

You see, we are part of that tremendous love, that wave of love.
We are one of them. Every drop is a part of the wave, part of
the ocean. So we are part of that wave of love.

Actually, love is within us, which reflects through others. If
we have no love within ourselves, we can never admire any love
outside. What is within us, we find that reflected in others.

496 *If we go within and see the radiant form of the master,*
may we ask him questions? Will we be told what to do and
given answers inside, so that we don't have to write letters
and come here and see you in your physical presence?

At that level of consciousness, what questions will you ask?
You're not interested in the world, you're not interested in this
creation at all. You're so much absorbed in your love and being
with your beloved, what questions will you ask? You may have a
list of a thousand questions in your hand, but you forget everything and all your questions are dissolved. Love helps you rise
above all those questions. Definitely he answers all your questions, but you will hardly have any question to ask.

A LOVING AND COMPASSIONATE HEART

497 *Do you love only your own disciples and not all humanity?*

We love the One who is in all of humanity, who is everywhere.
That is the Lord. It's not a question of just humanity – even

birds, animals and insects are part of the Lord. Wherever his refulgence is, we love him. In whomsoever he reflects, we love them. We don't love any particular person. We love the One who is in those persons.

498   Master, since it's natural to do things for people we love, and satsangis kind of naturally love each other, is there any harm in doing things for another satsangi?

Satsangis should have a loving habit, a loving nature. But to love somebody is different from having a loving, compassionate nature. Naturally one who is filled with love and devotion for the Father automatically will have compassion for everybody. He's not obsessed by certain persons, not attached to them, but he's loving to them and wants to do things for them. Having a loving heart is something very different from love.

Say you see an injured dog by the side of the road. You're so moved, you start weeping over the dog. You're not attached to the dog but you can't stand to see that dog suffer. You start shedding tears of misery for the dog. You're not in love with the dog, but you have a loving heart and your loving heart can't stand to see another person hurt. You have to develop that type of heart. It's not that you become obsessed with others or attached to them.

If you pass a car accident and you see that someone has died, you start weeping. You can't control your emotions because you have such a loving heart. You can't bear the people's suffering. You're not attached to them. You don't know them, you've never seen them before, and the moment you leave the situation, you will forget it. But you have a loving heart and so you can't stand to see people in pain. We have got to develop that type of love for one another.

499 Maharaj Ji, recently a distant relative in my family died of cancer. Her death was anticipated for many months, and she was very peaceful and gracious to her guests who came to visit until her last moment. But still, when I heard of her death, I wept. I was shocked that I should be so distraught, when the master always tells us that this is a play and that we should let people go peacefully. I don't understand why I should have been so upset.

Your weeping doesn't mean that you were attached to that person. Sometimes hearts are very kind, very loving, very soft. They cannot bear to see people miserable. Say, for example, you are driving, and you see a dog hit by a bus. Some people might stop their car and start weeping. It's not that they're attached to the dog – they've never even seen the dog before. But their heart is so soft and kind that they cannot see anybody in misery, anybody suffering. That doesn't mean that they were attached to the dog.

Actually, a satsangi's heart should be like that. We have a wrong concept if we think that our heart should not be soft. It should be very, very soft. Even if our enemy is suffering, there should be tears in our eyes. That doesn't mean we are attached to the person. That means we are so loving and kind and helpful to people that we cannot bear to see anybody suffering in this creation. This is not attachment. We think that if a tear comes when someone dies that perhaps we are attached to the person. We are not attached to the person. Say your neighbour dies and you see people weeping and crying – you automatically become soft to see them miserable. You never even knew the person who has died. But you see other people in tears, so your eyes become moist. You become very emotional. That doesn't mean that you are attached to the person. It's just that your heart is so soft and kind that you don't want to see anybody suffer. That should be the heart of a satsangi.

*500 Can you explain how one can feel sympathy or compassion
for other people without getting involved in their pain?*

If you have a kind heart, a loving heart, you are kind to everybody, you are loving to everybody, you are helpful to everybody.
When you are kind and loving and helpful to everybody, you're
not attached to any particular person – this has become your
nature. We have to develop that. It happens automatically if we
are filled with love and devotion for the Father. Then all such
qualities come like cream on milk. You don't have to strive for
them; they become part and parcel of you, because then you
see the Lord in everyone. You are humble before everyone, loving to everyone, because then what you see is the Lord – not a
particular person, but the Lord who is residing in everyone.

*501 Master, would you explain how we can love people with-
out being attached to them?*

You see, to have a loving heart is something very different from
being attached to somebody. An attachment more or less becomes
an obsession with you. You're always haunted by the memory of
a person, and then you are with him so much that you don't live
with yourself – you're always there, not within your own self. But
to have a loving nature is something very different. Then you love
everybody. To have a loving nature or to love everybody, practically speaking, means not to love anybody at all; it is to love that
being which is in everybody, and that is the Lord. So you are kind,
you are compassionate, you are noble and loving to everyone you
meet, because you love the Lord and so you love his creation – you
love the One who is in every one of us. You're not attached to
anybody in particular. But if you concentrate on one particular
person or two particular persons, and you are obsessed with their
memory and you cannot remain away from them – you're always
haunted by that relationship – that is attachment.

502 *How can people be detached and yet still be very loving?*
I find that advanced satsangis are very loving people.

You see, 'loving' means having a loving nature. They are loving
toward everybody. Their love does not run in a narrow channel
to one person. To love somebody is different from being loving
toward everybody. We should have a kind and loving nature and
try to be helpful to others, good and kind, loving to everybody.
Actually, when you love everybody, you don't love the individuals, you love the Lord who is in everybody. When you are filled
with love and devotion for the Father, you also develop a loving attitude towards his creation, even birds and animals. You
develop a loving and compassionate nature. Love is something
different when there is attachment in it. In a loving and sweet
nature, there is no attachment at all.

503 *Master, in regard to mental attitude, should a disciple*
maintain a disciplined, warrior-like attitude with no
emotions when confronting events in life, or should we
be less like a warrior and have a loving, compassionate,
understanding attitude?

Brother, we should have a very loving heart, very compassionate
heart, very kind heart. Even if our enemy is in trouble, there
should be tears in our eyes. We should be so compassionate, so
loving and so kind.

504 *In the last discourse that Professor gave, the saint whose*
poem he read said something like: If the disciple is not
moved with compassion by the suffering and misery of
others, he has a heart of stone and is not fit to be a dis-
ciple of the master. It's always been my impression, from
reading the books, that the saints have always said that

*this world has always been a place of suffering and mis-
ery and always will be, and that the disciple's job was to
rise above it and get out of the prison, once and for all.*

The statements are not contradictory. What Professor meant is
that our heart should be very kind, very compassionate, very
considerate of others' problems, others' miseries. But it doesn't
mean that you will be able to change the fate of this world. Even
by your becoming so compassionate, kind, loving and understanding, you cannot make this world a place of paradise. People
will still go through their destiny. But you should be very kind
and loving; your heart should be very, very kind and affectionate, and you should be helpful to others. There's absolutely no
contradiction about it.

It doesn't mean that satsangis are not bothered about what
is going on around them in this creation, and that they should
be self-centred and let people suffer right under their nose. That
is a wrong attitude. If we can do anything to help anybody, we
should. That is our duty – we are meant to help each other.
Humans are meant to help humans. Who else will help? Birds
and plants won't come to help you – you have to help each other.
We should be a source of strength to each other, but we should
not be so involved with the suffering of another person that we
ourselves suffer, that we ourselves become miserable. We must
be strong enough so as not to be affected by other people's misery
and suffering; but we have to be very, very helpful to them, very
kind and compassionate to them, to their problems.

Soami Ji says that your heart should be very, very soft to
other people and you should be very compassionate, very kind.*
You see, these qualities automatically come in you when you are
filled with the love and devotion for the Father, because then you

---

* *Komal chit daya man dharo.* Sar Bachan, p. 163.

see the Father in everybody. You are not attached to them, but you have a compassionate heart for people – a loving heart, a kind and helpful heart for people. It doesn't mean you are attached to them. You try to do your best to help them, but still you are not attached to anyone, because you see the Father in everyone.

505 *Master, if a satsangi has reached the level of being where he is attached to his master within, would he then begin to see the master in other people, to see the soul in them rather than the ego?*

He would see the love of his master in everybody. Seeing the master doesn't mean that a person sees the physical form of the master in everybody. He will see that love and devotion of the master in everybody.

You see, loving all is loving none – being attached to none. Attachment is created only when we channelize our emotions. Our emotions are channelled or grooved in a certain direction, which then takes the form of attachment. Otherwise, if you have a loving nature, compassionate nature, kind nature, that doesn't mean you are in love with everybody.

LOVE IS A GIFT FROM THE LORD

506 *Could you speak a little bit about love?*

Love? Well, if there's love, there is nothing to speak about, and if you speak, there is no love. Love loses its depth when you try to express it. The more you digest it, the more it grows. It is more to experience than to express. What do you want to know about love?

You see, love has two aspects. It raises our soul upwards; then passion pulls us down. So we are more concerned with the devotional part of love. Love means to lose your own identity, to become another being, to merge into another one, to do which pleases the other person and not to do anything which displeases the other person. That is love. The soul by instinct is in love with the Father. The tendency of the soul is always towards its own origin. It is full of love and devotion for the Father, but it is just helpless due to the mind. The mind has a weakness for the senses, so it has become a slave of the senses. There is such a great load on the soul that its love is just crushed under that weight.

The soul cannot help but love its own origin. So we have to lift the weight of the senses, of the mind, of karmas or sins, before we can experience that love. And we feel real love when we go beyond the realm of mind and maya, when there are no coverings on the soul, when the soul shines, when it knows itself. Then it experiences the real love for its own Father, for its own origin. Love has the quality of merging into another being, becoming another being. Ultimately, we lose our own identity and individuality and become one with the Father. And that is why we say that love is God and God is love.

The more love you give, the more it grows. It is something which doesn't decrease by sharing. All other things decrease if you share them, but this is something within us which always grows and grows, the more and more we give. And the only way to experience that love is to withdraw it from the senses by simran and dhyan and attach it to the divine melody within. Because the mind is fond of pleasures, when it gets a better pleasure than the sensual pleasures, it automatically leaves the sensual pleasures. So the more the mind is attached to shabd and nam within, the more the soul starts shining within – what we call a higher consciousness. That is our concept of love.

507 *In* Sar Bachan, Soami Ji *says, "If there be a bhakta with*
enough love and devotion, the testimony of the Lord can
be given. Nobody has enough love. What you are doing is
just imitation. But don't worry; such is the will this time,
the mauj." Can you say something about that part of the
disciple which is not imitation?

You see, Soami Ji is talking about a higher type of love. The
higher we go in the inner regions, the more we feel the depth
of the love. Now, at this level, we think we are absolutely filled
with love. But when we reach to that level of love, then we realize how insignificant our love was.

You see, the soul is always yearning towards the Lord. It
wants to become one with the Father; it is full of love for the
Lord. It is only the weight of the mind that makes it helpless.
The inclination of the soul is always towards its origin. But the
weight of the mind keeps it tied down to the creation. When
you go on lifting the weight, the soul will become lighter and
lighter. It will be filled with more and more love, more love,
more love, more love. The love starts growing, to the extent that
we become one with him. That is the higher type of love that
Soami Ji is talking about. But when the soul is dominated by
the mind, we just have emotion.

When there is no cover over an electric bulb, there is automatically so much light; but if we have many wrappings around
it, we don't see the light. If we start removing the wrappings, rays
of light start penetrating through the wrapping that remains.
So some sort of light is coming from the bulb. The more wrappings you remove, the brighter the light becomes. The light is
increasing and increasing and increasing, the more we remove
the wrappings.

That is how our love starts growing. The more time we
give to meditation, the more our love grows. And it grows

until we become one with the Lord. That is what Soami Ji is talking about.

508 *When we talk about loving our neighbours, loving God and loving ourselves, is that love also situated behind the eyes? Or is the heart chakra also the vital place where we should direct our attention?*

Sister, real love you only feel for the Father when you are able to withdraw your attention from the nine apertures of the body up to the eye centre, which is the spiritual heart centre, and become attached to the spirit or the voice of God within. Then you are actually on the path. The more you are on the path, the more love and devotion you will feel for the Father. The real love you will only feel when you are behind the eye centre, when you are one with the light, when you are one with the sound or spirit within. That creates devotion in us. That pulls us towards our destination. And the nearer we are to our destination, the more we are filled with the love and devotion for the Father.

509 *Maharaj Ji, speak to us about love.*

Love is to become another being, to lose your own identity, to lose your own individuality, to do something which pleases another person, to avoid doing which displeases another person. The ego has to be eliminated. Only then do you become another being, which is real love. Meditation creates love, it strengthens love, and by it love grows. The more you give, the more it grows. It grows to such an extent that we become one with the Father. That is love.

There's no other love in the world – the rest is all self-deception. Nobody belongs to us and we don't belong to anybody.

For some time we live in illusion, but soon we realize where we stand. Real love can only be for the Father. The pity is that what we see, we are not supposed to love, and what we don't see, we are supposed to love. What we see doesn't exist, what we don't see really exists, and that is the whole tragedy of our love. So we have to love him whom we don't see at all and who is everywhere. All that we see will perish; nothing of it is real.

510 What has the love of your neighbour to do with the love of God?

As you know, Christ gave us two commandments, the first being, thou shalt love the Lord thy God with all thy heart and with all thy soul and with all thy mind. This means you should be filled completely with his love. Every particle of your being should be in love with the Lord. And the second commandment was, thou shalt love thy neighbour as thyself.[67] The second commandment you can follow only if you have followed the first commandment. If you do not love the Father, it is not possible for you to love your neighbour. To love our neighbour means to love the Lord who is in every one of us. Then we see only the Lord and nothing else in this world. My 'neighbour' does not mean only the one who resides next to my house. Everyone is my neighbour. If I am living in a house, the next house is my neighbour. If I am living in one city, the next city is my neighbour. If I am living in one country, the next country is my neighbour. And if I am living on one continent, the other continents are my neighbours. It means the whole universe becomes my neighbour.

To love thy neighbour means to see the Lord in everyone, everywhere. And that you can do only if you have fulfilled the first commandment. When you see the Father within yourself, then wherever you look in this world, you will see the Father. Then, when you meet people, you do not see the people but the Creator who is in them. At that stage you are not attached to one particular person, one particular neighbour, because you are attached to the only One who is everywhere and who is in everyone. That is why Indian mystics tell us that this body is the temple of the living God. It means that you have to see the Father within your own body, and when you achieve that, then you can see the Father everywhere – wherever you look you see the Father.

511 Master, does trying to love our brothers and sisters help us to develop true love for the master?

It is just the reverse. If you are in love with the master, you'll automatically be in love with your brothers and sisters. Brothers' and sisters' love will not create love for the master in you. Love for the master will create love for your other fellow human beings, because then you will see the master in every disciple. You will like them, you will have a common aim, common love, and you will strengthen each other's love. But it's not that if you love each other, you will strengthen your love for the master. It is just the reverse. If we love the Lord, we'll be all nearer to each other, because we see the Lord in everyone. But if we love one another, it doesn't mean that we love the Lord. We may be involved with each other and remain involved just at this level. But if we love the Lord, then we love all the lovers of the Lord. They all become very dear and near to us.

Now, you see, we love our own master, we love the teachings, and so we also love the teaching of other mystics because they speak the same language of love and devotion for the Father. The other mystics have left us long, long ago, but we also look to their teaching with reverence because they speak the same language. So if we love the Lord, we'll love everyone.

*512 I think the most difficult part is the fact that by the way you
talk, we shouldn't really be loving people at all – we should
be isolated all the time and concentrating. If one feels love
for other people and wants to help them, is this wrong?*

Sister, my concept of love is different. I personally feel that the
more you love the Lord, the more you love his creation, the more
you're loving and helpful and kind to this creation. The more
you love the Lord, the nearer you are to him and the nearer you
are to his creation. The more you are away from the Lord, the
more you are away from his creation. You think you love people,
but actually you are not loving humanity at all. You are loving
certain individuals – attaching yourself to certain particular
persons – not loving his whole creation at all. The nearer you
will be to the Lord, the more you will be loving to his creation.
You'll be kind to everybody, you'll be good to everybody, you'll
be helpful and loving to everybody because then you will see
the Creator in every part of the creation. Then you won't be
attached to anybody. Attaching to everybody is attaching to
none. Attaching to the One who's in everybody is attaching to
the Creator.

I feel a love for everybody; is that all right?

Yes, that's perfectly all right. You see, we will develop that mood.
It will grow if we meditate. If we are in love with the Lord, our
love for humanity also will grow. We'll become more kind and
loving to everybody all around us. I don't think love for the Lord
will create hatred for others or indifference to others – certainly
not. We become more loving and kind to others then.

*Master, is it possible to learn to love the Lord by trying to
love the creation?*

No, to think that by loving the creation we will be able to love the
Creator would be a negative approach. You may become so much

involved in the creation and its attachments that you may absolutely forget the Creator. That concept has come in many organized religions – to serve humanity, while forgetting the Lord.

To serve humanity is a good thing; you are cleaning the
vessel. But our approach is that if you love the Lord, all good
qualities come in you like cream upon milk. If you love the Lord,
you become kind, loving, generous and helpful to all humanity.
But if you eliminate the Lord and try to help the creation, then
you just involve yourself and become attached to the creation,
which does not help you love the Creator at all.

513   Shouldn't disciples show love towards each other?

Well, brother, it's not a question of just disciples or one person or
another. There should be love towards everybody. We should try
to love everybody in the world. We should try to see the Creator in
everybody. The Lord has created all of us. The Lord is within every
one of us and we should try to see that Creator in every person.
So there should be no question of hating anybody or not living in
harmony with anybody. You should be loving to everybody.

*514   Master, I find that I reach out to the world for sweetness
        from others, and yet when I do that, it turns completely
        bitter. What do you really want from me?*

Sister, the problem is that we want people to be sweet to us; we
don't believe in being sweet to other people. You'll be happy with
yourself if you're sweet to others – you will never be unhappy.
We always want people to be good to us, kind to us, loving to
us, but we should be more kind and loving and compassionate
and sweet to other people. That very attitude of ours will make
us happy. We will never feel frustrated with anybody if we adopt
this attitude.

515 Master, could you please speak to us about the value of friendship?

A friend is someone with whom you have a clear understanding, who accepts you for what you are and whom you accept for what he is. There is a clear understanding between both of you. He wants to help you; you want to help him. That is friendship. It is very rare.

516 Master, how much proof, really, does the mind need before it believes how much the master really loves us?

Sister, love needs no proof. It comes from within and it comes with conviction. No logic, no reasoning will convince you. Something within you will convince you. And if you try to analyze what has convinced you, you will not be able to find any reason for it at all. There is something within which compels you, which convinces you. And that is all his grace and pull. No logic and reasoning can convince us about anybody's love. Love doesn't need any language to convince anybody. No language is required to express it. No reasoning is required to convince yourself that you are in love – you know when you are in love. Why are you in love? You have no explanation for it.

517 Language creates problems of communication?

That is right, but love has no language. You meet somebody and you do not understand each other's language, yet you are in love with each other. Do you need to explain with words? You both understand without saying anything. That is what I always say: Words are not the only means of communication. There is some understanding, some realization which comes with the help of love.

518 Master, love is very important on the path. Who helps to develop this love? Does the initiate really have to gener- ate this love himself for the master, or will the master himself help the disciple to generate love for the master?

Brother, it is the Lord's gift. He gives it. We think that we love. Actually, he gives us his love. We think we love the Lord, but it is he who gives us his devotion and his love. He is within us. He creates that love and devotion within us so that we love him. The love comes from that side, but we have to be receptive to that love. He has given us this bliss, this joy. Nothing comes without his grace. To be frank, it is he who gives us love.

519 Master, how will we get love and devotion?

Well, sister, to be frank, love is a gift from the Lord. Unless the Lord wishes, we can never think about him. Unless he pulls us towards himself, we can never seek him. We think we are loving the Lord, we are finding the Lord. Actually, he is the one who is pulling us from within. He is the one who gives us his love. Unless he so wills, we can never even think about him. So love is a gift given to us by him, and the more we love, the more it grows. The more effort we put in, the more love we feel and the greater his grace. These will always go side by side.

520 Maharaj Ji, it seems clear that the lover needs the Beloved. Does the Beloved have any need of the lover?

Yes. Who gives the love to the lover? It is the Beloved who gives love to the lover. The lover thinks he loves the Beloved. The pull in the lover's heart comes from the Beloved always. It gives the feeling to the lover that he is in love with the Beloved. Actually it is the Beloved who has put that pull in the lover's heart. Without that need, why should the Beloved give that pull to the lover?

Why should he create the seed of love in the lover's heart? The Beloved must be needing that love.

521 Master, how can we have more love for the master?

If you live the teachings, live the way of Sant Mat, attend to your meditation and are kind to everybody, in this way, every day, you are increasing your love for the master. All this will help your love for the master to grow.

522 Master, is love a form of grace?

The love by itself is grace. When you love a master, what more grace do you want? When you develop that love for a master, that itself is grace.

523 How does one learn to love more?

Well, sister, you don't try to learn to love. You only experience love. You only enjoy love. There's no school where they teach you how to love. It just grows from within; it just comes from within. The pull just comes from within. But sometimes there are positive means that we can adopt. Satsang, the company of good satsangis, reading Sant Mat literature – these help that love to grow. But they can't create love when the seed is not there. If the seed is there, the pull is there, then these things make you more receptive to that love. But it just grows from within. You don't have to learn anything about it.

524 Master, I feel I should be able to be happy all the time in your presence, but sometimes I just feel sad in your company. I don't understand.

So many of you tell me in interviews that you don't have love. I don't understand your concept of love and how you analyze and measure it. I have never been able to understand.

If you go on analyzing love, it leads you nowhere. It is something within which we can't describe, and if we every day try to analyze ourselves – how much love I have, whether it is faded out, whether it has grown deeper roots – then that's not the type of love we need. There is nothing to think about love. Love is just there. Our problem is that we compare ourselves with each other. We think that person is probably more in love than I am and I should be like him. But nobody knows anybody at all. We should never compare ourselves to anyone at all. But for love for the Father, nobody would come to the path. The pull is there to some extent, which brings us to the path, and without that love, we would not remain on the path. So we should try not to always analyze whether our love has deepened or become less, whether it has grown or is fading. We should never try to analyze these things.

Meditation creates love, meditation helps it to grow and the more we give, the more it grows. There's no limit to its growth, so how can we compare how much love we have when there's no limit to its growth?

525 Regarding love, I would like to ask you, Master, if a child that grows up without love – has no parents and gets no love in the early years – can that person feel love at all?

Well, normally you have to receive it, but the real lover never bothers whether he receives or not. He believes only in giving, because the more you give the more it grows. It's not that the more you get the more it grows. Love is in giving, not in taking. The one whose love is always reciprocated doesn't know the depth of love at all. Only the one whose love is not reciprocated knows the depth of love.

526 *Why do we often end up hurting the ones that we love so much?*

Love is not something which you possess – love is something you give. There's more pleasure in giving than accepting, in donating than accepting a donation, in giving a gift rather than taking a gift, in serving somebody rather than being served, in forgiving somebody rather than being forgiven. There's more pleasure in loving than in being loved. Try it.

527 *I've come across the statement that on a spiritual path, one must be gentle with oneself, in the sense of not becoming negative about oneself or disliking oneself intensely. Would you comment on that?*

You see, a loving and kind heart will always be gentle. In a heart which is full with love and devotion for the Father, all such qualities will come to the surface like cream on milk. You don't have to develop these qualities – they will take possession of you automatically. You'll be kind-hearted, loving, compassionate, very soft – all these qualities will come in you automatically, when you are filled with love and devotion for the Father.

528 *Can you tell us more about love and how we can develop it in ourselves?*

The more you give love, the more it grows. The more you share it, the more you will have it in abundance. The more we share it with his creation, the more he gives us and the more we feel nearer to him.

529 *Master, can you tell us how we can increase our love for the Lord?*

The main thing is that it is in the hands of the Lord. We get love when he gives it. But when we are attending to the meditation, the love comes automatically. And when actual love comes within us, all human qualities automatically come in us like cream on milk. You do not have to fight for those human qualities to get them. They just come. Love brings everything in us. Everybody has virtues in him. But love, the real spiritual love, brings out these virtues.

The difference between spiritual love and worldly love is this: In spiritual love you are not conscious of anybody except the object of your love, except your master or the Lord. In worldly love you are always conscious of others; there is an instinct of possession, and then jealousy comes in when you are conscious of others. In spiritual love there can be no jealousy, for you have forgotten the whole world; whether it exists for you or not, you are just in him. That is the difference.

530 How does one always act as the master's agent in order to avoid creating karma? How can he force his mind to stop and think in this manner before acting?

We have to submit to his will. And that we can do only if we meditate. The master's wish is that we should be firm on the four principles, which are prerequisites before we can travel on the path. So long as we are firm on that, we have submitted ourselves to the master. Then, automatically, our mind develops to that extent that it starts submitting rather than expecting, or not adjusting to a situation.

We will submit only if we have love. Without love, we cannot submit to anybody. Love is such a thing which makes one submit. Love drives out ego from us. That love we have within ourselves; it does not come from outside; it does not come from anybody; it comes from within. And when love comes in us, all the good qualities of a human being come up, like cream in milk. All that we have to fight for with ourselves now in order to be good, to be honest, to behave rightly, to do this or that, will automatically come in us when we feel that devotion within us for the Lord. Instead of trying to train our mind to pick up good qualities, one by one, the cream of all those qualities automatically will come in us. When we are devoted to him, we are devoted to everybody. We have no ego. Then we do not want to assert; then we do not want to offend. Automatically all those good qualities are manifested in us.

A GRATEFUL HEART

531 *Isn't it true that thankfulness and gratitude to the one who has brought us to the feet of the master has an immense power to take us even beyond the realm of existence?*

You see, the Lord has given us so much in life, but we don't have that thankful heart. Instead of asking the Father to give us the boons in life, we should ask him to give us that heart which is full of gratitude for what he has given to us. We need that understanding to thank him for what he has given, but we are always protesting what he has not given. We must believe that what he has not given is not meant for us, is not good for us, is not to our advantage. And for whatever he has given us in life, we should be grateful to him, we should be thankful to him. So we need a thankful heart, a heart full of gratitude, rather than praying for worldly things or to fulfil our worldly desires.

Everything is comparative. If we look to other people and start counting all the advantages we have over them, they're numerous. And for that we should be thankful to the Father.

Lala Munshi Ram had a very beautiful prayer – I don't know whether it's printed in his diary *With the Three Masters* or not. He said: O Lord, don't give me delicious food, but give me hunger. Don't give me cars and all that, but give me strength in my legs. Don't give me a comfortable bed, but give me sleep.

All these things are so meaningful. What will you do with all the delicious food around you if you have no hunger? And what will you do with the most luxurious bed if you cannot sleep in it? And what will you do with all the cars and all that if you have no strength in your legs to walk? All these things are comparative: Richness is comparative; beauty is comparative; health is comparative. So we should thank him for what he has given us rather than protest what he has not given us.

532 *Good afternoon, Master. My question is about anger. A year ago I had my right foot amputated, and I was really angry at God and I refused to meditate because I was so angry at the Lord and felt a lot of self-pity. But I wrote you a couple times and I started meditating a little bit, twenty minutes, maybe ten minutes at a time, and the self-pity and anger disappeared. I want to know if Kal is that powerful to still overcome me, even though I am initiated by you. It's so easy to blame God for any troubles in my life when it's my own destiny. And you teach that. I know that it's my own karma, and whatever I go through is for the best, but is Kal really that powerful to still allow me to be angry at the Lord?*

Brother, there's a beautiful story in Maulana Rum's *Masnavi* that we can all take lessons from. A beggar was walking on the sand in hot summer. He was just cursing the Lord: You have so much in this creation and for a poor man like me you don't have even a pair of shoes – I have to walk barefoot. When he went across the street, he saw a man without legs and without feet, rolling through the hot summer sand. He kneeled down and prayed to the Lord: Thank God, at least you have given me legs so that I can go into the shade.

So all our worldly problems are comparative. We don't realize what he has given us, how many blessings he has showered on us. If we look around, we can see how much better off we are than thousands and thousands of people in this life. Then we have nothing else left to do but to kneel down and thank him for what he has showered on us. And even those who appear to be the chosen ones, who look to us like perhaps they are the happiest people, may not be able to sleep at night and may be more miserable than us, even though they look like they are very well off and comfortable. We make ourselves miserable unnecessarily. We should try not to compare ourselves with others and then curse God. He has showered so many benefits on us that we have no tongue with which to thank him. When we look around in the world, we can see what misery people have to face. Go to the starving countries, the poor countries, the hospitals, the mental asylums. Then we know how much grace the Lord has showered on us and whether we should curse him or thank him.

533 *Something awful and frightening happened to me and some friends a few months ago, and we all came out of it safely, so we all sat down and wrote to our master and thanked him for looking after us. Was that our ego doing that?*

There is no ego in thanking the Lord for anything we go through in life. Actually, we have no words with which to thank him – we cannot thank him at all with this tongue, whatever the Lord or the master does for us in this life. We owe our very existence, all these privileges, just to the Father. This very human birth is nothing but his grace. So at every step we must thank him. We must find every excuse to thank him. There's no harm in it. After all, we take our master as a representative of the Father, as being one with the Father. Actually, we are passing on our thanks to the Father through the master.

534 What should be our approach to meditation?

Our approach to meditation should be of that of gratitude. The Lord has given us the opportunity of this human form and then the environment in which to attend to meditation. So we should always approach meditation with gratitude.

535 I have no specific question I want to ask you. I just want to thank you for your love.

To love is nothing but giving thanks. It is all his grace that he gives us his love, he gives us his devotion, and our words are too inadequate to express that feeling, that depth, that gratefulness to the Father. It is impossible.

A MIRACLE AT EVERY STEP

536 Master, it is said that a perfect saint does not perform miracles, so how can we believe in the miracles that Christ performed?

You see, I've said so many times, the purpose of the mystics is not to come here to perform any miracles. But miracles do happen in the lifetime of practically every mystic because they are very compassionate, kind-hearted, very soft-hearted. So miracles do happen in their lives. But performing miracles or attracting people by miracles is not their purpose of coming to this world. And a real miracle is something individual between the disciple and the master. It is not a public demonstration. Every disciple has an individual relationship with the master, and for him there may be many miracles. Sometimes they are exaggerated also.

Christ's miracles may have been exaggerated after some time, or may have been changed. Because if you read in sequence the whole Sermon on the Mount, first Saint Matthew explains that people from Jordan, Galilee, Syria and so many other places came to Christ for the purpose of getting healed. The sick came, lepers came. And Matthew says that, seeing the multitude, Christ went to the top of a hill and spoke, giving the people teachings.[7] He didn't perform miracles. Those people no doubt must have come to him just for miracles, for getting healed, for getting worldly boons and favours, but it was not Christ's mission to collect them for that purpose. And also somewhere in the Bible you will read that he healed somebody but told him to go and tell no one, and give your alms at the altar in the synagogue, so that those people may not say that I'm performing miracles. He said, don't tell anybody.[19] He didn't want to give any public demonstration of miracles.

He may have performed a few miracles but that is not the purpose of mystics coming to this world. Their real miracle is to change our very attitude of life, to detach us from this creation and attach us to the Creator. That is the greatest miracle they can perform. Our whole attitude and approach to life changes. Things for which we used to take credit and boast about, we feel ashamed of doing when we come into their company. As Christ said, I have come to make people blind, and give eyes to those who do not see.[103] That is the miracle mystics come to perform. Those who see only the world, see only the creation, are attached only to the creation – I have come to make them blind, meaning I have come to detach them from this creation. And I want to give them those eyes which see only the Father. I have not come to give eyes just to see the creation – but to those who are blind to the Father, who don't see the Father, I've come to give them eyes.

So these are not worldly miracles, they are spiritual miracles. We are awakened from deep slumber by the mystics – that is the miracle they perform. Healing a leper or sick person is no miracle – doctors do it every day. Mystics come to give their teachings, to change our attitude and approach to life. Their main purpose is to detach us from this creation and to attach us to the Creator. That is the miracle they perform. And this miracle is individual with every disciple. He feels that miracle within himself. It's not for any public demonstration.

537 Maharaj Ji, sometimes in our lives it appears that miracles occur, such as even being able to have the opportunity to be here with you. Do these things happen by our own faith, or is the master actively involved in them?

Well, brother, in our life, there's a miracle at every step. These are individual experiences, personal experiences; they have to be digested within ourselves. Call it a miracle, call it coincidence, call it our personal treasure, something which is very valuable to us, to which we give great significance. Give it any shape, any name. It's just a way of explaining. We actually do not know whether this was to happen with us or not. We can call it a miracle if we know our destiny, that this was not to happen with us and it has happened. When we are not in a position to know whether something was to happen, how can we say it is a miracle? Perhaps it was to happen in this very way. So these are just comparative words.

I don't think mystics come to perform miracles. To us, they may look like miracles. They may impress us, they may convince us – this may be a very strong means to pull us to the path – yet there may be no miracle at all. These events may be part of our destiny, part of how the Lord brings us to the path. Who are we to know whether something is a miracle or not? I am not conscious what my destiny is, so how can I know if something is a miracle? If I know both sides of a picture, both sides of a coin, only then can I know.

538 *I've been troubled reading Dr Johnson's book* The Path of the Masters, *where he gives criteria for knowing a true master. According to those criteria, Buddha and Christ would be disqualified because Christ performed some miracles and Buddha begged for a living.*

What Dr Johnson meant to say is that the purpose of saints is not to perform miracles. They come for a much higher purpose in this world.

Supposing you perform a miracle that you can fly in the air. Then what? Airplanes fly in the air every day. Or you take a pebble and turn it into a gold coin – then what? Treasuries are filled with gold coins. What is the use to the public of these tricks?

The real miracle of the mystics is that our whole outlook on life is changed, from downward and outward to inward and upward. Our mind doesn't run to the sensual pleasures now, we are yearning to be in touch with the divine bliss and we want to be filled with his love and devotion. That is the greatest miracle a mystic can perform – to change our whole attitude to life. Our concept of life, the whole purpose of our life, is changed. Otherwise, these miracles are just jugglery tricks.

But I don't say that saints don't perform miracles. They do happen in their lifetime because they are generally soft-hearted, very kind-hearted. If anybody comes to them with their woes, distress and miseries, they are very soft and kind, so sometimes it happens that their requests are granted, conceded. So you can call them miracles. For a satsangi, every day is a miracle; every step in life is a miracle for him.

539 *Master, it seems like a lot of little miracles happen in a disciple's life.*

What more important miracle can come in a disciple's life than that his whole attitude to life is changed? What is more of a miracle than that? His whole attitude of life changes. He becomes blind to the world and opens his eyes towards his home. First he was dead; now he's alive. What better miracle can there be than that?

People who were running after worldly things and worldly desires don't want to look at them anymore, don't want to see them and they have no time to talk to anybody. Day and night they are filled with love and devotion for the Father. What more of a miracle can a disciple have than this? His whole approach to life changes. Where people weep and cry, a disciple becomes happy. That is a miracle, which comes into every person's life when he comes to the path.

And some things happen also, just to convince a disciple to remain on the path. That is a miracle. If anything happens in anybody's life, he shouldn't broadcast it. He should digest those things within himself because that is his own personal experience. That's a personal miracle for him, a personal advantage from the master or the Lord. He must digest all that within, not broadcast it. At every step in a disciple's life, there is a miracle.

540 *Somebody once asked if it's possible for a satsangi to go inside in say, fifteen years, if it had been predestined for*

her to go inside in twenty years, and you said yes. Would
that be a miracle?

How do we know that it was not in her destiny to happen in that
way? How can we attribute it to a miracle? It may have been in
the destiny of that person to happen that way.

You see, we like to attribute everything to our love, because
we love so much. But the real definition of a miracle is that
which happens in spite of our destiny. If it is my destiny to be
cured and I am cured, well, I would like to thank my master,
but how can I call it a miracle? Miracles happen with satsangis
at every step in their lives. They're all individual miracles. A
miracle is something that happens within, not outside. How
our karmas are being taken care of, what we are supposed to
pay and how much remission we get – these are the miracles of
the mystics. Miracles are not that I was not supposed to have
a child and now I'm having a child. It may be in my destiny to
have a child after twenty years rather than just after marriage.
We call it a miracle because the person was craving a child for
nineteen years, but actually it may not be a miracle. A miracle
is the remission of our karmas – how much remission we get
inside, what help we get in meditation, what help we get to go
through our karmas in this life so that we are not affected by
the worst karmas which we have to face. These are the miracles
of the master. He gives us strength to face those karmas, so
they are just pinpricks for us now. When once we were wailing
and weeping and feeling miserable, now we just laugh. These
are the miracles.

What is already in our destiny, we can't call it a miracle.
But we love our master so much that anything that happens
to our liking, we call it a miracle. You can take it that way but
actually it's not a miracle. My concept of a miracle is something
very different.

Our concept of grace is also very different. Whatever happens to our liking, we say it is the grace of the master. Whatever happens that's not to our liking, we say it is not the grace of the master. But what doesn't happen to our liking may be the best grace of the master. That may turn our mind to meditation. Anything which pulls us towards meditation, that is the grace of the master. That which pulls us away from meditation, that's not the grace of the master. If I win a lottery, I say it's master's grace. But it may pull me back to this creation again. That money may pull me to the senses, to the attachments of the world. The grace of the master may be that I'm deprived of all that, and I am just pulled towards the Father and I give myself to meditation. We say that worldly fame, worldly profits, worldly achievements are the grace of the master. But those things may pull us back to the creation. Grace is only that which pulls us back from this creation and takes us back to the Father. What brings us back to the creation is not grace but condemnation, because that keeps us away from him.

The Lord knows best how to turn us away from the creation and how to create love for himself. That's his grace – detaching us from the creation and attaching us to the Father. Anything which makes us blind to the world and opens our eyes to his love and devotion is his grace. But we don't want that type of grace at all. We are so much in love with worldly things that when we get them, we feel that is the grace of the master. He has given me a good wife, a beautiful car, a beautiful house and so many friends, and we take these things as his grace. But those things may be pulling you back from your path, pulling you back from the Father.

So grace can be very bitter. Sometimes the medicine is very bitter, but it may be sugar-coated. It may be essential for the patient to take that bitter medicine. At the most, the doctor will sugar-coat it. So similarly, the master will give us strength to face that situation. So his grace is not always what we think.

TRUE AND ETERNAL HAPPINESS

541 *Master the word 'happiness' is sometimes defined as inner peace or calm or contentment. Is that what the masters mean when they say we should be happy?*

Happiness means perpetual happiness, perpetual bliss and peace within, not short-lived happiness or so-called sensual pleasures – those have terrible reactions. Happiness means that happiness which has no reverse reaction afterwards. That is perpetual peace and happiness.

542 *Does that mean you cannot be happy until you reach Sach Khand?*

We can be happy only when we go back and merge into the Father. We can be happy only when we are on the path to our home. The nearer we are to him, the happier we are becoming every day. The real happiness will come only when you merge back into him after meeting him face to face. When you are coming towards your home from a long distance, as you get nearer to your home you begin to have a little more sense of security within you. A sense of happiness starts coming within you as you come nearer, and a feeling that you will soon be there. When you see your home from a distance, you are happy that you have seen it, yet you are still away from your house. The actual peace you will get only when you enter your house, when you are in your home. Similarly, the nearer we are to the Lord, the nearer we are to our destination, the more contentment we feel within; the more bliss, the more peace, the more happiness we feel within. The true and eternal happiness, bliss, peace and contentment we can feel only when the soul is merged back into the Lord.

543 *This has always bothered me: How do we know that by reaching Sahansdal Kamal, by reaching Trikuti, by reaching Sach Khand, we are ascending? Everybody talks about going up, but how do we know we are going up?*

You feel it within. You sense it intuitively, and gradually you know. When you see a map of the country between here and New York, you are given all the information as to what you are going to see on the way, and when you are driving on that freeway and seeing all those things, how do you know that you are going to New York? When you see those signs on the way, the milestones and the scenery, they confirm that the path is right and that New York is only a few miles farther. You know that you are on the way to New York. Similarly, when all the saints explain to us that we will see so and so on our way up, and we see those things on the way, we feel we are going up. Besides, you yourself will know that you are going up. You have a certain bliss, certain contentment, certain happiness in those situations. You feel a certain joy and you dance within yourself in happiness. When you are on those planes, you radiate happiness. When you are going down, you know how miserable you feel. So, naturally, when you are away from such situations you can also feel or know if you are going up.

544 *Do I understand from what has been said that we cannot actually reach happiness or heaven on this earth in*

our present form and that actually our soul has to reach a higher plane in some other form before we can really have happiness?

No, brother. What I am trying to explain is that as long as our attention is rooted in this world, we will never be able to get happiness. Even if we achieve all the comforts of the world, we cannot be happy. We will be really happy only when the soul merges back into the Father. As long as the soul is separated from the Lord, it can never be happy.

For example, a child takes his father's hand and goes to see a fair. He's very happy, he's dancing. He thinks he is getting happiness from the fair. But if he loses his father's hand and becomes lost in the crowd, the child weeps and cries. The whole fair was a source of amusement and happiness to the child. But then he realizes that he was only getting happiness from the fair as long as he was holding his father's hand. The moment he lets go of the hand of his father, that whole fair becomes miserable, a place of agony for him.

We will get peace while in this world only when we are really devoted to the Lord within us. When we are working our way up, we are in tune with him, and we will also get happiness in this world. If we forget him, this whole world becomes a place of agony and misery for us. We will get happiness only in his devotion. If we forget him, we cannot get happiness from this world at all.

545 *I'm looking for a way to be happy, Master. How can I be content in life if I can't feel that whatever I may do, such as mistakes I'm making, are taking me closer to my goal?*

When you are happy within yourself you will radiate happiness everywhere. First we must obtain that peace within ourselves. Then our whole approach to life becomes happy. We will approach our daily activities in a happy mood if we obtain peace within ourselves. If we are at war with ourselves, then we are miserable within, no matter how much you try to show the world a happy face. You can't become happy by acting happy. Happiness must come from within.

We become happy by accepting what the Lord gives us, being content with what we have and by attending to meditation. You see, the more our mind is scattered in this creation, the more unhappy we are. The more our mind is one-pointed at the eye centre, the happier we are. The more it is scattered outside, the more unhappy we are. So we have to see that our mind doesn't scatter out into the world. The more it is concentrated at the eye centre, the more happiness and bliss you will feel. No matter what situation you are going through, you will feel that bliss and happiness within yourself.

546 *Maharaj Ji, you have said that Sardar Bahadur [Maharaj Jagat Singh] always lived at the eye centre, and I wondered if you could comment on this. I guess a satsangi can reach the stage where he is always at the eye centre, even when he's walking around during the day?*

What is meant by being at the eye centre? It means you don't let your mind scatter into the world at all. You don't lose your balance. Your mind is absolutely still, and you're always contented and feel happiness, and radiate happiness. That will be the effect of stilling the mind – you're always happy, nothing bothers you.

547 *When I'm not with you, I'm not very happy. What should I do about that?*

So why not always remain in the presence of the master? Be where the master is always there with you. Be in his presence always and always remain happy. We must bring ourselves to that level where we can always be with our master. Naturally if that gives you happiness, you'll remain happy. You know the way, you know the path, you know the route, you know the destination, so you have to work for it. Happiness comes from within, it doesn't come from anywhere outside at all. Happiness is always within. We have to help it to grow, grow, and grow from within, by meditation.

548 *Maharaj Ji, somebody suggested that we are all trapped into having to be happy. Could you please explain what that means – to be happy?*

Say a person who is mute eats sweets and you ask him: "What is the taste of that sweet?" What is he going to say? He cannot explain. You can't explain happiness. Happiness always radiates from your face, from your thoughts. If you are happy, you will radiate happiness. You will make other people happy. You will make your surroundings happy. But if you are asked to explain what happiness is, I don't think you can explain it. You can't explain why you are happy and how you are happy. It just reflects on your face, in your activities.

And we can be happy only when we are nearer to our source. The soul can be happy, really happy, only when it is nearer to its own source. In separation nobody is happy. In separation we are always miserable. In union we are happy. You can't explain the joy of that union. Many mystics have described it in their own way. They say to taste that joy is to believe it.

Sometimes, without any rhyme or reason, you suddenly feel you are very happy. And if you try to analyze what has given you that feeling of happiness – what especially you have gained at this moment which you were lacking a few minutes ago – I don't think you will be able to find out or explain it to yourself. When we cannot explain to our own self what happiness is, where it comes from, how it comes, how can we explain to others? We are just happy, we are just happy. That's all.

EPILOGUE

549 Is it true that a truly repentant sinner can't have a sense of humour?

I think a sense of humour is a God-given gift. He may give it to a sinner, or he may give to a pious man – that is for him to decide.

If the person recognizes that he is full of sin, wouldn't it mean that he couldn't laugh?

If the weight of his guilt is always on his conscience, then of course it may be difficult for him to laugh. But a man who is always happy within is always happy everywhere.

I sometimes wonder how we can laugh.

Then try to learn how to laugh. You must relax from within. When there is a weight on your conscience, when something is always weighing on your heart within, you can't laugh, you can't relax. You can only be humorous when you're relaxed within. If you are miserable within yourself, you can't smile and relax and be humorous.

Is the negative power frightened of laughter?

No, people go to merrymaking every day and they have so much good laughter and everything, and that is nothing but the negative power. The negative power is very happy at the laughter.

Is it desirable to be humorous? What does it mean to be humorous? Is it like a joke?

No, I'll tell you. It's not a joke. Everybody wants to be happy in this world. When you have happiness within, you want to share it with others. And that is humour, nothing else. Humour doesn't mean taunting anybody or making a fool of yourself. You see, enjoying a joke means that you enjoy it and the other person also enjoys it. You can't enjoy a joke at the cost of another person; that is no humour at all. That is taunting or ridiculing another person, which is wrong. Humour means the other person enjoys as much as you enjoy. And when you are happy within, you can't help radiating happiness and sharing it with others. You go to a miserable person, he'll make you miserable. You go to a happy person, he will automatically make you happy. He will relax you in two minutes.

Is humour a part of happiness?

Personally, I think it's a part of happiness. It may be otherwise with others, I don't know. Because you can't have calculated humour. You can't just enjoy a joke or be happy or relaxed if guilt is weighing on your conscience, if you are always suppressing something within you. You can hardly even smile. When you are light within, you like to be light everywhere.

Meditation leads to seriousness.

Seriousness in what way? Doesn't it lead to happiness?

It's withdrawing the mind from everything that is frivolous, everything that is worldly.

No, I don't agree. If meditation makes you sad and morose and miserable-looking, I don't think that is what meditation means. Meditation should make you absolutely light. Christ said, blessed are the peacemakers.[10] Peacemakers aren't those who go running about trying to create peace between warring countries. They are not peacemakers. Peacemakers are those who have attained peace within themselves and are sharing peace with others. Mystics are the peacemakers. If you have bliss and peace within, then naturally you will radiate peace and bliss anywhere you go. Seriousness means you see that you are not taking life very lightly. You are serious about your destination, your path, your principles – of course you are serious about them. But if you are happy and travelling on the road, you are travelling happily. Another person on the same road travels weepingly. Whom do you prefer?

But if one wants to meditate, he has to talk less, sleep less, enjoy things less, have less social company.

That is different. I'm not saying that you become happier by enjoying the sensual pleasures. You won't get happy that way, you'll become more miserable. That is no happiness, that is no bliss. It is in their nature that those things make you miserable.

So perpetual happiness is very different from this worldly happiness?

Certainly, certainly. You see, you have a servant in the house who may not even talk to you, but is always looking relaxed, smiling while moving about. You always like him. Another person is always looking miserable. He may be working harder, but when you see the misery on his face, you just shudder. Whom do you like better? We are all servants of the Father – whom would he like? He is pleased by the grateful person, the person who is happy to be his child.

If we are to be happy all the time, when do we get time for separation and longing?

This happiness will not come until there's union within, when you have attained peace and bliss within. It is not something that you can calculate, that you can manipulate. It comes naturally.

> *Maharaj Ji, even if we haven't attained union within, and we feel the separation, isn't it good for us to show joy for being initiated? To be thankful?*

Christ said that the bridegroom is happy because he has the bride. Friends of the bridegroom are also happy, not because they have the bride but because their friend has the bride. They are happy to see him happy.[81] They love him so much, so they enjoy his happiness, they share his happiness. It makes them happy to see their friend happy. The master is happy because he has the bride. People who come in his company automatically become happy because the bridegroom has the bride. That is why Christ said, blessed are the peacemakers, because they radiate peace.

> *You've been talking about calculating – I've never heard this on any tapes or in any writings before – and I think I do a lot of this calculating. Could you speak more about calculating? What do you mean? Trying to reach certain states through the intellect?*

Trying to intellectually act. For example, you say: I'd like to be happy today, I'm going to smile today – no matter how miserable you may be within.

> *It is never good to do that?*

No, and even if you try you can't succeed. If you are miserable within, your face will reflect that, your face will betray your feelings. I mean, we try to give smiling looks sometimes to people when we are miserable within. But our looks betray us. And people who are happy – even if they don't say a word – their face betrays that they are happy, howsoever they try to become serious. This is a certain expression which you can't conceal.

And master's always happy, even when we think he is unhappy with us?

That's what you want the master to feel?

Well, I don't want you to be unhappy.

I think after discussing happiness we shouldn't discuss anything else.

INDEX TO BIBLE QUOTES

According to the King James Version of the Bible

10   **Matthew 5:9** Blessed are the peacemakers: for they shall be called the children of God. [*i*.395, *i*.493, *iii*.417]

11   **Matthew 5:14** Ye are the light of the world. A city that is set on an hill cannot be hid. **15** Neither do men light a candle, and put it under a bushel, but on a candlestick; and it giveth light unto all that are in the house. **16** Let your light so shine before men, that they may see your good works, and glorify your Father which is in heaven. [*i*.381]

12   **Matthew 5:17** Think not that I am come to destroy the law, or the prophets: I am not come to destroy, but to fulfil. [*i*.322]

13   **Matthew 5:18** For verily I say unto you, Till heaven and earth pass, one jot or one tittle shall in no wise pass from the law, till all be fulfilled. [*i*.308]

14   **Matthew 5:21** Ye have heard that it was said by them of old time, Thou shalt not kill; and whosoever shall kill shall be in danger of the judgment: ... [*ii*.59]

15   **Matthew 5:23** Therefore if thou bring thy gift to the altar, and there rememberest that thy brother hath ought against thee; **24** Leave there thy gift before the altar, and go thy way; first be reconciled to thy brother, and then come and offer thy gift. [*iii*.134, *iii*.261]

16   **Matthew 5:25** Agree with thine adversary quickly, whiles thou art in the way with him; lest at any time the adversary deliver thee to the judge, and the judge deliver thee to the officer, and thou be cast into prison. [*i*.124, *i*.399, *iii*.257]

17   **Matthew 5:28** But I say unto you, That whosoever looketh on a woman to lust after her hath committed adultery with her already in his heart. [*i*.113]

18   **Matthew 5:39** But I say unto you, That ye resist not evil: but whosoever shall smite thee on thy right cheek, turn to him the other also. [*i*.302, *i*.314, *iii*.363]

19   **Matthew 6:1** Take heed that ye do not your alms before men, to be seen of them: otherwise ye have no reward of your Father which is in heaven. **2** Therefore when thou doest thine alms, do not sound

a trumpet before thee, as the hypocrites do in the synagogues and in the streets, that they may have glory of men. Verily I say unto you, They have their reward. [*iii*.156, *iii*.403]

20   **Matthew 6:6** But thou, when thou prayest, enter into thy closet, and when thou hast shut thy door, pray to thy Father which is in secret; and thy Father which seeth in secret shall reward thee openly. **7** But when ye pray, use not vain repetitions, as the heathen do: for they think that they shall be heard for their much speaking. **8** Be not ye therefore like unto them: for your Father knoweth what things ye have need of, before ye ask him. [*ii*.134]

21   **Matthew 6:10** Thy kingdom come. Thy will be done in earth, as it is in heaven. **11** Give us this day our daily bread. **12** And forgive us our debts, As we forgive our debtors. [*i*.497, *i*.505, *ii*.437]

22   **Matthew 6:21** For where your treasure is, there will your heart be also. [*i*.275, *i*.392, *i*.490, *iii*.297, *iii*.299, *iii*.331]

23   **Matthew 6:22** The light of the body is the eye: if therefore thine eye be single, thy whole body shall be full of light. [*i*.209, *i*.239, *i*.299, *i*.309, *i*.333, *i*.388, *i*.476, *ii*.15]

24   **Matthew 6:24** No man can serve two masters: for either he will hate the one, and love the other; or else he will hold to the one, and despise the other. Ye cannot serve God and mammon. [*ii*.105, *ii*.111, *ii*.302, *iii*.10, *iii*.161, *iii*.299]

25   **Matthew 6:25** Therefore I say unto you, Take no thought for your life, what ye shall eat, or what ye shall drink; nor yet for your body, what ye shall put on. Is not the life more than meat, and the body than raiment? **26** Behold the fowls of the air: for they sow not, neither do they reap, nor gather into barns; yet your heavenly Father feedeth them. Are ye not much better than they? **27** Which of you by taking thought can add one cubit unto his stature? **28** And why take ye thought for raiment? Consider the lilies of the field, how they grow; they toil not, neither do they spin: **29** And yet I say unto you, That even Solomon in all his glory was not arrayed like one of these. **30** Wherefore, if God so clothe the grass of the field, which to day is, and to morrow is cast into the oven, shall he not much more clothe you, O ye of little faith? **31** Therefore take no thought,

saying, What shall we eat? or, What shall we drink? or, Wherewithal shall we be clothed? 32 (For after all these things do the Gentiles seek:) for your heavenly Father knoweth that ye have need of all these things. [*i*.263, *i*.380, *ii*.131, *ii*.133, *ii*.144, *ii*.451, *iii*.201]

26   **Matthew 7:1** Judge not, that ye be not judged. [*iii*.250]

27   **Matthew 7:3** And why beholdest thou the mote that is in thy brother's eye, but considerest not the beam that is in thine own eye? [*iii*.244]

28   **Matthew 7:6** Give not that which is holy unto the dogs, neither cast ye your pearls before swine, lest they trample them under their feet, and turn again and rend you. [*ii*.254]

29   **Matthew 7:7** Ask, and it shall be given you; seek, and ye shall find; knock, and it shall be opened unto you: … [*i*.288, *i*.329, *i*.476, *ii*.159]

30   **Matthew 7:11** If ye then, being evil, know how to give good gifts unto your children, how much more shall your Father which is in heaven give good things to them that ask him? [*iii*.202]

31   **Matthew 7:17** Even so every good tree bringeth forth good fruit; but a corrupt tree bringeth forth evil fruit. 18 A good tree cannot bring forth evil fruit, neither can a corrupt tree bring forth good fruit. [*i*.121]

32   **Matthew 7:21** Not every one that saith unto me, Lord, Lord, shall enter into the kingdom of heaven; but he that doeth the will of my Father which is in heaven. [*iii*.80]

33   **Matthew 10:8** Heal the sick, cleanse the lepers, raise the dead, cast out devils: freely ye have received, freely give. 9 Provide neither gold, nor silver, nor brass in your purses,… [*i*.312]

34   **Matthew 10:16** Behold, I send you forth as sheep in the midst of wolves: be ye therefore wise as serpents, and harmless as doves. [*iii*.178]

35   **Matthew 10:19** But when they deliver you up, take no thought how or what ye shall speak: for it shall be given you in that same hour what ye shall speak. 20 For it is not ye that speak, but the Spirit of your Father which speaketh in you. [*i*.317]

answered and said unto him that told him, Who is my mother? and who are my brethren? **49** And he stretched forth his hand toward his disciples, and said, Behold my mother and my brethren! **50** For whosoever shall do the will of my Father which is in heaven, the same is my brother, and sister, and mother. [*iii*.221, *iii*.280, *iii*.292, *iii*.294, *iii*.303, *iii*.306]

48   **Matthew 13:3** And he spake many things unto them in parables, saying, Behold, a sower went forth to sow. **4** And when he sowed, some seeds fell by the way side, and the fowls came and devoured them up. **5** Some fell upon stony places, where they had not much earth: and forthwith they sprung up, because they had no deepness of earth. **6** And when the sun was up, they were scorched; and because they had no root, they withered away. **7** And some fell among thorns; and the thorns sprung up, and choked them. **8** But other fell into good ground, and brought forth fruit, some an hundredfold, some sixtyfold, some thirtyfold. [*i*.424, *i*.440, *ii*.420, *ii*.421]

49   **Matthew 13:13** Therefore speak I to them in parables: because they seeing see not; and hearing they hear not, neither do they understand. [*i*.403, *i*.408, *i*.415, *ii*.370]

50   **Matthew 13:24** Another parable put he forth unto them, saying, The kingdom of heaven is likened unto a man which sowed good seed in his field. **25** But while men slept, his enemy came and sowed tares among the wheat, and went his way. **26** But when the blade was sprung up, and brought forth fruit, then appeared the tares also. **27** So the servants of the householder came and said unto him, Sir, didst not thou sow good seed in thy field? from whence then hath it tares? **28** He said unto them, An enemy hath done this. The servants said unto him, Wilt thou then that we go and gather them up? **29** But he said, Nay; lest while ye gather up the tares, ye root up also the wheat with them. **30** Let both grow together until the harvest: and in the time of harvest I will say to the reapers, Gather ye together first the tares, and bind them in bundles to burn them: but gather the wheat into my barn. [*ii*.438, *iii*.6, *iii*.121, *iii*.372]

51   **Matthew 15:4** For God commanded, saying, Honour thy father and mother: and, He that curseth father or mother, let him die the death. [*iii*.307]

52   **Matthew 15:24** But he answered and said, I am not sent but unto the lost sheep of the house of Israel. [*ii.*7]

53   **Matthew 16:23** But he turned, and said unto Peter, Get thee behind me, Satan: thou art an offence unto me: for thou savourest not the things that be of God, but those that be of men. [*i.*505]

54   **Matthew 17:12** But I say unto you, That Elias is come already, and they knew him not, but have done unto him whatsoever they listed. Likewise shall also the Son of man suffer of them. 13 Then the disciples understood that he spake unto them of John the Baptist. [*i.*467]

55   **Matthew 17:20** And Jesus said unto them, Because of your unbelief: for verily I say unto you, If ye have faith as a grain of mustard seed, ye shall say unto this mountain, Remove hence to yonder place; and it shall remove; and nothing shall be impossible unto you. [*ii.*124]

56   **Matthew 18:3** And said, Verily I say unto you, Except ye be converted, and become as little children, ye shall not enter into the kingdom of heaven. [*iii.*205]

57   **Matthew 18:12** How think ye? If a man have an hundred sheep, and one of them be gone astray, doth he not leave the ninety and nine, and goeth into the mountains, and seeketh that which is gone astray? [*i.*404, *ii.*428, *iii.*4, *iii.*6, *iii.*18, *iii.*132]

58   **Matthew 18:13** And if so be that he find it, verily I say unto you, he rejoiceth more of that sheep, than of the ninety and nine which went not astray. 14 Even so it is not the will of your Father which is in heaven, that one of these little ones should perish. [*iii.*4]

59   **Matthew 18:20** For where two or three are gathered together in my name, there am I in the midst of them. [*iii.*106, *iii.*115, *iii.*126]

60   **Matthew 18:26** The servant therefore fell down, and worshipped him, saying, Lord, have patience with me, and I will pay thee all. [*iii.*258]

61   **Matthew 19:24** And again I say unto you, It is easier for a camel to go through the eye of a needle, than for a rich man to enter into the kingdom of God. [*i.*267, *i.*392, *iii.*143, *iii.*146]

62   **Matthew 19:30** But many that are first shall be last; and the last shall be first. [*i*.97, *i*.430, *ii*.274, *ii*.350]

63   **Matthew 20:16** So the last shall be first, and the first last: for many be called, but few chosen. [*ii*.275, *ii*.421, *ii*.423]

64   **Matthew 20:28** Even as the Son of man came not to be ministered unto, but to minister, and to give his life a ransom for many. [*i*.498]

65   **Matthew 22:14** For many are called, but few are chosen. [*i*.429]

66   **Matthew 22:21** They say unto him, Caesar's. Then saith he unto them, Render therefore unto Caesar the things which are Caesar's; and unto God the things that are God's. [*i*.47, *i*.83, *i*.89, *i*.103, *i*.109, *i*.499, *iii*.225, *iii*.354]

67   **Matthew 22:36** Master, which is the great commandment in the law? **37** Jesus said unto him, Thou shalt love the Lord thy God with all thy heart, and with all thy soul, and with all thy mind. **38** This is the first and great commandment. **39** And the second is like unto it, Thou shalt love thy neighbour as thyself. **40** On these two commandments hang all the law and the prophets. [*i*.174, *i*.393, *i*.485, *ii*.58, *ii*.102, *ii*.450, *iii*.130, *iii*.261, *iii*.389]

68   **Matthew 26:42** He went away again the second time, and prayed, saying, O my Father, if this cup may not pass away from me, except I drink it, thy will be done. [*iii*.73]

69   **Mark 8:18** Having eyes, see ye not? and having ears, hear ye not? and do ye not remember? [*i*.284, *i*.289, *i*.468, *ii*.30, *ii*.206]

70   **Luke 6:48** He is like a man which built an house, and digged deep, and laid the foundation on a rock: and when the flood arose, the stream beat vehemently upon that house, and could not shake it: for it was founded upon a rock. [*ii*.397]

71   **Luke 11:21** When a strong man armed keepeth his palace, his goods are in peace: ... [*ii*.298]

72   **John 1:1** In the beginning was the Word, and the Word was with God, and the Word was God. **2** The same was in the beginning with God. **3** All things were made by him; and without him was not any thing made that was made. **4** In him was life; and the life

was the light of men. 5 And the light shineth in darkness; and the darkness comprehended it not. [*i*.27, *i*.29, *i*.116, *i*.175, *i*.178, *i*.284, *i*.298, *ii*.14, *ii*.230]

73   **John 1:6** There was a man sent from God, whose name was John. [*i*.428, *i*.443, *ii*.14]

74   **John 1:14** And the Word was made flesh, and dwelt among us, (and we beheld his glory, the glory as of the only begotten of the Father) full of grace and truth. [*i*.451, *i*.464]

75   **John 1:27** He it is, who coming after me is preferred before me, whose shoe's latchet I am not worthy to unloose. [*i*.516]

76   **John 2:16** And said unto them that sold doves, Take these things hence; make not my Father's house a house of merchandise. [*i*.315]

77   **John 3:3** Jesus answered and said unto him, Verily, verily, I say unto thee, Except a man be born again, he cannot see the kingdom of God. [*i*.309, *i*.517, *ii*.16, *ii*.23, *ii*.24, *iii*.352, *iii*.377]

78   **John 3:8** The wind bloweth where it listeth, and thou hearest the sound thereof, but canst not tell whence it cometh, and whither it goeth: so is every one that is born of the Spirit. [*i*.298, *i*.309, *i*.476]

79   **John 3:14** And as Moses lifted up the serpent in the wilderness, even so must the Son of man be lifted up: 15 That whosoever believeth in him should not perish, but have eternal life. [*ii*.234]

80   **John 3:17** For God sent not his Son into the world to condemn the world; but that the world through him might be saved. 18 He that believeth on him is not condemned: but he that believeth not is condemned already, because he hath not believed in the name of the only begotten Son of God. [*i*.428, *iii*.11, *iii*.16, *iii*.26]

81   **John 3:29** He that hath the bride is the bridegroom: but the friend of the bridegroom, which standeth and heareth him, rejoiceth greatly because of the bridegroom's voice: this my joy therefore is fulfilled. [*iii*.418]

82   **John 4:14** But whosoever drinketh of the water that I shall give him shall never thirst; but the water that I shall give him shall be in him a well of water springing up into everlasting life. [*i*.200, *iii*.151]

83 John 4:23 But the hour cometh, and now is, when the true worshippers shall worship the Father in spirit and in truth: for the Father seeketh such to worship him. [*i*.344, *ii*.24]

84 John 4:24 God is a Spirit: and they that worship him must worship him in spirit and in truth. [*i*.305]

85 John 5:14 Afterward Jesus findeth him in the temple, and said unto him, Behold, thou art made whole: sin no more, lest a worse thing come unto thee. [*i*.201, *i*.409, *ii*.22, *ii*.155]

86 John 5:25 Verily, verily, I say unto you, The hour is coming, and now is, when the dead shall hear the voice of the Son of God: and they that hear shall live. [*i*.477]

87 John 5:27 And hath given him authority to execute judgment also, because he is the Son of man. [*i*.448]

88 John 5:30 I can of mine own self do nothing: as I hear, I judge: and my judgment is just; because I seek not mine own will, but the will of the Father which hath sent me. [*i*.418, *i*.443, *ii*.348]

89 John 5:35 He was a burning and a shining light: and ye were willing for a season to rejoice in his light. [*i*.467]

90 John 6:27 Labour not for the meat which perisheth, but for that meat which endureth unto everlasting life, which the Son of man shall give unto you: for him hath God the Father sealed. [*i*.448]

91 John 6:38 For I came down from heaven, not to do mine own will, but the will of him that sent me. 39 And this is the Father's will which hath sent me, that of all which he hath given me I should lose nothing, but should raise it up again at the last day. [*i*.444]

92 John 6:40 And this is the will of him that sent me, that every one which seeth the Son, and believeth on him, may have everlasting life: and I will raise him up at the last day. [*i*.439, *i*.465, *ii*.29, *ii*.396, *iii*.34, *iii*.352]

93 John 6:44 No man can come to me, except the Father which hath sent me draw him: and I will raise him up at the last day. [*ii*.6, *ii*.10]

94 John 6:53 Then Jesus said unto them, Verily, verily, I say unto you, Except ye eat the flesh of the Son of man, and drink his blood, ye have

no life in you. 54 Whoso eateth my flesh, and drinketh my blood, hath eternal life; and I will raise him up at the last day. [*iii*.43]

95   John 6:63 It is the spirit that quickeneth; the flesh profiteth nothing: the words that I speak unto you, they are spirit, and they are life. [*iii*.46]

96   John 7:37 In the last day, that great day of the feast, Jesus stood and cried, saying, If any man thirst, let him come unto me, and drink. 38 He that believeth on me, as the scripture hath said, out of his belly shall flow rivers of living water. [*i*.329, *i*.408, *i*.416]

97   John 8:28 Then said Jesus unto them, When ye have lifted up the Son of man, then shall ye know that I am he, and that I do nothing of myself; but as my Father hath taught me, I speak these things. [*iii*.38, *iii*.40]

98   John 8:32 And ye shall know the truth, and the truth shall make you free. [*iii*.260]

99   John 8:34 Jesus answered them, Verily, verily, I say unto you, Whosoever committeth sin is the servant of sin. 35 And the servant abideth not in the house for ever: but the Son abideth ever. [*i*.151]

100   John 8:50 And I seek not mine own glory: there is one that seeketh and judgeth. [*i*.518]

101   John 9:1 And as Jesus passed by, he saw a man which was blind from his birth. 2 And his disciples asked him, saying, Master, who did sin, this man, or his parents, that he was born blind? 3 Jesus answered, Neither hath this man sinned, nor his parents: but that the works of God should be made manifest in him. [*i*.98]

102   John 9:4 I must work the works of him that sent me, while it is day: the night cometh, when no man can work. 5 As long as I am in the world, I am the light of the world. [*i*.191, *i*.466, *i*.475]

103   John 9:39 And Jesus said, For judgment I am come into this world, that they which see not might see; and that they which see might be made blind. [*i*.486, *i*.505, *iii*.403]

104   John 10:4 And when he putteth forth his own sheep, he goeth before them, and the sheep follow him: for they know his voice. [*i*.404, *i*.405, *i*.406, *i*.407, *ii*.322, *iii*.43]

116 **John 14:2** In my Father's house are many mansions: if it were not so, I would have told you. I go to prepare a place for you. [*i*.276, *i*.329, *i*.476]

117 **John 14:3** And if I go and prepare a place for you, I will come again, and receive you unto myself; that where I am, there ye may be also. [*ii*.216, *iii*.35]

118 **John 14:4** And whither I go ye know, and the way ye know. [*iii*.31, *iii*.67, *iii*.69, *iii*.72]

119 **John 14:9** Jesus saith unto him, Have I been so long time with you, and yet hast thou not known me, Philip? he that hath seen me hath seen the Father; and how sayest thou then, Shew us the Father? [*i*.464, *ii*.55]

120 **John 14:10** Believest thou not that I am in the Father, and the Father in me? The words that I speak unto you I speak not of myself: but the Father that dwelleth in me, he doeth the works. 11 Believe me that I am in the Father, and the Father in me: or else believe me for the very works' sake. [*i*.81, *i*.404, *i*.462, *i*.478, *ii*.55]

121 **John 14:16** And I will pray the Father, and he shall give you another Comforter, that he may abide with you for ever; 17 Even the Spirit of truth; whom the world cannot receive, because it seeth him not, neither knoweth him: but ye know him; for he dwelleth with you, and shall be in you. 18 I will not leave you comfortless: I will come to you. 19 Yet a little while, and the world seeth me no more; but ye see me: because I live, ye shall live also. 20 At that day ye shall know that I am in my Father, and ye in me, and I in you. 26 But the Comforter, which is the Holy Ghost, whom the Father will send in my name, he shall teach you all things, and bring all things to your remembrance, whatsoever I have said unto you. [*i*.307, *iii*.33, *iii*.69]

122 **John 14:20** At that day ye shall know that I am in my Father, and ye in me, and I in you. 21 He that hath my commandments, and keepeth them, he it is that loveth me: and he that loveth me shall be loved of my Father, and I will love him, and will manifest myself to him. 23 Jesus answered and said unto him, If a man love me, he will keep my words: and my Father will love him, and we will come unto him, and make our abode with him. [*ii*.194, *ii*.225, *ii*.231, *iii*.29, *iii*.37, *iii*.42, *iii*.44, *iii*.46, *iii*.95, *iii*.294]

123   **John 15:4** Abide in me, and I in you. As the branch cannot bear fruit of itself, except it abide in the vine; no more can ye, except ye abide in me. [*i*.474]

124   **John 15:20** Remember the word that I said unto you, The servant is not greater than his lord. If they have persecuted me, they will also persecute you; if they have kept my saying, they will keep yours also. [*iii*.248]

125   **John 15:22** If I had not come and spoken unto them, they had not had sin: but now they have no cloke for their sin. [*i*.93]

126   **John 16:7** Nevertheless I tell you the truth; It is expedient for you that I go away: for if I go not away, the Comforter will not come unto you; but if I depart, I will send him unto you. [*iii*.66, *iii*.67, *iii*.72]

127   **John 16:16** A little while, and ye shall not see me: and again, a little while, and ye shall see me, because I go to the Father. 17 Then said some of his disciples among themselves, What is this that he saith unto us, A little while, and ye shall not see me: and again, a little while, and ye shall see me: and, Because I go to the Father? 18 They said therefore, What is this that he saith, A little while? we cannot tell what he saith. 19 Now Jesus knew that they were desirous to ask him, and said unto them, Do ye enquire among yourselves of that I said, A little while, and ye shall not see me: and again, a little while, and ye shall see me? 20 Verily, verily, I say unto you, That ye shall weep and lament, but the world shall rejoice: and ye shall be sorrowful, but your sorrow shall be turned into joy. 21 A woman when she is in travail hath sorrow, because her hour is come: but as soon as she is delivered of the child, she remembereth no more the anguish, for joy that a man is born into the world. 22 And ye now therefore have sorrow: but I will see you again, and your heart shall rejoice, and your joy no man taketh from you. 23 And in that day ye shall ask me nothing. Verily, verily, I say unto you, Whatsoever ye shall ask the Father in my name, he will give it you. 24 Hitherto have ye asked nothing in my name: ask, and ye shall receive, that your joy may be full. 25 These things have I spoken unto you in proverbs: but the time cometh, when I shall no more speak unto you in proverbs, but I shall shew you plainly of the Father. [*i*.47, *i*.475, *ii*.127, *ii*.235, *iii*.59, *iii*.62, *iii*.99, *iii*.190]

128   **John 17:9** I pray for them: I pray not for the world, but for them which thou hast given me; for they are thine. [*i*.405, *i*.416, *i*.426, *i*.427, *ii*.355, *ii*.369, *ii*.371]

129   **John 17:11** And now I am no more in the world, but these are in the world, and I come to thee. Holy Father, keep through thine own name those whom thou hast given me, that they may be one, as we are. **22** And the glory which thou gavest me I have given them; that they may be one, even as we are one: **23** I in them, and thou in me, that they may be made perfect in one; and that the world may know that thou hast sent me, and hast loved them, as thou hast loved me. [*i*.110, *i*.305, *i*.405]

130   **John 20:9** For as yet they knew not the scripture, that he must rise again from the dead. [*i*.477, *i*.506]

131   **1 Corinthians 15:31** I protest by your rejoicing which I have in Christ Jesus our Lord, I die daily. [*ii*.226, *ii*.244, *ii*.245, *ii*.246, *ii*.247]

132   **2 Corinthians 6:16** And what agreement hath the temple of God with idols? for ye are the temple of the living God; as God hath said, I will dwell in them, and walk in them; and I will be their God, and they shall be my people. [*i*.174, *i*.239, *i*.329, *i*.476, *iii*.170]

133   **Galatians 6:7** Be not deceived; God is not mocked: for whatsoever a man soweth, that shall he also reap. [*i*.50, *i*.54, *i*.56, *i*.75, *i*.115, *i*.125, *i*.132, *i*.138, *i*.151, *ii*.59, *iii*.224, *iii*.260]

134   **Ephesians 1:3** Blessed be the God and Father of our Lord Jesus Christ, who hath blessed us with all spiritual blessings in heavenly places in Christ: ... [*i*.494]

135   **Ephesians 2:18** For through him we both have access by one Spirit unto the Father. [*i*.29]

136   **1 John 4:8** He that loveth not knoweth not God; for God is love. [*i*.284, *i*.461, *ii*.97]

137   **1 John 4:16** And we have known and believed the love that God hath to us. God is love; and he that dwelleth in love dwelleth in God, and God in him. [*i*.289, *ii*.102]

138   **Exodus 20 (The Ten Commandments)** 1 And God spake all these words, saying, 2 I am the LORD thy God, which have brought thee out of the land of Egypt, out of the house of bondage. 3 Thou shalt have no other gods before me. 4 Thou shalt not make unto thee any graven image, or any likeness of any thing that is in heaven above, or that is in the earth beneath, or that is in the water under the earth. 5 Thou shalt not bow down thyself to them, nor serve them: for I the LORD thy God am a jealous God, visiting the iniquity of the fathers upon the children unto the third and fourth generation of them that hate me; 6 And shewing mercy unto thousands of them that love me, and keep my commandments. 7 Thou shalt not take the name of the LORD thy God in vain; for the LORD will not hold him guiltless that taketh his name in vain. 8 Remember the sabbath day, to keep it holy. 9 Six days shalt thou labour, and do all thy work: 10 But the seventh day is the sabbath of the LORD thy God: in it thou shalt not do any work, thou, nor thy son, nor thy daughter, thy manservant, nor thy maidservant, nor thy cattle, nor thy stranger that is within thy gates: 11 For in six days the LORD made heaven and earth, the sea, and all that in them is, and rested the seventh day: wherefore the LORD blessed the sabbath day, and hallowed it. 12 Honour thy father and thy mother: that thy days may be long upon the land which the LORD thy God giveth thee. 13 Thou shalt not kill. 14 Thou shalt not commit adultery. 15 Thou shalt not steal. 16 Thou shalt not bear false witness against thy neighbour. 17 Thou shalt not covet thy neighbour's house, thou shalt not covet thy neighbour's wife, nor his manservant, nor his maidservant, nor his ox, nor his ass, nor any thing that is thy neighbour's. [*i*.448, *i*.479, *ii*.54, *ii*.58]

Subject Index

calamity. *See* karmas, types of, group
calculation, *iii*.68, *iii*.239
  in meditation, *ii*.108, *ii*.447
castes, creeds and colours
  Maharaj Charan Singh's memories
    of caste distinction, *iii*.124
  no distinctions of, *i*.289, *i*.299,
    i.322, *ii*.110, *iii*.94, *iii*.145,
    iii.150
celibacy, *ii*.92, *ii*.96
chakras
  analogy of starting at middle of
    hill, *ii*.160, *ii*.161, *ii*.163, *ii*.167,
    ii.180
Charan Singh Maharaj
  describing village life of olden
    days, *iii*.270
  his nephew becoming vegetarian,
    ii.70
  memories of caste distinction,
    iii.124
  pushed into world after love for
    master grew, *iii*.160
charity, *i*.105, *i*.382, *ii*.442, *iii*.154–58.
  See also helping others
  accepting, *iii*.184
  deception of, *i*.74, *iii*.156, *iii*.157
  expectation of reward, *iii*.183,
    iii.184, *iii*.239
chaurasi. *See* cycle of eighty-four
children, *i*.134, *iii*.320–30
  born with handicaps, *i*.98, *i*.101,
    iii.154
  born with special knowledge, *i*.138
  death of, *i*.67, *i*.72, *i*.98
  discipline of, *iii*.329
  duty towards parents, *iii*.301
  explaining Sant Mat to, *iii*.321,
    iii.323–25, *iii*.327

  influence of initiated parents,
    iii.322, *iii*.323, *iii*.325
  on vegetarian diet. *See* vegetarian
    diet, children and
  responsibility to, *ii*.282, *iii*.320,
    iii.328
  when life enters into, *i*.186
choices, *i*.118, *i*.137, *i*.412, *i*.425,
  ii.429. *See also* free will
chosen people. *See* soul(s), marked
Christ, teachings of, *i*.296, *i*.302,
  i.319, *i*.322, *i*.329, *i*.338, *i*.474
circumstances. *See* life,
  circumstances
citizens, good, *ii*.429, *iii*.180
civilization, *i*.267, *i*.376–78. *See also*
  worldly achievements
clear thinking. *See* discrimination
coincidence. *See* path, coming to
Comforter. *See* shabd
communication, *i*.376–77, *iii*.393
communion, *iii*.82
company
  good, *iii*.246
  of mystics, *i*.443
  of satsangis, *ii*.434, *iii*.116, *iii*.186
  our own, *iii*.93, *iii*.276
compassion, *iii*.289, *iii*.379–85,
  iii.397
concentration, *i*.112, *ii*.171, *ii*.173,
  ii.199, *ii*.244–45, *ii*.314, *ii*.395
  analogy of rolling stone gathers no
    moss, *ii*.269
condemnation, *i*.428
conditioned free will. *See* free will,
  limited
conflict, human. *See* creation,
  imperfections of
conscience, *i*.241, *i*.254, *ii*.399

of lust, *i.*225, *ii.*93, *iii.*168, *iii.*295
*surat, i.*298
surat shabd yoga. *See* yoga, types of
surrender, *iii.*214–21
  and idea that everything belongs
    to master, *iii.*216
  intellectual, *iii.*218
  unconditional, *iii.*153, *iii.*215,
    *iii.*216, *iii.*219

talents, *iii.*274
teachings
  arrested into religion, *i.*299–318
  commercialization of, *i.*312
  distortion of, *i.*294, *i.*296, *i.*321,
    *i.*328, *i.*338
  how masters convey, *i.*308,
    *i.*335–42, *i.*369, *i.*449, *i.*478,
    *i.*480, *i.*485, *ii.*224, *iii.*109
  in traditions, *i.*310
  meant only for marked souls, *i.*403
  not forcing on others, *ii.*51, *iii.*314,
    *iii.*318
  remain the same, *i.*308
  understanding of, *i.*408, *iii.*103
  universal, *i.*302, *i.*308, *i.*311, *i.*326
telepathy, *i.*259
temptations, inside, *i.*255
  analogy of house with five stories,
    *ii.*211
Ten Commandments, *i.*310, *i.*385,
    *i.*479, *ii.*53–54, *ii.*58
tension, *ii.*115, *ii.*116, *iii.*198.
    See also worry
thankfulness. *See* gratitude
third eye. *See* eye centre
thoughts
  controlling, *ii.*387, *ii.*389–91.
    See also simran, doing all day

spreading out, *ii.*152
throat centre, *ii.*305–10
time, lacking, *iii.*180. *See also* worldly
  achievements
tolerance, *ii.*416. *See also* forgiveness
tragedy. *See* karmas, types of, group
transmigration, *i.*113, *i.*151, *i.*154,
    *i.*157, *i.*168, *i.*188, *i.*190, *i.*191.
    See also cycle of eighty-four;
    reincarnation
Trikuti, *i.*82, *i.*210, *i.*237, *ii.*213,
    *ii.*216–19
trust, *iii.*193
truth
  as excuse to humiliate another,
    *iii.*247
  rarely accepted, *i.*446
  sharing, *i.*381
twins, *i.*73. *See also* karmic
  relationships

ultimate goal, *i.*169, *i.*238, *i.*344,
    *ii.*431, *ii.*439, *iii.*368. *See also*
    soul(s), returning to God
understanding. *See also* discrimination
  as gift, *ii.*375
universal mind, *i.*228, *i.*237. *See also*
  Brahm; mind
urge for following path. *See* path,
  coming to

vacuum, *ii.*174, *ii.*188, *ii.*192, *ii.*196.
    See also meditation, dry
vegetarian diet, *ii.*56–78
  animals and, *ii.*74, *ii.*75, *ii.*76
  children and, *i.*69, *i.*71, *ii.*70, *ii.*71,
    *ii.*78, *iii.*326
  hair-splitting and, *ii.*72
  health of soul, *ii.*62

ADDRESSES FOR
INFORMATION AND BOOKS

INDIAN SUB-CONTINENT

INDIA
The Secretary
Radha Soami Satsang Beas
Dera Baba Jaimal Singh
District Amritsar, Punjab 143204

NEPAL
Capt. S.B.B. Chhetri (Retd.)
Radha Soami Satsang Beas Nepal
Gongabu 7, P. O. Box 1646
Kathmandu
☎ +977-1-435-7765

PAKISTAN
Mr. Sadrang Seetal Das
Lahori Mohala, Larkana, Sindh

SRI LANKA
Mr. Chandroo Mirpuri
Radha Soami Satsang Beas
No. 45 Silva Lane
Rajagiriya, Colombo
☎ +94-11-286-1491

SOUTHEAST ASIA

FOR FAR EAST
Mrs. Cami Moss
RSSB-HK
T.S.T., P.O. Box 90745
Kowloon, Hong Kong
☎ +852-2369-0625

MALAYSIA
Mr. Bhupinder Singh
Radha Soami Satsang Beas
29 Jalan Cerapu Satu, Off Batu 3 ¼
Jalan Cheras, Kuala Lumpur 56100
☎ +603-9200-3073

THAILAND
Mr. Harmahinder Singh Sethi
Radha Soami Satsang Beas
58/32 Ratchadaphisek Road, Soi 16
Thapra, Bangkok Yai, Bangkok 10600
☎ +66-2-868-2186 / 2187

INDONESIA
Mr. Ramesh Sadarangani
Jalan Pasir Putih IV/16, Block E 4
Ancol Timur, Jakarta
DKI Jakarta 14430

Yayasan Radha Soami Satsang
Jalan Transyogi KM. 5, Jatikarya
Pondok Gede, DKI Jakarta 17435
☎ +62-21-845-1612

Yayasan Radha Soami Satsang
Jalan Bung Tomo
Desa Pemecutan Raya
Denpasar, Barat 80116
☎ +62-361-438-522

PHILIPPINES
Mr. Kay Sham
Science of the Soul Study Center
9001 Don Jesus Boulevard
Alabang Hills, Cupang
Muntinlupa City, 1771
☎ +63-2-772-0111 / 0555

SINGAPORE
Mrs. Asha Melwani
Radha Soami Satsang Beas
19 Amber Road, Singapore 439868
☎ +65-6447-4956

ASIA PACIFIC

AUSTRALIA
Mr. Pradeep Raniga
Science of the Soul Study Centre
1530 Elizabeth Drive
Cecil Park, New South Wales 2178

NEW ZEALAND
Mr. Tony Waddicor
P. O. Box 5331, Auckland

Science of the Soul Study Centre
80 Olsen Avenue, Auckland
☎ +64-9-624-2202

GUAM
Mrs. Hoori M. Sadhwani
115 Alupang Cove
241 Condo Lane, Tamuning 96911

HONG KONG
Mr. Manoj Sabnani
Radha Soami Satsang Beas
3rd Floor, Maxwell Centre
39-41 Hankow Road
Tsim Sha Tsui, Kowloon
☎ +852-2369-0625

JAPAN
Mr. Jani G. Mohinani
Radha Soami Satsang Beas
1-2-18 Nakajima-Dori
Aotani, Chuo-Ku, Kobe 651-0052
☎ +81-78-222-5353

KOREA
Mr. Haresh Buxani
Science of the Soul Study Group
613, Hopyeong-Dong
R603-18604 Sungbo Building
Nam Yangju, Gyeong Gi-Do
Nam Yangju Kyung-gi
☎+822-315-117-008

TAIWAN, R.O.C.
Mr. Haresh Buxani
Science of the Soul Study Group
Aetna Tower Office, 15F., No. 27-9
Sec.2, Jhongjheng E.Rd.
Danshuei Township, Taipei 25170
☎+886-2-8809-5223

NORTH AMERICA

CANADA
Mr. John Pope
5285 Coombe Lane
Belcarra, British Columbia V3H 4N6

Mrs. Meena Khanna
149 Elton Park Road
Oakville, Ontario L6J 4C2

Science of the Soul Study Centre
2932 -176th Street
Surrey, B.C. V3S 9V4
☎ +1-604-541-4792

Science of the Soul Study Centre
6566 Sixth Line, RR 1 Hornby
Ontario L0P 1E0
☎ +1-905-875-4579

MEXICO
Radha Soami Satsang Beas
Efrain Gonzalez Luna
2051 Col. Americana
Guadalajara, Jalisco 44090
☎ +52-333-615-4942

Radha Soami Satsang Beas
Circuito Universidad S/N
Lomas Del ProgresoEL Pitillal CP 48290
☎ +52-322-299-1954

UNITED STATES
Mr. Hank Muller
P.O. Box 1847, Tomball, TX 77377

Dr. Vincent P. Savarese
2550 Pequeno Circle
Palm Springs, CA 92264-9522

Dr. Frank E. Vogel
275 Cutts Road
Newport, NH 03773

Dr. Douglas Torr
P.O. Box 2360
Southern Pines, NC 28388-2360

Science of the Soul Study Center
4115 Gillespie Street
Fayetteville, NC 28306-9053
☎ +1-910-426-5306

Science of the Soul Study Center
2415 Washington Street
Petaluma, CA 94954-9274
☎ +1-707-762-5082

CARIBBEAN

FOR CARIBBEAN
Mr. Sean Finnigan
R.S.S.B. Foundation
P. O. Box 978
Phillipsburg, St. Maarten, N. A.

Mrs. Jaya Sabnani
1 Sunset Drive South
Fort George Heights
St. Michael BB111 02, Barbados

BARBADOS, W.I.
Mrs. Mukta Nebhani
Science of the Soul Study Center
No. 10, 5th Avenue
Belleville BB11114
☎ +1-246-427-4761

CURACAO, N.A.
Mrs. Hema Chandiramani
Science of the Soul Study Centre
Kaya Seru di Milon 6-9
Santa Catharina
☎ +599-9-747-0226

ST. MAARTEN, N.A.
Mr. Prakash Daryanani
R.S.S.B. Foundation
P. O. Box 978, Phillipsburg
☎ +599-547-0066

GRENADA, W.I.
Mr. Ajay Mahbubani
P.O. Box 820, St. Georges

GUYANA
Mrs. Indu Lalwani
155, Garnette Street
Newtown Kitty, Georgetown

HAITI, W.I.
Ms. Mousson Finnigan Pierre
P.O. Box 2314, Port-au-Prince

JAMAICA, W.I.
Mrs. Reshma Daswani
17 Colombus Height
First Phase, Ocho Rios

ST. THOMAS
Mrs. Hema Melwani
P.O. Box 600145
USVI-VI00801-6145

SURINAME
Mr. Ettire Stanley Rensch
Surinamestraat 36, Paramaribo

TRINIDAD, W.I.
Mr. Chandru Chatlani
20 Admiral Court
Westmoorings-by-Sea, Westmoorings

FOR CENTRAL & SOUTH AMERICA

Mr. Hiro W. Balani
Paseo De Farola, 3, Piso 6
Edificio Marina
Malaga, Spain 29016

CENTRAL AMERICA

BELIZE
Mrs. Milan Hotchandani
4633 Seashore Drive
P.O. Box 830, Belize City

PANAMA
Mr. Ashok Tikamdas Dinani
P.O. Box 0301
03524 Colon

SOUTH AMERICA

ARGENTINA
Ms. Fabiana Shilton
Leiva 4363 Capital Federal
C.P. 1427 Buenos Aires

BRAZIL
Mr. Guillerme Almeida
RUA Jesuino Arrvda 574/51
Sao Paulo 04532-081

CHILE
Mr. Vijay Harjani
Pasaje Cuatro No. 3438
Sector Chipana, Iquique

Fundacion Radha Soami Satsang Beas
Av. Apoquindo 4770, Oficina 1504
Las Condes, Santiago

COLOMBIA
Mrs. Emma Orozco
Asociacion Cultural
Radha Soami Satsang Beas
Calle 48 No. 78A-30, Medellin 49744
☏ +574-234-5130

ECUADOR
Dr. Fernando Flores Villalva
Radha Soami Satsang Beas
Calle Marquez de Varela
OE 3-68y Avda. America
P.O. Box 17-21-115, Quito
☏ +5932-2-555-988

PERU
Mr. Carlos Fitts
P.O. Box 18-0658, Lima 18

Asociacion Cultural
Radha Soami Satsang Beas
Av. Pardo #231
12th Floor, Miraflores, Lima 18

VENEZUELA
Mrs. Helen Paquin
Radha Soami Satsang Beas
Av. Los Samanes con
Av. Los Naranjos Conj, Res. Florida 335
La Florida, Caracas 1012

EUROPE

AUSTRIA
Mr. Hansjorg Hammerer
Sezenweingasse 10, A-5020 Salzburg

BELGIUM
Mr. Piet J. E. Vosters
Driezenstraat 26, Turnhout 2300

BULGARIA
Mr. Deyan Stoyanov
Radha Soami Satsang Beas
P. O. Box 39, 8000 Bourgas

CYPRUS
Mr. Heraclis Achilleos
P. O. Box 29077, 1035 Nicosia

CZECH REPUBLIC
Mr. Vladimir Skalsky
Maratkova 916, 142 00 Praha 411

DENMARK
Mr. Tony Sharma
Sven Dalsgaardsvej 33, DK-7430 Ikast

FINLAND
Ms. Anneli Wingfield
P. O. Box 1422, 00101 Helsinki

FRANCE
Mr. Pierre de Proyart
7 Quai Voltaire, Paris 75007

GERMANY
Mr. Rudolf Walberg
P. O. Box 1544, D-65800 Bad Soden

GIBRALTAR
Mr. Sunder Mahtani
RSSB Charitable Trust, 15 Rosia Road
☏ +350-200-412-67

GREECE
Mr. Themistoclis Gianopoulos
6 Platonos Str., 17672 Kallithea, Attiki

ITALY
Mrs. Wilma Salvatori Torri
Via Bacchiglione 3, 00199 Rome

THE NETHERLANDS
(HOLLAND)
Mr. Henk Keuning
Kleizuwe2, Vreeland 3633AE

Radha Soami Satsang Beas
Middenweg 145 E
1394 AH Nederhorst den Berg
☎ +31-294-255-255

NORWAY
Mr. Manoj Kaushal
Langretta 8, N - 1279 Oslo

POLAND
Mr. Vinod Sharma
UL. Szyprow 2M12, 02-654 Warsaw

PORTUGAL
Mrs. Sharda Lodhia
CRCA Portugal
Av. Coronel Eduardo Galhardo
No.18 A-B
Lisbon 1170-105

ROMANIA
Mrs. Carmen Cismas
C.P. 6-12, 810600 Braila

SLOVENIA
Mr. Marko Bedina
Brezje pri Trzicu 68, 4290 Trzic

SPAIN
Mr. J. W. Balani
Fundacion Cultural RSSB
Fca Loma del Valle S/N
Cruce de Penon de Zapata
Alhaurin De la Torre, Malaga 29130
☎ +34-952-414-679

SWEDEN
Mr. Lennart Zachen
Norra Sonnarpsvägen 29
SE-286 72 Asljunga

SWITZERLAND
Mr. Sebastian Züst
Weissenrainstrasse 48
CH 8707 Uetikon am See

UNITED KINGDOM
Mr. Narinder Singh Johal
Radha Soami Satsang Beas
Haynes Park
Haynes, MK45 3BL Bedford
☎ +44-1234-381-234

AFRICA

BENIN
Mr. Jaikumar T. Vaswani
01 Boite Postale 951,
Recette Principale Cotonou 01

BOTSWANA
Dr. Krishan Lal Bhateja
P. O. Box 402539, Gaborone

CONGO
Mr. Prahlad Parbhu
143 Kasai Ave., Lubumbashi

GHANA
Mr. Murli Chatani
Radha Soami Satsang Beas
P. O. Box 3976, Accra
☎ +233-242-057-309

IVORY COAST
Mr. Veerender Kumar Sapra
Avenue 7, Rue 19, Lot 196
Trechville, Abidjan 05

KENYA
Mr. Surinder Singh Ghir
Radha Soami Satsang Beas
P.O. Box 15134
Langata 00509, Nairobi
☎ +254-20-890-329

LESOTHO
Mr. Sello Wilson Moseme
P. O. Box 750, Leribe 300

LIBYA (G.S.P.L.A.J.)
Mr. Abhimanyu Sahani
P.O. Box 38930, Bani Walid

MADAGASCAR
Mr. Francis Murat
Lote 126B
Amnohiminono, Antanetibe
Antananarivo 101

MAURITIUS
Dr. I. Fagoonee
Radha Soami Satsang Beas Trust
69 CNR Antelme /Stanley Avenues
Quatre Bornes
☎ +230-454-3300

NAMIBIA
Mrs. Jennifer Carvill
P. O. Box 449, Swakopmund 9000

NIGERIA
Mr. Nanik N. Balani
G.P.O. Box 5054, Marina, Lagos

RÉUNION
Ms. Marie-Lynn Marcel
5 Chemin 'Gonneau, Bernica
St Gillesles Hauts 97435

SIERRA LEONE
Mr. Kishore S. Mahboobani
82/88 Kissy Dock Yard
P.O. Box 369, Freetown

SOUTH AFRICA
Mr. Gordon Clive Wilson
P.O. Box 1959
Randpark Ridge, Gauteng 2156

Radha Soami Satsang Beas
P.O. Box 5270, Cresta 2118
☎ +27-11-792-7644

SWAZILAND
Mr. Mike Cox
Green Valley Farm, Malkerns

TANZANIA
Mr. Manmohan Singh
99 Lugalo Street
Dar-Es-Salaam 65065

UGANDA
Mr. Sylvester Kakooza
Radha Soami Satsang Beas
P. O. Box 31381, Kampala

ZAMBIA
Mr. Surinder Kumar Sachar
6 Mutondo Crescent
Riverside, Copper belt, Kitwe

ZIMBABWE
Mr. Gordon Clive Wilson
P.O. Box 1959
Randpark Ridge
Gauteng 2156, South Africa

MIDDLE EAST

BAHRAIN
Mr. Iqbal Kundal
P.O. Box 76091 - Juffair

ISRAEL
Mr. Michael Yaniv
Moshav Sde Nitzan 59
D.N. Hanegev 85470

KUWAIT
Mr. Vijay Kumar
Yousef AL Badar Street
Bldg 28, Block 10, Flat #8, Salmiya

U.A.E.
Mr. Daleep Jatwani
P.O. Box 37816, Dubai
☎ +971-4-339-4773

BOOKS ON THIS SCIENCE

SOAMI JI MAHARAJ
　　Sar Bachan Prose
　　Sar Bachan Poetry

BABA JAIMAL SINGH
　　Spiritual Letters

MAHARAJ SAWAN SINGH
　　The Dawn of Light
　　Discourses on Sant Mat, Volume I
　　My Submission
　　Philosophy of the Masters (5 volumes)
　　Spiritual Gems
　　Tales of the Mystic East

MAHARAJ JAGAT SINGH
　　Discourses on Sant Mat, Volume II
　　The Science of the Soul

MAHARAJ CHARAN SINGH
　　Die to Live
　　Divine Light
　　Light on Saint John
　　Light on Saint Matthew
　　Light on Sant Mat
　　Quest for Light
　　The Path
　　Spiritual Discourses (2 volumes)
　　Spiritual Heritage
　　Spiritual Perspectives (3 volumes)

BOOKS ABOUT THE MASTERS
　　Call of the Great Master – Daryai Lal Kapur
　　Heaven on Earth – Daryai Lal Kapur
　　Treasure beyond Measure – Shanti Sethi
　　With a Great Master in India – Julian P. Johnson
　　With the Three Masters (3 volumes) – Rai Sahib Munshi Ram

MYSTICS OF THE EAST SERIES
　　Bulleh Shah – J. R. Puri and T. R. Shangari
　　Dadu: The Compassionate Mystic – K. N. Upadhyaya
　　Dariya Sahib: Saint of Bihar – K. N. Upadhyaya
　　Guru Nanak: His Mystic Teachings – J. R. Puri
　　Guru Ravidas: The Philosopher's Stone – K. N. Upadhyaya
　　Kabir: The Great Mystic – Isaac A. Ezekiel
　　Kabir: The Weaver of God's Name – V. K. Sethi
　　Mira: The Divine Lover – V. K. Sethi
　　Saint Namdev – J. R. Puri and V. K. Sethi
　　Sant Paltu: His Life and Teachings – Isaac A. Ezekiel
　　Sarmad: Martyr to Love Divine – Isaac A. Ezekiel

BOOKS ON THIS SCIENCE

Sultan Bahu – J. R. Puri and K. S. Khak
The Teachings of Goswami Tulsidas – K. N. Upadhyaya
Tukaram: The Ceaseless Song of Devotion – C. Rajwade
Tulsi Sahib: Saint of Hathras – J. R. Puri and V. K. Sethi

SPIRITUALITY AND SANT MAT
Honest Living – M. F. Singh
In Search of the Way – Flora E. Wood
The Inner Voice – C. W. Sanders
Liberation of the Soul – J. Stanley White
Living Meditation: A Journey beyond Body and Mind
  – Hector Esponda Dubin
Message Divine – Shanti Sethi
The Mystic Philosophy of Sant Mat – Peter Fripp
Mysticism: The Spiritual Path – Lekh Raj Puri
The Path of the Masters – Julian P. Johnson
Radha Soami Teachings – Lekh Raj Puri
A Spiritual Primer – Hector Esponda Dubin

THE MYSTIC WAY AND WORLD RELIGIONS
Adventure of Faith – Shraddha Lietz
Buddhism: Path to Nirvana – K. N. Upadhyaya
The Divine Romance – John Davidson
The Gospel of Jesus – John Davidson
The Holy Name: Mysticism in Judaism – Miriam Caravella
Jap Ji – T. R. Shangari
The Odes of Solomon – John Davidson
The Prodigal Soul – John Davidson
The Song of Songs – John Davidson
A Treasury of Mystic Terms,
  Part I: The Principles of Mysticism (6 volumes) – John Davidson, ed.
Yoga and the Bible – Joseph Leeming

BOOKS ON MISCELLANEOUS THEMES
Empower Women: An Awakening – Leena Chawla
Life Is Fair: The Law of Cause and Effect – Brian Hines
One Being One – John Davidson
A Soul's Safari – Netta Pfeifer

VEGETARIAN COOKBOOKS
Baking Without Eggs
Creative Vegetarian Cooking
The Green Way to Healthy Living
Meals with Vegetables

BOOKS FOR CHILDREN
The Journey of the Soul – Victoria Jones
One Light Many Lamps – Victoria Jones

For Internet orders, please visit: www.rssb.org

For book orders within India, please write to:

Radha Soami Satsang Beas
BAV Distribution Centre, 5 Guru Ravi Dass Marg
Pusa Road, New Delhi 110 005